D0762938

OMENS OF ADVERSITY

OMENS OF ADVERSITY

Tragedy, Time, Memory, Justice

David Scott

Duke University Press   Durham and London   2014

Designed by Heather Hensley
Typeset in Warnock Pro by Tseng Information
Systems, Inc.

Library of Congress Cataloging-in-Publication Data
Scott, David, 1958–
Omens of adversity : tragedy, time, memory, justice /
David Scott.
p. cm
Includes bibliographical references and index.
ISBN 978-0-8223-5606-6 (cloth : alk. paper)
ISBN 978-0-8223-5621-9 (pbk. : alk. paper)
1. Grenada—History—American Invasion, 1983.
2. Grenada—Politics and government—1974–1983.
3. New Jewel Movement (Grenada) I. Title.
F2056.8.S36 2014
972.9845—dc23
2013025660

For Anju
and the generations of her time

CONTENTS

AFTERMATHS

The future diminishes as the past grows, until the future has
completely gone and everything is past.
—SAINT AUGUSTINE, *Confessions*

At one level, my central concern in *Omens of Adversity* is with
time or, rather, with *temporality*, with the lived experience of time
passing—the social relation, more precisely, between past (the
time of memory), present (the time of conscious awareness), and
future (the time of anticipation). It seems to me that, though in a
still inchoate way, a new time-consciousness is emerging everywhere in contemporary theory.[1] Not surprisingly, perhaps, a fresh
resonance has attached itself to Augustine and his perplexed anguish in the face of the unyielding *aporias* of temporal experience—the nonexistence of the past, the not-yet of the future,
the fleeting instant of the present—by contrast with the divine
transparency and constancy of eternity. In the memorably obsessive reflections that comprise book eleven of the *Confessions*,
which trace his motivated and exacting path of existential self-
questioning, these aporias constitute for him the immeasurable
and ineliminable paradox of the being and nonbeing of time. And,
of course, at least in the picture he draws of the soul's temporal
distention (*distentio animi*) across the three dimensions of pres-
entness—the presence of the past, the presence of the present,
and the presence of the future—Augustine does not so much re-

solve the seemingly intractable problems of time as render them, in a *vivid* phenomenological way, all the more eloquent, all the more intense.[2]

Admittedly, though, my concerns in *Omens of Adversity* are not with the *whole* of this ontology of temporal presence (even though Augustine's anxious sense of diminishing futures, captured in my epigraph, haunts the conceptual landscape of my preoccupations here).[3] Inevitably, perhaps, I have a somewhat narrower focus than this—namely, the temporality of the aftermaths of political catastrophe, the temporal disjunctures involved in living *on* in the wake of past political time, amid the ruins, specifically, of postsocialist and postcolonial futures past. What interests me about these catastrophic aftermaths is above all the untimely experience they have provoked of a more acute *awareness* of time, a more arresting *attunement* to the uneven *topos* of temporality. They have provoked, if not an experience of time as such (whatever that might mean), then certainly an accentuated experience of temporality, of time as *conspicuous*, as "out of joint" (as Hamlet unnervingly put it). It is an experience of time standing *away*, so to speak, from its conventional grounding and embeddedness in history, its modern handmaiden, so that time and history, once barely distinguishable, seem no longer synchronized, much less synonymous—as though time had found itself *betrayed* by history, or that history now confronted us as inauthentic time, the irreversibly lapsed time of our former anticipations of political futurity.

I have written before—in *Conscripts of Modernity*—of something of this sense of the out-of-jointness of time, in reference to the seeming waning of the "longing for total revolution" that framed and animated the great modernist politics of emancipation, including (indeed, especially) its anticolonial and socialist forms.[4] Skeptical of the historicism that plotted the story of past–present–future as a kind of Romance (in terms Hayden White made famous),[5] I suggested that perhaps what our present solicits from us most urgently is an attunement to *tragedy*, to the sort of appreciation of contingency, chance, *peripeteia*, and catastrophe that a sensibility for the tragic aims to cultivate and enliven. The occasion for that thinking was my rereading of C. L. R. James's classic story of the Haitian Revolution in *The Black Jacobins* and his late re-rendering (in the second, revised edition of that book) of the figure of his protagonist, Toussaint Louverture as an explicitly tragic hero. In *Omens of Adversity*, I turn this sense of the out-of-jointness of time to connected but extended purposes. The idea and importance of tragedy, we will see, remain crucial to my concerns, but here I am interested less in tragedy's place in an overall reading of colonial and postcolonial history than in its usefulness for thinking about the *temporality of action*—the temporality of *political* action, especially. In the earlier book, I was concerned more with reading tragedy as a strategy of historical criticism; here I want to mobilize its resources and sensibilities for an approach to the pervasiveness of collisions in human actions in time. And where in the earlier book I was anxious to construct the space of visibility, so to speak, for the work of tragedy as such, here, by contrast, I take much of that work to be done and *begin* with tragic time to open a discursive space for a wider critical labor and a broader dispersion of concerns—with ruin and memory and generations, for example, as well as justice and forgiveness. But still, as in *Conscripts of Modernity*, it is revolution and revolutionary action that hold my attention in *Omens of Adversity*, that provide the essential conceptual-political terrain for my theoretical preoccupations. This is so because, as James says in his preface to *The Black Jacobins*, revolution offers an ideal, if rare, vantage from which to consider the nature of historical-political action since "society is at boiling point and therefore fluid," and so renders human action, not so much more true as more vivid.[6] But it is also because, as Hannah Arendt says in *On Revolution*, the idea of revolution has been a founding paradigm for the modern organization of political time, for connecting old endings to new beginnings and, therefore (I would add), connecting our dissatisfactions with the past to our hopes for alternative futures.[7]

In *Omens of Adversity*, I take as my historical occasion another Caribbean revolution, one that while less remote, temporally, than the Haitian Revolution, is still, perhaps, less present to our political memories and theoretical imaginations—namely, the Grenada Revolution (1979–83). If the Haitian Revolution is treated in some quarters now as though it were part of a story of universal freedom, the Grenada Revolution, by contrast, has largely been relegated to the margins of historical amnesia. The rise in the Grenada of the 1970s of the New Jewel Movement (NJM) as a revolutionary political organization aiming at state power is part of a wider story of the rise of Marxist-Leninist political formations in the Caribbean region during this period.[8] Indeed, it is part of an even wider story of the radicalization of the Bandung project in the Third World, as postindependence political movements opted for the revolutionary overthrow of existing neocolonial regimes.[9] These were years when revolutionary futures were not merely possible but *imminent*; not only imminent, but *possible*. Thus, the success of Maurice Bishop and his comrades in the leadership of the NJM in overthrowing the tyrannical rule of Eric Gairy in March 1979 was, in its way, a world-historical *event* in the modern history of revolutions, and certainly an unprecedented event in the political history of the Anglophone Caribbean. It was a revolutionary beginning, undoubtedly, a euphoric leap into the future. Like many Caribbeans of my generation I have a vivid memory of exactly where I was on the morning of 13 March 1979 when the news broke in on us: I was sitting in a lecture at the University of the West Indies, Mona, where I was working toward my undergraduate degree. But it was the beginning, also, though we could not see it then, of a sort of *end*. Not merely the beginning of the end of the particular story of the Grenada Revolution itself (although in retrospect it can be argued that the seeds of that were sown early), but the beginning of the end of a whole *era* of revolutionary socialist expectation—indeed, of revolutionary socialist possibility. Because when in October 1983 the Grenada Revolution collapsed, as a consequence of party conflict within and US military intervention from without (another moment vividly inscribed in my generational memory), the global conditions of possibility for *any* postcolonial socialism were already in steep—irreversible—decline. The 1980s marked the effective end of Bandung in any of its varied postures of nonaligned sovereignty.[10] It was almost already the "end of history," as it would come to be called. The leadership of Ronald Reagan in the United States and of Margaret Thatcher in the United Kingdom had given impetus to a reformed and smugly confident liberalism—neoliberalism—armed with the militant determination and the military re-territorializing power to roll back what was now perceived as the "moral evil" of communism. And in the wake of their evident success—the irreversible collapse of the Soviet Union and its system of allied states—there arose, as a seemingly single and natural horizon, the new utopia of liberal democracy, its dogma of human rights, and the disciplining and governmentalizing technologies to urge and enforce its realization. In a real sense, the Grenada Revolution was the first casualty of the rise in the Reagan era of a belligerent neoconservative anticommunism. Therefore, in 1984, as the prison doors at Richmond Hill closed on the Grenada 17 (those of the party and army leadership of the Grenada Revolution accused of, and tried and convicted for, plotting and carrying out the murder of Prime Minister Maurice Bishop and his colleagues on 19 October 1983), they also *foreclosed* any possibility of return to the Cold War structure of ideological antagonisms that shaped their Marxist politics of anti-imperialism and socialism.[11] Their era had vanished, and now they were like leftovers from a former future stranded in the present. So that paradoxically, perhaps, in the wake of their trial—an explicitly Cold War event—these former revolutionaries would be obliged to undertake to save themselves from hanging and, subsequently, to seek to have their sentences overturned in a political world *redefined* in a new jargon of authenticity that no longer admitted the legibility, much less recognized the legitimacy, of their former political ambitions, their former political languages, their former political lives.

Thus, from the tragic action that brought about the downfall of the revolution to the regime of transitional justice that refigured the revolutionaries as criminals (the arc of my preoccupations in this book), the collapse, and aftermaths of the collapse, of the Grenada Revolution seem to me an exemplary instance of a larger phenomenon of global transformation and, therefore an exemplary terrain on which to think through aspects of the contemporary aporia of the crisis of political time. This is the discursive space of *Omens of Adversity*.

For moderns, temporality preeminently has been an experience of the unfolding of *historical* time. As is well enough known, modern historical time—the collective time of nations and classes and subjects and populations—has been organized around a notion of discrete but continuous, modular change, in particular, modular change as a linear, diachronically stretched-out *succession* of cumulative instants, an endless chain of displacements of before and after. Such succession, moreover, is progressive: change *is* improvement. Change, therefore, not only has a formal, built-in rhythm of movement and alteration but also a built-in *vector* of moral direction. Secular Enlightenment change is pictured as temporal movement in which, with regular periodicity, the future overcomes the past, and in which the present is a state of expectation and waiting for the fulfillment of the promise of social and political improvement. In the modernist Hegelian-Marxist version of this story of the march of historical time, change is imagined not only as successive and progressive, but also as *revolutionary*. That is to say, it is governed by a logic of dialectical reason (however de-spiritualized and upended); the gradual evolution of successive forms of the present gives way in an eschatological moment to a utopian future in which the alienated, reified time of capitalism is overcome, and socialist humanity finally coincides with the time of its historical destiny. This is the awaited end of history, when time is at once realized and canceled. I believe that a deep *rupture* has occurred in this form of experience. There is, I think, a profound sense in which the once enduring temporalities of past–present–future that animated (indeed, that constructed, even *authorized*) our Marxist historical reason, and therefore organized and underwrote our ideas about historical change, no longer line up quite so neatly, so efficiently, so seamlessly, so instrumentally—in a word, so *teleologically*—as they once seemed to do. That old consoling sense of temporal *concordance* is gone. The present as time, as a temporal frame of meaningful experiential reference, no longer appears—as it was once prominently pictured as appearing—as the tidy dialectical negation of an oppressive or otherwise unwanted past, and it is hard to continue imagining the present as though it were merely waiting for its own dialectical overcoming in a Hegelian-Marxist story of futurity understood as the ready horizon of Universal History. The existential rhythms of that enduring relation between past, present, and future have been broken—or, at least, they somehow have been very significantly interrupted. So much so that now remains from the past stick unaccountably to the hinges of the temporality we hitherto relied on to furnish ourselves with the confidence that we are in fact going somewhere—somewhere other and maybe *better* than where we currently are. Time, in short, has become less yielding, less promising than we have grown to expect it should be. And what we are left with are *aftermaths* in which the present seems stricken with immobility and pain and ruin; a certain experience of temporal *afterness* prevails in which the trace of futures past hangs like the remnant of a voile curtain over what feels uncannily like an endlessly extending present.[12]

This sense of a stalled present, a present that stands out in its arrested movement, is no doubt one reason that Walter Benjamin has become a literary-philosophic figure of such resonance, and his work has seemed so prescient, so evocative, and so timely for contemporary discussions about time and history. For Benjamin, as we know, as the European 1930s grew more perilous, a central, urgent intellectual-political task was to subvert the prevailing historicist philosophy of time and the conformist assumptions about change drawn from it (by social democrats and Marxists alike) and to provoke—indeed, to will—an *untimely* temporal sensibility for the future in the present. This is the role played in his thought by the theological idea of the "messianic" and "messianism," especially in that memorable work, "Theses on the Philosophy of History," where its function is to help disabuse the present of the illusion of a future that is waiting elsewhere than the possible, graspable, *now*.[13] The Benjaminian intuition was of the out-of-jointness of time in history, or of time *with* history. Indeed, one way to elaborate the sense I am pointing to of a conspicuous, arresting disjuncture between history and time—or between historicity and temporality as phenomenal planes of experience—is to pay attention to a curiously under-discussed early essay by Giorgio Agamben on time that draws inspiration precisely from this Benjaminian attunement to the contingencies of event and temporality.[14] Not surprisingly, in this essay the starting point for Agamben's reflections on time in Western philosophy (part of a larger reflection on catastrophe and modern experience) is the distinction Benjamin makes between the progressive, empty, and homogeneous time of versions of historicism and the ecstatic, momentous, and untimely time of the messianic coming. Agamben appreciates that in this work, Benjamin is pointing to an uncanny sense of divergence between the *experience of time* and the *expectations of history* and, more than this, to the hegemonic *occlusion* of temporality by rigid conventions of historicity. For Agamben, this disjuncture has broader philosophic implications for thinking time and history. "Every conception of history," he writes, "is invariably accompanied by a certain experience of time which is implicit in it, conditions it, and thereby has to be elucidated."[15] Notably, then, the problem of time and the problem of history are thought of here as *irreducible* to each other; they are connected, undeniably, but not necessarily identical. A distinctive temporality is always embodied in—while not being the simple mirror of—each imaginary of history. The assumption that time and history are identical—or, anyway, that what plainly matters is time *as* history, as opposed to some other plane of temporality—has been a pervasive one in modern political thought, including, of course, Marxist political thought. Indeed, this is partly what is at stake here for Agamben. "Even historical materialism," he laments, "has until now neglected to elaborate a concept of time that compares with its concept of history."[16] And this omission has had profound conceptual implications for Marxism as a practice of criticism (and therefore for such Marxist revolutionary movements as will concern me in this book) inasmuch as it has "been unwittingly compelled to have recourse to a concept of time dominant in Western culture for centuries, and so to harbour, side by side, a revolutionary concept of history and a traditional experience of time."[17]

Now, Agamben's exploration of the question of time and of the discordance between time and history (much like Paul Ricoeur's later, more systematic inquiry into time and narrative) is meant to be *philosophic* in the sense that he is principally concerned with developing a more adequate normative account of time than currently exists.[18] What account of time, for example, might do justice to Marx's exemplary conception of history? This is Agamben's question. Thus, he hopes to find, "scattered among the folds and shadows of the Western cultural tradition," the elements of a different and more active and decisive conception of time.[19] Scanning that tradition, he thinks he can just about discern some of these elements, for example, in ancient Gnosticism, in which there is an experience of time that is radically opposed to both the Greek idea of a circular time (now largely defunct as experience) and the Christian notion of a linear time (the modern secularization of which is crucial to Enlightenment conceptions of time, including Marxism's). The time of Gnosticism, Agamben says, is "an incoherent and unhomogeneous time, whose truth is in the moment of abrupt interruption when man, in a sudden act of consciousness, takes possession of his own condition of being resurrected."[20] It is easy to see in this formulation the pursuit and playing out of a whole Benjaminian motif of "now-time," the *kairos* in which a favorable moment is grasped in its finite, unrepeatable potentiality.[21] It opens a conceptual path that enables Agamben to solicit allusive intimations of Heidegger's way (owing famously to Augustine and Kierkegaard and Dilthey) of displacing the continuous time of "vulgar historicism" and of gesturing, at least, at a notion of being as "primordial temporalization," as having the capacity for seizing the moment as an "authentic" experience of *temporalizing* time.[22] Thus, for Agamben, a new conception of time will have to be built not only out of Gnostic and Stoic sources but out of Benjaminian and Heideggerian elements, as well.[23] Yet within the frame of this preoccupation, Agamben is less interested in whether or to what extent Benjamin's insight of temporal out-of-jointness might be inextricably linked to his particular historical-political *context* of crisis; that it may be something about the nature of his *problem-space* that made time stand out in the conspicuous way that it did. To be sure, Agamben is explicitly aware of Benjamin's context of catastrophe (he cites the moment of the Nazi–Soviet nonaggression pact of 1939 that is well known to be the immediate political context of "Theses on the Philosophy of History"), but this awareness forms only a *muted* background to his reading of the philosophic content of Benjamin's grappling with time.[24] Agamben is not, for example, interested in drawing a connection or contrast with the temporal sensibility of his own historical conjuncture. For me, by contrast, the historical question is crucial because that cognitive-political context of Benjamin's registers precisely the sense in which time has become conspicuous to him as discontinuity with history, as no longer assimilable by history, in a moment of revolutionary failure and attendant social-political catastrophe.

Benjamin's catastrophic present is, of course, not ours. But something of the unease about time, and about the uncertainty of just how to think productively about the temporality of past–present–future in the wake of the fin de siècle collapse of the communist project, can be discerned in a number of theoretical discussions in more recent decades that nevertheless bear a Benjaminian trace. Consider, for example, Jacques Derrida's memorable intervention—in *Specters of Marx*, and "Marx & Sons" especially—concerning the haunting presence of ruined time, "messianicity without messianism," and its corollary, the indestructible futurity of a "justice-to-come."[25] Here, turning self-consciously toward the question of the spectral *afterlife* of Marx in the very moment of the visceral, global crisis of the inheritance of Marxism, Derrida brings together a number of themes that are directly pertinent to my concerns throughout this book. Among them are the tragic out-of-jointness of the present as time and the conspicuousness of temporality relative to history it has engendered; the loss of the promise of communist revolution as the horizon of political emancipation; and the relation between the modern longing for revolution and the prospect of social, political, and economic justice.[26] Needless to say, I am not going to rehearse here the whole prolix discourse that constitutes the already widely commented-on reflections in *Specters of Marx* or the reply to his critics in "Marx & Sons." And I am also not going to offer anything like an "interpretation" of Derrida's views on time and history.[27] What interests me, rather, is the *registration* in this work of the palpable sense of dissolution of the political temporality of former futures and the profound indication we have of Derrida *groping*, uncertainly, toward the answer to an implicit demand for a new sensibility of time, politics, and justice that responds to his new, unsettled present. Consequently, it is unimportant to my concerns whether we agree or not with his specific formulation, what the truth-values might be of his final answer to the problem of time.

Not unlike for Agamben, but in a very different conjuncture from the one that framed *Infancy and History*, for Derrida in *Specters of Marx* and "Marx & Sons" modern political thought (especially Marxist thought) has been constrained by a model of time as "conjoined"—that is, as linear, homogeneous, teleological time. Against this conventional conception (and again, not unlike Agamben), Derrida commends a model of "disjointed" time, "time out of joint," that disrupts the dependable linearity of chronological time (the "objective" time, say, of Marxist historicism) and urges the prospect of an *atemporal* futurity—that is, the time of untimely events, of futures to come that are irreducible to any ontology of time.[28] If we adopt this perspective, he suggests, futures will always be open—yet undecidable and heterogeneous—possibilities. The conception of time that governs this open futurity, Derrida calls "messianic" or, more precisely (to underscore its paradoxical character), "messianicity without messianism." Note, then, that while this "messianicity" connotes a "universal structure of experience" in relation to events that are "to come," it is, Derrida insists, nevertheless non-utopian, which is to say that it does not conform to the teleology of historical materialism. Rather, messianicity is said to refer, "in every here-now, to the coming of an eminently real, concrete event, that is, to the most irreducibly heterogeneous otherness. Nothing is more 'realistic' or 'immediate' than this messianic apprehension, straining toward the event of him who/that is coming."[29] So conceived, messianicity describes a "waiting without expectation" that is also an "active preparation, anticipation against the backdrop of a horizon, but also exposure without horizon, and therefore an irreducible amalgam of desire and anguish, affirmation and fear, promise and threat."[30] In whatever way we gloss the precise meaning of Derrida's idea of messianism here, what seems to me most compelling about the *speech act* that constitutes his carefully wrought intervention is his inchoate apprehension, first, of the *loss* of the old metaphysical security of futures to come (an apprehension without nostalgia, of course, given the demeanor of deconstruction); and the speculative apprehension, second, that the present as ruined time establishes a philosophic *demand* to reassert (for Derrida is not constructing an argument in these texts so much as he is offering a number of perspicuous propositions) a *futural* claim. The idea of messianicity without messianism is Derrida's tentative *answer* to this perceived philosophic-political demand.

Especially interesting here to readers of Benjamin's own wrestling with the problem of time and history is Derrida's resolute disavowal that his non-utopian way of thinking about messianicity owes something of generative significance to Benjamin's idiom.[31] This may seem puzzling. Derrida maintains, first, that whereas Benjamin's messianism retains the trace of its specifically Jewish sources, his conception of messianicity without messianism is instead a secular idea, clearly disconnected from any theological resonances.[32] Secular and *therefore* "what?" one is tempted to ask. It is far from clear. Derrida holds, second, that whereas Benjamin's conception of "weak messianism" can be linked to a particular historical context (the Hitler–Stalin pact), his messianicity without messianism is *beyond* history. It constitutes, Derrida writes, a "universal, quasi-transcendental structure" that is "not bound up with any particular moment of (political or general) history or culture (Abrahamic or any other); and it does not serve any sort of alibi, does not mime or reiterate any sort of messianism, does not confirm or undermine any sort of messianism."[33] Some may well doubt this motivated reading of Benjamin's "Theses on the Philosophy of History," but from the point of view of my circumscribed concerns here, what is useful to note is the way in which Derrida marks his difference with, and distance from, Benjamin and the performative force with which he does so. For Derrida, Benjamin's messianic idea of a temporality that is irreducible to any ontology of homogeneous, empty time is limited by its Jewish metaphysics, and by the urgent circumstances of the historical moment. But it may not be obvious to even the most sympathetic readers that the genealogy of Derrida's own formulations (here and elsewhere in his oeuvre) could be devoid of some trace of the Judeo-Christian tradition within which his philosophic project as a whole is formed. And it will be plain to any attentive reader of *Specters of Marx* that it is itself framed by a (self-consciously) determinate occasion for speaking—namely, the collapse of "really existing socialism" and the triumphalism with which it was met by philosophic ideologues such as Francis Fukuyama, whose *The End of History* can be read as offering a panoramic picture of its ideological age, the aspiration to a final assimilation of time into Universal History.[34] Because what is hard *not* to recognize about the respective catastrophes of political time inhabited by Benjamin and Derrida is that in some relevant sense where Benjamin's personal and figurative ending was followed by an "after" of philosophic and political renovation (one instance of which is Derrida's thought itself), it is as yet uncertain what possibilities of "afterness" might follow, or might be extracted from, the historical conjuncture of Derrida's ends.[35]

Again, I want it to be clear that my point in reflecting on Derrida in this way is not to challenge the ambiguous suggestiveness of his idea of messianicity without messianism so much as to underline the *strain* with which it registers the apprehension that time is out of joint and therefore has become visible as a philosophic and political *problem*. We may now better appreciate Agamben's earlier prescient (explicitly Benjaminian) reflection that embodied in the conception of history that we moderns have taken for granted, and by which we have ordered our experience of past–present–future, there is an unexamined conception of time. Once self-evidently convergent, time and history—or temporality and historicity—now seem to be diverging from each other. In a certain respect, one might say that in the very moment that history has seemed so resistant to change, so unyielding, time has suddenly become more discernible, more conspicuous, more at odds, more palpably *in question*—as though the ends of history somehow marked the beginnings of time. *Omens of Adversity* aims to engage this apprehension of temporal insecurity and uncertainty.

It seems to me that the sense of the present as ruined time has had profound and far-reaching implications for how we think about our moral-political predicament—including, of course, our postcolonial and post-socialist predicament, my main concern in this book. Indeed, across a wide swath of contemporary intellectual discussion there have been significant—more or less subtle—shifts in theme and emphasis that signal this peculiar crisis (or, at least, conspicuousness) of time. Witness, for example, the rise to some prominence over the past two decades or so of the scholarly preoccupation with "memory" and "trauma" and their connection with each other. A large and rapidly growing literature deals with precisely this theme.[36] Now, obviously neither memory nor trauma is a new area of intellectual concerns in itself—it is enough to call to mind the names Henri Bergson and Sigmund Freud, and respective work such as *Matter and Memory* (1911) and *The Interpretation of Dreams* (1900), to recognize this. But it seems to me that the problem of memory and trauma, and of their interconnection, has received a new impetus and urgency—and, perhaps, a new conceptual *pertinence* and *orientation*—in the current historical conjuncture. Curiously, it is precisely when the future has *ceased* to be a source of longing and anticipation that the past has become such a densely animated object of enchantment.[37] After all, not so long ago, in comparative terms, the past was largely conceived as a storehouse of *disenchantment*; it existed to be *overcome*, not to be excavated and memorialized. *Then*, the past had temporal significance only insofar as it was tethered to the engine of history driving inexorably toward the future. *Now*, by contrast, the past has loosed itself from the future and acquired a certain quasi-autonomy; far from being dependent upon any other time, it seems now to exist for its own sake, as a radiant source of wisdom and truth. Now it is not the future that stands in need of liberation from the present, but the past. It is, of course, in such a context of seeming temporal reversal that the concern with the generative effects of psychic trauma becomes entirely intelligible, even unavoidable. In a sense, psychological trauma is nothing but a past that will not go away, a past that returns, unbidden, involuntarily, to haunt or unsettle or somehow mangle the present. As Freud suggested, trauma is a memory disorder. Again, not so very long ago, what the past produced was social oppression and inequality, economic exploitation, and political discrimination—that is, forms of injustice in the relations that constitute a community. Then, the past was a *social* fact; now, however, it is a *pathological* one. The past is a wound that will not heal. What the past produces now are inward, psychic harms and injuries to an individual sense of self and a collective sense of identity.

The rise of a preoccupation with memory and trauma as pivotal concepts for discerning the lineaments of the temporal relation between past and present is itself connected to—is in some sense, in fact, a *condition* for—another crucial shift in contemporary theoretical discussion central to this book's concerns: the rise to prominence of the idea of *reparatory* or *restorative* justice (alongside the more established dimensions of distributive and punitive or criminal justice) and, with it, the techniques of "truth and reconciliation" and political forgiveness. Memory and trauma, and their temporal coordinates, are at the center of the idea of reparatory justice, itself an aspect of the larger tectonic shift that has produced our age as one defined by human rights.[38] In the wake of the vaunted end of the ideological battle of the Cold War era and the rise of liberal democracy as the single, absolute horizon of political civilization, the human rights project of reparatory justice has seemed an essential, inescapable element in settling intractable conflicts of the past in the present and facilitating the "transition" from varieties of authoritarian rule. Indeed, reparatory justice is often seen precisely as a dimension of *transitional* justice.[39] During the era of the ideological and political rivalry between capitalism and communism, the justice or injustice of political actions was often described and adjudicated (in part, at least) by reference to a systemic social-moral imaginary that established a normative standard of right and wrong. Justice was not unconnected to moral truth, of course, but such moral truth inhabited a world of explicitly competing universalities. Now, by contrast, all of this seems self-evidently unacceptable; indeed, it all seems patently mistaken. The only truth today is that every human being has the right to a *perspective* on what is true. Therefore, arguably, there is no single point of view that can monopolize or guarantee the truth for all. What counts now is each *story* of what is true. Truth, so it is said, is "socially constructed" within narratives of identity and community, with varying relations to structures and powers of authorization.[40] Consequently, since there is no longer an overarching meta-truth by which to judge the injustice of the past (no master narrative, for example, of the class determination of social injury), victims and their persecutors are urged to adopt an attitude of reconciliation toward each other; they are urged to reconstruct the past in such a way as to enable them to conjure a reasonable, shareable, *modus vivendi*. Reconciliation is the *summum bonum* of reparatory justice. To put it another way, because the present can no longer be overcome for a future of emancipation, there has to be an *accommodation* with the past. Truth and reconciliation and its central idiom of "forgiveness" are the names of a moral politics for an age characterized by being stranded in the present.

To say all this, of course, is not to dismiss outright the scholarly interest in memory and trauma and reparatory justice and political forgiveness as mere ideological false consciousness or, for example, as the mere theoretical self-consciousness of our neoliberal age. It may be this too, but it may not be *only* this. To my mind, the preoccupation with trauma and memory and justice and forgiveness are symptoms of the larger crisis of time and temporal experience. Therefore, whatever our suspicions, hesitations, they need to be argued over, argued *through*, reflexively, to determine what their critical, untimely, yield can be. This, anyway, is a task I undertake in *Omens of Adversity*.

Revolutions are consummately about time. So too, perhaps, are their collapse and destruction. As I have said, in *Omens of Adversity* I take up these concerns with time and ruin and aftermaths on the historical-political terrain of the collapse of one revolution: the Grenada Revolution, in many ways the world-historical revolution of my Caribbean generation.

On 19 October 1983, the Grenada Revolution came to a sudden, violent end. It was barely four-and-a-half years old. The relatively small group of revolutionaries who constituted the leadership of the Marxist-Leninist party, the NJM—among them, Maurice Bishop, Bernard Coard, George Louison, Unison Whiteman, Kendrick Radix, Hudson Austin, and Selwyn Strachan—had ushered in the revolution on 13 March 1979 by forcibly toppling the repressive and tyrannical regime of Eric Gairy, who had dominated Grenadian politics almost uninterruptedly since he burst upon the scene in the early 1950s.[41] Gairy was a shrewd, charismatic, and self-regarding leader who had made a name for himself in the early years when he confronted the British colonial authorities, demanding better working conditions for poor, largely agricultural workers; organizing demonstrations and strikes; and inspiring the burning of the detested estate great houses, that painful legacy of colonial plantation slavery—"sky red," as the blazes from these incendiary acts of popular indignation were called.[42] But once power accumulated in his hands, initially as a member of the Legislative Council (1951–57), then as chief minister (1961–62), premier (1967–74), and, finally, prime minister of independent Grenada (1974–79), Gairy had shown himself to be a corrupt and openly self-aggrandizing politician inclined to rule the country by patronage, when possible, and by fear and intimidation and violence when necessary.[43] The NJM's revolution brought Gairy's tyranny to an end.[44] Under the leadership of the People's Revolutionary Government, a range of social, economic, and political reforms were inaugurated that are widely regarded as having had a significantly positive impact on the country's development.[45] By all accounts, the revolution was immensely popular with the urban and agricultural working poor. In particular, its undisputed leader, Maurice Bishop, was said by virtually everyone to possess to a remarkable degree a dynamic and magnetic personality, an ability to translate hard political concepts into ordinary language, and, above all, an ability to inspire people with a sense of urgency and purpose and of historic destiny.[46] More than anything else, revolutionary Grenada was an unprecedented symbol of the possibility of breaking with the colonial and neocolonial Caribbean past, and of hope for egalitarian change and social and political justice. Nothing like it had taken place in the Anglophone Caribbean. The Grenada Revolution was an *event*, and Grenada soon came to stand as an inspiring instance of a small nation-state willing to defy the dictates of US imperialism in defense of its right of self-determination. As Bishop put it in one of the many speeches for which he became justly famous, "No country has the right to tell us what to do or how to run our country, or who to be friendly with. We certainly would not attempt to tell any other country what to do. We are not in anybody's backyard, and we are definitely not for sale."[47] It was ordinary language spoken to ordinary people. But it was a radical declaration of defiant purpose.

By 1982, however, signs of stress and strain had started to show. Internal dissent met with draconian measures from the revolutionary state, especially in the wake of the terrible bomb blast at Queen's Park, St. George's, on 19 June 1980, which killed three schoolgirls and injured a large number of people. It was a graphic indication of the lengths to which the revolution's political enemies were willing to go, and the revolution had powerful enemies from the outset. Indeed, the administration of US President Ronald Reagan, which had succeeded that of Jimmy Carter in early 1981, was openly hostile to the People's Revolutionary Government, actively blocking foreign aid, refusing diplomatic recognition, fomenting destabilization, and even planning invasion.[48] It was an open secret that the United States wanted to destroy the Grenada Revolution.

However, the deeper problems lay within the revolutionary party itself. By late summer of 1983, a crisis around the structure of leadership was paralyzing the internal organs of the NJM and disabling its capacity to function coherently as the vanguard of the revolution. A sharp debate emerged that—obliquely at first, then, eventually, very pointedly—implicated Prime Minister Maurice Bishop as lacking the requisite qualities of a *party* leader. Given the Leninist nature of the party, none of this internal quarreling was public knowledge. But when the hugely popular Bishop was placed under effective house arrest for allegedly spreading a false rumor that his colleagues Bernard and Phyllis Coard had threatened his life, the conflict was thrown into the open. It precipitated mass protests and demonstrations in support of Bishop and *against* the party, and especially against those associated with Bernard Coard, the presumed mastermind of a subversive plot to undermine and displace Bishop. Freed by one of these organized demonstrations on the morning of 19 October 1983, Bishop and a large number of his supporters converged on the headquarters of the People's Revolutionary Army at Fort Rupert (subsequently returned to its colonial name, Fort George), where they proceeded to relieve the soldiers of their arms and to open the armory and distribute weapons among civilians. Meanwhile, from another base—Fort Frederick, a short distance away—the army's leaders sought to enter into talks with Bishop's associates, but after being rebuffed, the young day-to-day commander Ewart Layne made a decision to dispatch troops to retake Fort Rupert. When they arrived at the steep entrance to the fort, however, the soldiers (many riding on the outside of the armored vehicles, evidently not expecting serious resistance) came under fire, which killed their commanding officer, Cadet Conrad Meyers. A fierce gun battle ensued in which scores of men, women, and children were killed or wounded, until Bishop ordered one of his associates to negotiate a surrender to avoid further bloodshed. Having brought the fort back under their control, members of the army detained Bishop and seven of his associates—namely, Unison Whiteman, Jacqueline Creft, Fitzroy Bain, Norris Bain, Evelyn Bullen, Evelyn Maitland, and Keith Hayling—who were taken to the inner courtyard of the fort and, under circumstances that have not yet been incontrovertibly established, shot to death.

This catastrophe effectively brought the Grenada Revolution to an end. As people, staggered at the thought of their beloved prime minister being killed by his own soldiers, and bewildered and terrified at what the immediate implications might be for their lives and livelihoods, sought to digest what had taken place, the army established a ruling military council (the Revolutionary Military Council) under the command of General

Hudson Austin. The council's immediate concern was to restore calm and order (if not quite legitimacy) and try to stave off the military invasion from the United States they knew was being planned in Washington. Their diplomatic efforts were to no avail, however. On 25 October 1983, against the express wishes of his close political and ideological ally Margaret Thatcher, the prime minister of the United Kingdom, President Reagan ordered the launch of Operation Urgent Fury, ostensibly to rescue US citizens studying at the medical college and to restore democracy.[49] The invading forces (some ten thousand) met more resistance from the remnants of the Grenadian army and militia than they expected, taking fully a week to gain effective control of the country and to announce the official cessation of hostilities, which occurred on 2 November 1983.[50] Having established military ascendancy, the US forces began to round up and detain the remaining leaders of the NJM and of the People's Revolutionary Army. By the end of the first week of November, they had all been arrested and taken into custody. The principals of the party and army were initially held incommunicado aboard a US naval vessel and in packing crates at the airport under the supervision of the Caribbean Peacekeeping Forces brought in to do police work for the United States.[51] Subsequently, they were turned over to the authorities at the prison at Richmond Hill, not far from the capital, St. George's.

The capture of the party and army leadership, who would soon come to be called the Grenada 17, marked not only the official end of the Grenada Revolution but also the formal beginning of the investigation into the killing of Maurice Bishop and his colleagues on 19 October. This was undertaken in conditions of widespread shock as a consequence of the collapse of the revolution and the US invasion, as well as in a context of intense Cold War "psychological" propaganda conducted by the US Armed Forces Psychological Operations department, which sought systematically to negate the popular experience of the Grenada Revolution; criminalize and vilify the detained leaders of the party and army; and, as Richard Hart puts it, create "a state of mental, and consequently physical, resignation to the domination of the region by imperialism."[52] Military personnel from the Caribbean Peacekeeping Forces carried out the preliminary questioning of the prisoners. There is strong evidence that torture was used to extract confessions from the prisoners.[53]

In April 1984, twenty members of the NJM and the People's Revolutionary Army were charged with the murder of Maurice Bishop and seven others, and in August of that year, after a preliminary examination, nineteen of the accused were committed to stand trial in the Grenada High Court. Eventually, seventeen would be brought to trial. At the preliminary inquiry, the prosecution offered evidence that Bishop and his associates had been shot to death by members of the People's Revolutionary Army. But it was clear from the beginning that these soldiers were not the principal targets of the judicial proceedings. Their main purpose, rather, was to secure the criminal conviction of the surviving leaders of the revolution, "thereby teaching the people of the region a lesson," as Hart puts it, "and ensuring that, in the foreseeable future, no revolutionary overthrow of an established government would be attempted."[54] The prosecution alleged that the members of the Central Committee of the NJM went to Fort Frederick after Bishop was released from house arrest and there decided that he—Bishop—should be killed. The problem, however, was that there was no credible evidence to support this allegation. The only evidence was the testimony of Cletus St. Paul, Bishop's former chief security guard, who was being held in custody in connection with the charge that he had attempted to create unrest by circulating a false rumor on Bishop's behalf. According to St. Paul, he saw Central Committee members give the directive to retake the fort and liquidate Bishop and his colleagues. As the presiding judge underscored, this testimony was the principal basis of the prosecution's case, even though no one besides St. Paul told the story he did.

Nevertheless, it was precisely on the basis of St. Paul's evidence and such "confessions" as were extracted from the detainees that the jury was invited to find that the Central Committee members had met and decided that Bishop should be eliminated. Notably, the accused did not participate in their trial; early on, they instructed their defense team to withdraw from the case on the grounds that the court before which they were ordered to stand trial, the Grenada High Court, was unconstitutional and that the proper forum for hearing the case was the Eastern Caribbean Supreme Court. On 4 December 1986, at the conclusion of a trial shot through with blatant partiality and systematic legal irregularities and in an atmosphere of ideological coercion in which the accused were painted as little more than vile political thugs, the main defendants (Hudson Austin, Dave Bartholomew, Callistus Bernard, Bernard Coard, Phyllis Coard, Leon Cornwall, Liam James, Ewart Layne, Colville McBarnette, Cecil Prime, Lester

Redhead, Selwyn Strachan, Christopher Stroude, and John Ventour) were found guilty of multiple counts of murder and sentenced to hang. This had been almost a foregone conclusion. The rank-and-file soldiers alleged to have fired the fatal shots (Andy Mitchell, Vincent Joseph, and Cosmos Richardson) were convicted of multiple counts of manslaughter and sentenced to fifteen years of imprisonment for each count, with certain of the sentences to be served consecutively.

The Grenada 17 launched and waged a long, difficult campaign to have their convictions quashed and to vindicate themselves of the crime of which they were convicted. Needless to say, from within their confinement, the resources at their disposal were meager, and the pro-US political climate in the region following the wider collapse of the socialist project was resolutely unsympathetic to their efforts. For their part, the political members of the Grenada 17 maintained that while they clearly bore *part* of the moral and political responsibility for the events that led to the deaths of Bishop and his associates, they did not bear the whole responsibility and, most important, they were not *criminally* liable. This is a position they have consistently held throughout their ordeal. On 14 August 1991, the death sentences of the fourteen principal defendants were commuted to life in prison. On 7 February 2007, after a long struggle to have their case heard, the Judicial Committee of the Privy Council in the United Kingdom impugned the constitutionality of the original death sentences and ordered the resentencing of the thirteen named appellants.[55] And on 4 September 2009, the last of the Grenada 17—among them, Bernard Coard—walked free from Richmond Hill Prison, having served more than a quarter of a century for a crime that is still to be diligently investigated and impartially adjudicated.

On a Caribbean scale, anyway, the Grenada Revolution of 13 March 1979 was world-historical (in a way, one might imagine, that the Haitian Revolution was in 1804 and the Cuban Revolution was in 1959). More important, perhaps, it was *generationally* historic in the sense that, for the generation who made it or who recognized their identity in it (the Caribbean generation of 1968, so to call it), the revolution was not merely the vindication of an ideological truth—say, the doctrinal truth of Marxism. It was also, and more poignantly, the vindication and culmination of a certain organization of temporal expectation and political longing.[56] Generations, we will see, form a crucial dimension of temporal experience of past-present-future. Consequently, the collapse of the Grenada Revolution in October 1983, and the US-led invasion that followed it and that laid the basis for the trial and conviction of the Grenada 17, are not merely incidental moments in Caribbean political history. They constitute a *watershed* event in the generational experience of time and history—a traumatic ending and an aftermath without end. This apprehension of its significance shapes the overall approach I adopt in this book. Thus, in *Omens of Adversity* it is not my purpose to try to reconstruct a whole history of the revolution or of the circumstances that surrounded its demise; the violent death of its popular leader and his associates; or the trial, conviction, and eventual release of those who were found guilty of murder and conspiracy to commit murder on 19 October 1983. The definitive political history of these catastrophic events is waiting to be written. Whether it will be—whether it *can* be—written, remains to be seen. This book has a different, perhaps a somewhat more circumscribed, project. It aims, in an admittedly partial way, to be a contribution, written through selective aspects of this particular Caribbean catastrophe, to a wider critical discussion of the ethical-political experience of the temporal "afterness" of our postcolonial, postsocialist time.

I have divided the four chapters that constitute *Omens of Adversity* into two parts. This is not to suggest any deep discontinuity; it only registers certain affinities between the two chapters in each part of the book that, to my mind, draw their preoccupations together more intimately. Time, of course, is my overall theme throughout, because, as I have already suggested, it is the alteration in our experience of time, the reorganization of our sense of the temporal relation between anticipated futures and remembered pasts that has seemed to me fundamental for thinking through a range of contemporary issues. But the question of time and the experience of temporality arise differently in each of the chapters as I range across an arc of preoccupations from tragedy to justice that is itself pertinent to me. For tragedy and justice undoubtedly are connected. After all, the greatest fictive models of literary tragedy—Sophocles, say, or Shakespeare—are deeply concerned with the problem of justice. What else is Oedipus's action of self-blinding in the wake of his unwilled murder of his father and marriage to his mother, or Antigone's defiance of Creon in burying her brother, but acts that open and problematize the question of justice? And what else is Hamlet's dilemma, the moral-intellectual fatigue that seems simultaneously to drive and paralyze him, if not his inability to decide whether or how justly to avenge his father's murder?

Part I, "Tragedy, Time," is concerned overall with time, mimesis, tragedy, and action. That action unfolds in time is one fundamental and intractable source of tragedy, and revolutionary action unfolding in time—the multiple, public, passionate, polyvalently motivated actions initiated in specific political conjunctures—is especially vulnerable to tragic collision. But the intelligibility of action's temporality is a function of mimesis in the sense that the time that unfolds an action is assimilated into experience insofar as it is rendered as a narrative.

Chapter 1, "Revolution's Tragic Ends: Temporal Dimensions of Political Action," is an exploration of the relation between tragedy and the temporal frame of political action. Tragedy arises from the fact that the well-intentioned actions of willing and self-determining agents are pervasively vulnerable to contingency and therefore to outcomes that are never predictable or entirely knowable in advance. Tragedies, in other words, do not merely *happen*, although they do seem very much to befall us; they are a consequence of action or, rather, of a plurality of concatenating actions. Tragedies, moreover, are often not merely the outcome of just any action or type of action but of the collision of actions that are *one-sided* in their attachment to their own justifications (their pathos, as Hegel would say) and consequently unyielding to the justifications of others. By their very nature, Raymond Williams and C. L. R. James suggested in different ways, revolutions are political fields of such collisions of action and, consequently, of potential tragedy. It may not be surprising, then, that the collapse of the Grenada Revolution is widely regarded as a tragic event. But curiously, even in the work of the most important and acute of its scholarly analysts, the idea of tragedy is largely decorative; it has no generative *conceptual* content—it does no discernible *theoretical* work. Part of the problem, it seems to me, is that in this work, the register of the historical analysis of the structure and practices that brought about the catastrophe of the revolution, however illuminating in its own right, nevertheless has tended to obscure another vital one—namely, the register of the *temporality of action* and, therefore, the constitutive fragility and instability of human action in time. (This is, recognizably, a line of thinking that owes variously to Benjamin and Arendt.) Thus, for example, the question of the moral and political emotions (hubris, hamartia, anger, shame, resentment, envy, fear) and accidental temporalities (reversals, contingency, luck) has been overlooked as merely incidental to the inquiry into what brought down the four-and-a-half-year-old revolution. Yet it is precisely these dimensions of human action—the *alterities* of the moral and political emotions, the colliding contingencies of acting in time—that show that our ineluctable inability to shield ourselves from tragedy by our reasons may be a pervasive feature of human action, and of *political* action more so than any other. So it seems to me that the intuition that the conflict between Maurice Bishop and the Central Committee of the NJM can be thought about in terms of tragedy is worth fuller exploration. Certainly, the collision of reasoned actions that led to the deadlock around the unanimous decision on joint leadership, and the subsequent equally reasoned actions that conducted these actors into an armed confrontation that led to their personal and political doom, invite an inquiry into the temporality of tragic action. This is what this chapter is concerned with; it redescribes the final weeks of the Grenada Revolution, paying close attention to the conundrums and predicaments of action among actors whose pathos disabled insight into their one-sided wills and drove them inexorably to a tragic collision. But it is also propelled by a wider speculation—namely that, paradoxically, tragedy may be a price for our political freedom, and therefore that modesty and responsibility ought to be central elements of a critical political sensibility.

Chapter 2, "Stranded in the Present: The Ruins of Time," is concerned with the artifices and figurations of temporality by which we order our experiences of endings, especially *catastrophic* endings, such as the sudden, violent collapse of a popular revolution. At the center of my concerns here therefore is the relation between narrative and time, or with narrative (as Paul Ricoeur would have it) as an exemplary response to irresolvable aporias in the experience of time. Principally, I am interested in fictive models of temporal experience. The chapter engages the problem of fictive temporality through a reading of two successive novels by Merle Collins, *Angel*, published in 1987, and *The Colour of Forgetting*, published in 1995. Both novels are concerned with the traumatic collapse of the Grenada Revolution, but each approaches this untimely event through a different model of narrative time and therefore shapes a different "sense of an ending."

In *Angel*, a Bildungsroman with resonant affiliations with a tradition of West Indian women's writing, Collins constructs a social-realist story of progressive (but also generational) time leading up to the triumph of the revolution and followed soon after by its reversal or peripeteia in catastrophic implosion. The protagonist of the story, the eponymous Angel, is a self-conscious revolutionary participant and a survivor of the disorienting demise of the revolution and the violence of the US military invasion that comes in its wake, and she finds herself in the end at a sort of temporal *standstill*, stranded in a postrevolutionary present that has nowhere to go. By contrast, we will see that *The Colour of Forgetting*, as though responding to the temporal dilemmas of the first novel, is shaped by different generic affiliations—namely, allegory, and fundamentally recasts the sense of the ending of the revolution. Its narrative temporality is driven less by the linear mimesis of character development than by the metaphysical or symbolic order of *repeating* time. Within its allegorical economy, the collapse of the Grenada Revolution is conceived not as the catastrophic end of a teleological history of progressive crisis and change but, rather, as merely one signal episode in a larger and recurrent story of generations of conflict and perseverance and survival in what is now figured as the cyclic pattern of a history whose very *logic* and *grammar* is catastrophic. My aim in drawing this contrast, I should say, is not to offer up allegory as intrinsically superior (whatever that might mean) to the Bildungsroman in its fictive organization of time, but to suggest why paying attention to generic dimensions of mimesis might enable us a wider range of temporal dispositions and story forms in the face of catastrophic ends.

In Part II, "Memory, Justice," I turn my attention in the direction of other renderings of the aftermaths of political catastrophe. Time remains the inexorable existential context of my inquiry. And tragedy's trace still lingers. But memory now figures the temporality of the experience of loss and mourning and hope, and the question of justice frames my horizon. I take these to be conjoined, for not only might there be justice in the persistence of remembrances of harmful pasts, but in some quarters of contemporary political theory, memory is now seen as a crucial aspect of what justice demands as a measure of repair.

Chapter 3, "Generations of Memory: The Work of Mourning," is concerned with thinking about the contrast between mourning and melancholia in relation to generations of remembering the catastrophic loss of a political project. (In a certain sense, this carries on the theme of generations and the temporality of generations that is crucial to the previous chapter.) Specifically, I am interested in the contrast between a generation that lives the (political, personal) loss as its own immediate experience and memory and a generation that lives it at a generational *remove*, in an existentially mediated way. How do successive generations remember the same catastrophic event? This is my principal question. I focus in this chapter on one figuration of loss that exemplifies the traumatic *after*-life of the collapse of the Grenada Revolution—namely, the loss that centers on the haunting absence of the disappeared body of Maurice Bishop. More than any other single person, Bishop embodied the ideals and hopes of the Grenada Revolution. In death as in life, his body is a political emblem, and the absence of its remains is a tangible reminder of the cruel unresolvedness of the revolution's collapse. Without it, there seems no possibility of bringing closure to the terrible end of October 1983, at least for the generation that lived the rise of the revolution as the horizon of its longing and for whom its collapse is remembered in embittered disappointment and melancholic fixation—at best, in painfully ambivalent nostalgia, and at worst, in a blind desire for revenge. In this chapter, I contrast this generation's paralysis with what I take to be the work of reparative remembering and mourning represented by the endeavor of a small booklet titled, *Under the Cover of Darkness*, written by a group of secondary-school boys in Grenada, the Young Leaders, and published in 2002. This remarkable booklet documents the students' project to find out what happened to the bodies of Bishop and his seven colleagues killed at Fort Rupert on 19 October 1983; they were hastily burned and buried by members of the People's Revolutionary Army and vanished shortly after their exhumation during the US invasion and occupation. What interests me about *Under the Cover of Darkness* is not only the astonishing investigative labor that turned up hitherto unknown (or forgotten) facts about the sequence of events concerning the bodies, and the clear implication of a plot to conceal or disappear Bishop's remains especially, but also the text's status as an intervention in an abject memorial space. I read the booklet as a kind of *speech act*, as the performance by these schoolboys of a refusal to surrender to the paralysis and doomed silence of their parents' generation. By reopening the question of the missing bodies from a generational location defined by "postmemory," the Young Leaders initiate a kind of remembering drained of their parents' melancholic affective demands and suggestive of what a reparative mourning for that terrible loss might now entail in postrevolutionary circumstances.

Chapter 4, "Evading Truths: The Rhetoric of Transitional Justice," is concerned with thinking about aspects of the post–Cold War regime of liberalism and the ways in which it frames talk about what justice demands in the wake of the collapse of forms of so-called illiberal rule. These, we ought to remind ourselves, are the aftermaths not only of right-wing military dictatorships or exclusionary racial authoritarianisms but also of the Bandung project, those uncertain attempts by postcolonial states to imagine and pursue modes of self-determination beyond the dictates of empire (whether the former colonial powers or the contemporary US imperium). Since the end of the Cold War, the distinctions among them have almost completely vanished, *all* now being subsumed in the new totalizing category of "totalitarianism," liberalism's catchall for its political Others. Now that fascist and communist forms of totalitarianism have been vanquished, we are told, liberal democracy has emerged as the only acceptable direction of political futures—as the *single*, indisputable standard of civilization by which political legitimacy can be judged. This, of course, is not merely the outcome of the global assimilation of liberal democracy as a new ethical-political norm, the new self-image of the age; it is the outcome of the credible military force of the United States of America that has adopted the role of imperial evangelist for liberal democracy. *This* is the ideological space of the rise of "transitional" justice as the legal mechanism by which to engineer the transformation of non-liberal or illiberal predecessor regimes into liberal ones. In the new context of liberal transition, what justice demands may indeed entail legal punishment for the commission of particular crimes, but this punishment will be directed not merely at the legally culpable individuals but also at the political regime itself, of which these alleged perpetrators are only representatives. Whereas the crimes committed by representatives of liberal democratic regimes—torture, for example, or mass murder—are deemed mere exceptions perpetrated by rogue individuals, the crimes committed by representatives of non-liberal regimes are deemed to define the illiberal character of the regimes themselves. Here it is the form of state that is rogue. Transitional justice is the name of a post–Cold War development in liberal justice that, through the political technologies of successor trials and, above all, historical truth commissions, aims to draw a line between the illiberal past and the *liberalizing* present. Commissioned remembering to construct the truth of what happened in the past, it is argued, is the basis for the "reconciliation" of victims with their perpetrators within a liberalizing political time. Against the backdrop of this (to my mind, often cynical) rhetoric of transitional justice, chapter 4 considers the case of the Grenada 17, the former members of the revolutionary regime and army who stood trial for, and were convicted of, the crimes of murder and conspiracy to commit the murder of Maurice Bishop and his colleagues on 19 October 1983. They were, as Amnesty International aptly described them, among the last Cold War prisoners. I suggest that this successor trial was little more than a show trial, a politically motivated exercise aimed not at impartially investigating the truth of the killings but at sending an unambiguous warning to Grenada and the wider Caribbean about the consequences of pursuing revolutionary self-determination. Then, taking up the truth and reconciliation process that followed the trial by a decade and a half (while the Grenada 17 were still in prison), I suggest that this exercise was not only an implicit acknowledgment of the failure of the prior trial to determine the truth of the events of October 1983 and bring closure to that historical period, but also little more than an exercise in politically motivated evasion. It certainly served neither the purpose of disclosing a full and truthful account of what took place on that fateful day and why, nor that of justly reconciling an admittedly conflicted society.

Finally, to shape at least one sense of an ending to *Omens of Adversity*, the epilogue, "The Temporality of Forgiving," offers a brief reflection on forgiveness, a virtue that has become a kind of leitmotif in contemporary moral-political discussions of catastrophic aftermaths. I take up Hannah Arendt's well-known suggestion that the nature of human action, specifically its constitutive *uncertainty* and *irreversibility*, invites us to regard forgiveness as a necessary moral virtue. Forgiveness, it seems to me, brings the temporality of action very much into relief—not as the means of repressing unreconciled resentments, but as a reflexive attitude of critical recognition of the intractable agonism and risk of action, especially political action. The members of the Grenada 17 have all now been released from prison. But have they been released from their moral debt? Are *we* so certain of owing nothing to *them*? As I point out, the Grenada 17 have apologized for their role in the events of 19 October 1983 and sought forgiveness for the pain and suffering they caused by their actions while they led the revolution. But what of their suffering and pain? If, as I and others have suggested, the trial of the Grenada 17 was an utter travesty of justice, who bears responsibility for what *they* have endured? With whom does the moral burden of forgiveness lie? Who decides?

These chapters, it is easy to see, are meant to be exploratory. They constitute, together, an effort to capture *dimensions* of the political present that in some significant measure are the protracted aftermaths of the catastrophic collapse of revolutionary futures past and the re-hegemonization of the world by a cynical imperial and neoliberal agenda. These chapters seek to work in and through the experience of time, the temporality of past-present-future, because it seems to me that one arresting, if not altogether transparent, feature of our present is the strange out-of-jointness of time—an out-of-jointness that makes time itself pervasively conspicuous. The ghost of Augustine wanders among us. We are suddenly more aware than before that action—political action, say—is not merely historical in the familiar contextual senses. It takes place in time, is temporal, temporalizes, and is therefore always vulnerable to contingency and conflict that are not always reversible. We are suddenly more aware than before of just how much, and how uncannily, fictive models of time shape our experience of the past in the present and our expectations for the future. We are suddenly more aware than before of the temporality of generations, of experiences shaped by successive and overlapping locations within the passage of social time. We are suddenly more aware of how the collapse of emancipatory futures frames our imagining of what justice entails. So that in some respects, at least, these chapters form an arc of interconnected preoccupations stitching together the time of tragic action with the time of just repair. Finally, these chapters invite us to remember the Grenada Revolution. Written less as a comprehensive reconstruction of its historical rise and fall than through aspects of its catastrophic collapse and aftermaths, they invite us to unlearn some of our most cherished conceits about what counts in the scholarly scales of geopolitical relevance. We are obliged to remember the cynical "success" of truth and reconciliation in postapartheid South Africa, not its cynical failure in postrevolutionary Grenada. Yet an island, too, is a world and therefore world-*historical*.

The Grenada Revolution was undoubtedly flawed. It was politics, after all: on the whole, worthy men and women acting in concert and in conflict and in full exposure of the public realm to shape a more just and egalitarian world out of the colonial and neocolonial past, and with limited resources to hand. They succeeded. They failed. It was revolution, timely and untimely—a past revolution of our better selves.

PART I | TRAGEDY, TIME

Time is the most profound and the most tragic
subject which human beings can think about.
One might even say: the only thing that is tragic.
All tragedies which we can imagine return in
the end to the one and only tragedy: the passage
of time.

—SIMONE WEIL, *Lectures on Philosophy*

ONE

REVOLUTION'S TRAGIC ENDS

Temporal Dimensions of Political Action

> That men start a course of events but can neither calculate nor
> control it, is a *tragic* fact.
> —A. C. BRADLEY, *Shakespearean Tragedy*

In A. C. Bradley's elegantly stated paradox about human action in
time lies the whole of my preoccupation in this chapter with a certain reading of the collapse of the Grenada Revolution in October
1983. Tragedy arises, in Bradley's Hegelian view of it (and here, at
least, his chief concern is with Shakespearean tragedy specifically)
from the unavoidable fact that the reasoned and well-intentioned
actions of self-determining agents acting in time are pervasively
subject to contingency, and therefore to outcomes that are never
entirely predictable or guaranteed in advance.[1] One consequence
of this incalculableness of human actions is that they can never
be entirely shielded from conflicts and collision; action in collision, for Bradley (underlining Hegel), forms the generative epicenter of any tragedy. If in tragedy what we typically see depicted
is a story of exceptional suffering that leads ultimately toward the
destruction or death of a person of prominence whose calamity
registers as a disaster with resonant public meaning and social
significance, it is not the suffering or misery or even death as
such that summons the tragic effect (Aristotle's moral emotions,

fear and pity) but, rather, the characteristic structure of *action* in human conduct that propels the hero with irreversible momentum toward it. The point, in other words, is that tragic disaster does not merely *befall* the hapless hero; tragedies do not simply *happen*. They stem from the actions of agents acting in a field of potentially rival actions and in circumstances over which they can, in the end, exercise only partial and unstable control.

The specific problem with which I am concerned in this chapter is the unintended tragic consequences of moral agents acting, and colliding, in an expressly political field—as Max Weber put it, the "tragedy in which all action is ensnared, political action above all."[2] More specifically still, I am interested in revolutionary action where the consequences of tragic collision are considerably magnified. As Hannah Arendt and C. L. R. James in their different ways have helped us to appreciate, the modern social imaginary of revolution organizes itself around the idea of an *exceptional time* of crisis and dislocation in which human action, in its capacity to intervene, stands out starkly against established patterns, past action now congealed to automatism and repetition.[3] But revolutions are not only an extraordinary time of social and political upheaval. They are also a time of *exceptional human beings* who stand—momentarily—at the animating center of political affairs; whose actions are of unusual intensity and urgency; and who therefore inspire, by turns and sometimes together, awe and sympathy, admiration and terror; and whose errors, misjudgments, or conceits can bring ruin not only upon themselves but also upon the whole of which they are the leading part, and often upon the very ideal in whose service their actions were initiated. These would be Weber's charismatic leaders whose sometimes blind commitments to valuable causes expose them to a tragically debilitating vanity.[4] In the upheaval of modern revolution, you have one of those rare historical moments in which, because the old is rejected as intolerable and the new is as yet uncertain and unfamiliar—and, moreover, unwanted and resisted by the prevailing powers—human action is even more *exposed* than usual to the risks and hazards and treacheries of political affairs and therefore more vulnerable to the collisions that can lead to tragedy. Revolution, in short, is a time when everything seems at stake and, consequently, when everything can—and sometimes does—go wrong. Crises, mutations, transitions: these, as Karl Jaspers says, are the "zones" of tragedy.[5]

Revolutions and tragedy, therefore, have between them an uncanny but nevertheless adhesive intimacy. And few, perhaps, have been more alert to this intimate connection between tragedy and modern revolution than Raymond Williams was. "The tragic action, in its deepest sense," he wrote in that much-neglected book *Modern Tragedy*, first published in 1966, "is not the confirmation of disorder, but its experience, its comprehension, and its resolution. In our own time, this action is general, and its name is revolution."[6] Williams wrote *Modern Tragedy* in the midst of considerable political upheaval, social crisis, and mass violence (defined by the immediate aftermaths of the revelations about Stalin, the Hungarian Revolution and its crushing defeat by Soviet troops, and the escalating Algerian war of national liberation that underlined the poignancy and urgency of the unfolding anticolonial revolution). He also wrote it as a response to George Steiner's provocatively antimodernist (and anti-Marxist) death-of-tragedy narrative in which tragedy seemed severed not only from modern, but also from personal and historical-political, experience.[7] As was typical of the movement of his thinking, Williams sought in *Modern Tragedy* to connect the personal and historical-political experience of his time and, in particular, the senses of political temporality that grew out of his earlier book *The Long Revolution*, to the modes of intelligibility of tragedy.[8] The rise of revolutionary politics in the twentieth century, he suggested, had altered significantly the conditions of our experience and comprehension of tragedy (made it at once more ordinary and more acutely *social* in its significance), and fundamentally challenged the normative preeminence of the individualist structure of feeling embodied in the subgenre he called "liberal tragedy."[9] Needless to say, for Williams it was Marx who pointed the direction in which to rescue the idea of revolution from its reductive understanding as mere violence or as the mere overthrow of a standing government. Directly contrary to Steiner, for whom Marx was the paradigmatic anti-tragic figure, Williams saw in Marx precisely a thinker who grasped the long revolution as a "whole action," as a change in the "form of activity of a society, in its deepest structure of relationships and feelings," as he put it.[10] To comprehend revolution as a whole action in this way, Williams argued, was not to be blind to the inherent dangers of exposure to social and political disorder. After all, as the author of a dramatic tragedy centered on Stalin's political career, Williams was keenly aware that even authentic revolutionary commitments can congeal into nightmare regimes in which people are reduced to being merely the means to abstract, instrumental ends—so much so that, as he dryly put it, they can be "killed from lists."[11] Rather, Williams's point was to get us to see that the liberation and the terror are neither unconnected nor synonymous, but stood nevertheless pervasively in danger of being drawn together. This is why he concludes on the cautionary note that the "final truth in this matter seems to be that revolution—the long revolution against human alienation—produces, in real historical circumstances, its own new kinds of alienation, which it must struggle to understand and which it must overcome, if it is to remain revolutionary."[12]

But even such cautiously optimistic faith as Williams had in the future of revolution (however long the process of the whole action) has considerably dimmed in the more than forty years since he first published *Modern Tragedy*. The world upon which Williams gazed as he wrote that book at the end of the 1950s and beginning of the 1960s (notably, the same years in which James composed his revisions for the second edition of *The Black Jacobins* and Arendt wrote *On Revolution*) was still one that nurtured and sustained the hope and longing for revolution.[13] After all, the Grenada Revolution, for example, was yet to come; its dramatis personae were all young men and women, the inspired Caribbean generation of 1968, cultivating the dream of a self-determining island republic free of the tyranny and subjection that had defined its continuing colonial history. Williams's sobering sense of the intimacy between revolution and tragedy was meant to provide a moral compass for this generation's anticipated future to come, to temper the anti-tragic inclinations of revolutionary enthusiasm and ambition. By contrast, the world upon which I gaze, from within the historical experience of my own time, is a *disenchanted* world, a world defined precisely by the loss of that promise of revolution, a world of temporal aftermaths. The Grenada Revolution ended more than two decades ago, in a brutal catastrophe. Therefore, the question of the intimacy between revolution and tragedy is for me less a matter of immediate prospect than of *retrospect*, of recollection of the defeated and the dead; and the moral point of reading this intimacy is less to secure (in however tempered a form) the overall direction of the whole action of revolutionary politics than to suggest that what bears scrutiny more than before is our understanding of the *propensities* and *limits* of political action itself, political action in time: in *failure* and ruin as much as in success.[14] It may well be, as Arendt so often suggested, that "remembrance" is no idle cognitive-affective function, but the exercise of a critical mode of sustaining not only the hopes of the vanquished and the common world to which we—and they—belong but, perhaps, the only way to engage the possibility of reflecting on their conduct and that common world in new and unexpected ways.[15] This is why—to my mind, anyway—Bradley's aphoristic remark concerning the relation between action and tragedy is so worthwhile a thought with which to think.

Readers of Arendt's political theory, particularly the often pondered work *The Human Condition*, will no doubt be attuned to her "tragedy-inflected" conception of action; her characterization of the intrinsic "frailty" of the public realm, its constitutive vulnerability to tragic hazards, given action's unending and ineradicable temporality, boundlessness, contingency, and unreliability.[16] For Arendt, to act politically in time (which for her is to act disclosively and in freedom) is unavoidably to expose oneself to the potential collision of actions embodying rival ends, competing interests. This is the thought that inspires me: tragedy may be the price of freedom. And this tragic fact about political action invites reconsideration of the demands of political judgment and political responsibility. I suggest, in what follows, that the lessons to be derived from the terrible collapse of the Grenada Revolution are not to be sought in the registers of ideology or ambition as such, but in our understanding of the risk of tragedy that pervasively accompanies political action—our understanding of the fact, in other words, that tragedy is often the price of freedom.

My itinerary is as follows: First, I consider the story of the demise of the Grenada Revolution told by Brian Meeks in "Grenada: The Pitfalls of 'Popular' Revolution from Above," which forms a chapter in his *Caribbean Revolutions and Revolutionary Theory*.[17] Published two decades ago, it remains to my mind the best scholarly account that exists of those terrible events. Not only is it nuanced in its understanding of the social, historical, and political context of the revolution's emergence, and attentive to the tensions and paradoxes that beset the revolution's project, what is especially interesting to me is Meeks's intuition that the revolution's collapse can profitably be seen in terms of "tragedy," at least in the sense of a succession of events that seem to conduct the protagonists ineluctably and irreversibly toward a catastrophic end. Notably, though, Meeks is not interested in drawing out the implications of this sense of tragedy's theoretical claim on his narrative. Instead, he is concerned, as the title of his essay suggests, with laying emphasis on the dangers of elite populism to the integrity and progress of the revolutionary enterprise. By contrast, I am principally interested in enlisting the resources of tragedy as a guide for an inquiry into the problem of the temporality of action, especially the temporality of political action. Second, therefore, I sketch in outline Hegel's idea of tragic collision in such a way as to highlight the underlying phenomenology of action in time and the conceptions of contingency, pathos, and conflict that shape it. I mean to urge that Hegel offers an especially instructive perspective from which to begin to think about human finitude, the limits of certainty, and their tragic implications. Third, and against the background of this rehearsal of the problem of tragic action in Hegel, I redescribe the final collapse of the Grenada Revolution as a tragic collision—the collision, that is, of two substantive positions, neither of them altogether unjustified but each pursued with a heedless and mutually reinforcing blindness to the validity of the other. Finally, bringing the discussion of tragic action together with the redescription of the political-ethical collision among the revolutionaries in Grenada, I draw on Arendt's tragic conception of action and freedom to consider some of the implications of tragic collision for retrospectively examining political action—political action in the "living past."[18] Arendt does not acknowledge the influence of Hegel in her conception of action, but sufficient convergences exist between them to suggest that however critical she was of his thought, she was also, perhaps, indebted to it in important ways.[19] In any event, Hegel and Arendt develop comparable, if not identical, conceptions of action that are especially attuned to its constitutive temporality and therefore its intractable vulnerability to contingency and conflict. For both, tragic consequences are an ineradicable dimension of human action in time, and for the very reason that Bradley gives—namely, that human action consists of the initiation and conduct of activities over the course of which complete control is never possible.

My overall aim, it may reasonably be suspected, is not to offer a comprehensive explanation for the downfall of the Grenada Revolution that rivals or surpasses those accounts of political intrigue or ideological struggle that hitherto have dominated. As I have said, that story is still waiting to be written in all its multifaceted historical and political detail. My more circumscribed aim is to open up such events in the recent political past to an inquiry in which the ineliminable contingency of action and its implications can be more fruitfully considered. For it seems to me that such an exploration can provide one way to better appreciate the constitutive role of blindness in human knowledge and conflict in human action, and consequently affords a better vantage from which to think about the ethics of political judgment and responsibility.

Reading Revolutionary Failure

In the immediate aftermath of the collapse of the Grenada Revolution on 19 October 1983, and the invasion led by the United States that followed just days after, on 25 October 1983, a flurry of books sought to describe and explain what had taken place. Much of this work was overtly, unapologetically anticommunist, seeking merely to denigrate the revolution and to justify the invasion.[20] Some of it, however, was more balanced and thoughtful, attempting to offer more nuanced and sympathetic accounts of the internal political disaster that had overtaken the revolutionaries.[21] As I have suggested, by far the best account of the rise and fall of the revolution is the chapter by Meeks in his comparative study, *Caribbean Revolutions and Revolutionary Theory*. We will see in a moment that I disagree in some measure with the progressivist cast of the overall frame of his analysis, but what is instructive is that Meeks offers an account that displaces the persistent theme of "personality" and "conspiracy" that dominates the literature on the revolution's collapse.[22] Against this, he endeavors, as he says, to "place a more important role on the social formation within which the personalities operated and to raise serious questions on the nature and content of the personality and ideological clashes as they did occur."[23] In doing so, he develops an insightful account attuned to what he sees as the generative paradoxes that simultaneously shaped and constrained the conditions in which the revolutionaries acted and which they seem to have been unable to overcome. This, as I will show, is where he registers his sense of the Greek tragedy-like character of the catastrophe of the collapse of the Grenada Revolution.[24]

The central feature of the Grenada social formation around which Meeks's story of the making and unmaking of the revolution turns is the entrenched "paternalism" that derived historically from the "vast social, educational and linguistic gap" that existed between those at the top of the society and those at the bottom.[25] This paternalism was reinforced under the long modernizing, authoritarian rule of Eric Gairy. Meeks argues, however, that during the revolution, this tendency was not reversed or undone. To the contrary, it was strengthened and reinscribed in a more fatal social and political dynamic. This paternalism enhanced tendencies toward the political monopoly of power and therefore authoritarianism.

When the New Jewel Movement (NJM) was formed in March 1973 out of the merger of two existing political formations—Joint Endeavour for Welfare, Education, and Liberation (JEWEL) and Movement for Assemblies of the People (MAP)—it adopted what Meeks characterizes as a "Jamesian" approach to radical politics. As he describes it, this is an approach inspired by C. L. R. James's thinking about revolutionary political action that resisted hierarchical party structures (thus, the joint leadership of Maurice Bishop from MAP and Unison Whiteman from JEWEL), that valued inclusion and openness rather than exclusion and secrecy in political organization, and that criticized vanguardist conceptions of political action in favor of the spontaneity of mass action.[26] But with the revolutionary "upsurge" of late 1973–74, as the struggle against Gairy's increasingly brutal and tyrannical regime intensified (and as it seemed that the British colonial authorities would allow constitutional independence to go forward in 1974 despite the protests), there was a growing sense in the party that this mode of leftist organization and political opposition was less than effective.[27] As a strategy for the capture of the state, something else was needed. Thus, largely under the inspiration of Bernard Coard, the NJM began to transform itself into a Leninist vanguard party, on the view that what was required was a more tightly knit, more disciplined, and more doctrinally focused party form. Meeks is careful to underline that while the move toward Leninism was undoubtedly *initiated* by Coard— and did, indeed, provoke some opposition from party stalwarts such as Teddy Victor, Lloyd Noel, and Kendrick Radix—the majority, including Bishop, in fact endorsed it. The caution is crucial because in the wake of the revolution's collapse, Coard would be vilified as a power-hungry conspirator who maneuvered his supporters into key positions in the party in order to subvert Bishop's authority. Indeed, this became the almost unshakable narrative center of standard accounts of the collapse of the revolution. Moreover, as Meeks rightly argues, there was a wider regional (and in some sense *global*) context of intelligibility for the rise of Leninism: in the 1970s, leftist formations across the Third World were increasingly seeking to position themselves to take state power, not merely to agitate around popular causes. In this atmosphere, Leninism as an arguably successful party form was "not so much a choice but an irresistible current for bright, thinking persons."[28]

The shift to a vanguard political formation meant, of course, the rejection of the Jamesian model of the party as an agitational tribune with a relatively antihierarchical and inclusive organizational structure. This was now replaced by what Meeks describes as a "conspiratorial and hierarchical command structure with restricted membership and a hidden ideology."[29] Here a paradox emerged that would eventually prove fateful for the revolutionary project. The only way to capture state power in the specific conditions of Grenada (small size; largely rural, underdeveloped economy; relatively small educated class, and so on—the usual markers of a lack of revolutionary readiness) was by clandestine preparation and surprise attack. But this seemed to require a form of organization in which accountability and internal democracy could be, at best, only shallow, formal commitments. The one political value seemed to preclude the other. It appeared impossible to have both at the same time. As Meeks cogently writes, "Each Leninist measure which made the party more capable of taking power, also increased its tendency toward hierarchical decision-making and enhanced the autonomy of the leadership both from ordinary party members and the people."[30] Thus, for example, the creation of a military wing in 1975 at once improved the party's readiness for insurrection *and* "increased the tendency toward secrecy."[31] Or again, the introduction in 1978 of an "organizing committee" within the political bureau at once increased the party's efficiency *and* amplified the relative position of Bernard Coard vis-à-vis Maurice Bishop within the party.[32]

The internal restructuring of the NJM, then, was largely hidden from public view. Whereas in 1974 the party program, structure, and leadership were a matter of public knowledge (published in the party's newspaper, *New Jewel*), with the conversion to Leninism only the leadership was now privy to knowledge about decisions regarding direction, policy, and comrades. The public knew nothing about the internal decision to transform the party; thus, to them the party of the late 1970s was still the popular tribune of 1974. As Meeks neatly summarizes it, "This both eroded the popular connection and increased the sense of sectarianism in those few privileged to possess the knowledge or 'science.' It also had the potential to generate distrust and betrayal, depending on the manner in which this divergence was revealed as, it is suggested, was the case at the time of the 1983 crisis and fall of the revolution."[33] Moreover, this entire scenario of accumulating contradiction would be further complicated when in 1976 the anti-Gairy coalition, the People's Alliance (consisting of the NJM, the old Grenada National Party, and the newly formed United People's Party), won six of fifteen seats in the House of Assembly, and Bishop formally became the leader of the opposition.[34] For now, supplementing the party's hierarchical form, there was a new dimension of potential conflict. As Meeks describes it, two poles were now emerging within the NJM, "one centred around the party with Coard at its head and the other, with Bishop as its leader, on the question of national leadership. In 1976, this was embryonic, but in retrospect it is difficult to deny that there was the potential for further tension in this divergence of command."[35] This tendency would only be exacerbated when, in the wake of the revolution, Bishop became the head of state.

Indeed, in late 1983, it is precisely this tension that led down the road to catastrophe. In the summer of that year, an internal crisis concerning the structure of leadership was becoming more and more acute. And in September and October, as the crisis unraveled, the leadership took a familiar path: "accustomed to ruling from above, they sought to resolve the crisis from above, by tinkering with the structure and form of leadership."[36] But, Meeks laments,

> Such an approach failed to recognize that two diverging "logics" had been at work, at least since the 1976 elections, and certainly since 13 March 1979. These were: the logic of the supreme leader and the logic of the vanguard party. Both logics operated within the parameters of "rule from above," and as the differences intensified in September, both trends at first sought to keep them within the leadership and resolve them in a manner in harmony with hierarchy and bureaucracy. In the end, it was only the logic of the leader which could and did appeal to

the people, but it did so without rupturing the structures and norms of the deeply entrenched paternalist relationship.[37]

This is an enormously insightful observation. And Meeks goes on to add:

> It is my belief that there was no established conspiracy, there were no substantial ideological or tactical differences and, although personality differences did, of necessity, intercede, the overarching issue was the growing disconnection of the leadership tout court from the people, which, coupled with the depth of the crisis and the physical strain of paternalist rule, drove them to take irretrievable decisions. Once these were taken, the "gridlock of events" followed its own logic, in which pride, misunderstanding, innuendo, external intervention and further rash action, each served to stoke the fire, leading like a Greek tragedy to the eventual *dénouement*. If this approach is not simple, for me it is the only satisfying one, able to explain that rapid transition from fraternity to antagonism which I noted in 1983, and have not forgotten.[38]

Here, to my mind, is an account of profound sensibility and critical illumination. Tinged with the melancholy of revolutionary regret, it is unmarred by disenchanted dogma or reductionism, and attuned analytically to the internal contradictions of the unfolding political crisis and the intractable conundrum that seemed to propel the revolutionaries to their doom. There is about Meeks's narrative of the collapse of the Grenada Revolution the haunting spirit of C. L. R. James and Raymond Williams and Karl Jaspers, the moving apprehension of the loss of so much that was so possible for so many of undoubted virtue.

Significantly, though, Meeks does not press his intuition about the *tragedy* of the collapse of the revolution, as James might have, or Williams, or Jaspers. As mobilized here, "tragedy" seems invoked to add a merely *literary* allusion to the otherwise discursive account, gesturing at a generic caption for the catastrophic end of insoluble paradox. It does not, though, shape in any *generative* way the conceptual structure of the narrated event or organize our understanding of its implications. It does not, perhaps most significant for our purposes here, interrupt the conventional notion of history and its conceit of a seamless identity with the temporality of human action. Indeed, as though drawing back from the possible abyss of tragedy's unmasterable temporal warrant, Meeks reverts to the familiar progressivist axiomatics of revolutionary "failure" and the consoling, anticipatory teleology of the future promise of revolution: "the fall of the revolution was essentially a crisis of democracy and the failure of the leadership to escape from a deeply-entrenched structure of hierarchy which it inherited. The lessons for the future of the Caribbean can easily be derived from this."[39] And of course the principal lesson to be learned from the Grenada catastrophe for a future revolutionary moment is that a more subaltern approach, a more authentically *popular* populism, a more genuine democracy, a more *something* might have saved the revolution from devouring itself. I am not so sure.[40] I am not sure whether there are not other lessons that run directly counter to this confidence in history's promises, however subaltern they may be. One is reminded here of Giorgio Agamben's very Benjaminian observation (discussed in the prologue) that revolutionary conceptions of history very often harbor the most conventional notions of time and action; and the disjunctures in which history and time no longer coincide are likely to be those of crisis and catastrophe, when human action takes the most surprising, sometimes fatal turns.[41] One is reminded, further, of Arendt's reflections on how easy it has been (in our zeal to envision ourselves as sovereign "makers" of history) to disdain and distrust the more unstable and unpredictable realm of human action in time.[42] So it may be, then, that the more instructive lesson to be learned from tragedy—from Greek tragedy especially, with its attunement to moral and political emotions (hubris, hamartia, anger, shame, resentment, envy, fear) and to accidental temporalities (reversals, contingency, luck)—is that there is a register that is often overlooked by the influential philosophic history that supports Meeks's account, namely, the dramatic register of human action.[43] This lesson might suggest that precisely those dimensions of human action to which Meeks draws our attention almost as an inadvertent aside ("pride, misunderstanding, innuendo, external intervention and further rash action") are more significant than he is willing to allow, more complexly at work in the motivations, decisions, and judgments that shaped (or misshaped) the unintended consequences of the tragic events his narrative so eloquently describes. These dimensions of human action, moreover—the alterities of the moral and political emotions, the colliding contingencies of acting in time—suggest that our vulnerability to tragedy (or, at any rate, our inability to completely shield ourselves from it by our reasons) may be a pervasive feature of human action, and of *political* action more so than any other.

Action, Agonism, Finitude, Tragedy

Through A. C. Bradley, we have already caught a glimpse of Hegel's idea of tragic collision. The place of this idea in Hegel's thought—in particular, its place in the distinction between Aristotle's concern with a "poetics" of tragedy, the proper compositional elements of a dramatic form, on the one hand, and Hegel's with a "philosophy" or theory of the tragic, of a particular kind of experience, on the other—has been the topic of some very illuminating and provocative reflections. These discussions to a very considerable degree have shaped the direction of my preoccupations.[44] For my purposes, however, it is enough to bear in mind that from his earliest writings (the so-called Frankfurt theological writings) through the *Phenomenology of Spirit* (of the Jena years), and most prominently and systematically in the late *Lectures on Aesthetics* (from the Heidelberg and Berlin periods), the question of tragedy was a pervasive and generative (if not always explicit or direct) one for Hegel.[45] For my purposes, too, it is as well to note that the political-historical moment in which tragedy's impact on Hegel's philosophic inquiry emerges is that of revolution, a fact that Williams might have found significant.[46] At the center of Hegel's emerging preoccupation with the tragic as a form of experience was the problem of *conflict*. While it is true that there was a deep and abiding interest in tragedy and, moreover, adumbrations of a focus on conflict as the *essence* of tragedy among his near-contemporaries in the post–Kantian German Romantic movement (think of Schelling's idea of tragedy as a conflict between freedom in the subject and objective necessity, or Hölderlin's idea of tragedy as a conflict between art and nature), Hegel's is arguably the first significant critical exposition of tragedy *systematically* understood in terms of contradiction, self-division, incommensurability, strife, and struggle.[47] Prior to Hegel's reflections on the subject, Michelle Gellrich suggests, for example, accounts of tragedy—guided in large part by an agonistic engagement with Aristotle's formal and thematic concerns in the *Poetics*—are typically muted, if not silent, on the deep problem of the otherness of conflict.[48] In Hegel's thought, by contrast, the idea of tragic conflict is more constitutively generative—indeed, foundationally so—for understanding the disjunctures and discontinuities in the life of Spirit. As Peter Szondi has insightfully argued, the origin of Hegel's speculative thought on the tragic is "at one" with the origin of his thought on dialectic. In Hegel's thought, Szondi writes, "the tragic and the dialectic coincide"—or, put somewhat differently, "The tragic process is the dialectic of ethics."[49] Consequently, the idea of the tragic—and tragic conflict—comes to have a pervasive presence in his philosophy. Hegel turns to the idiom of tragedy—just as Nietzsche, Heidegger, Benjamin, and others in the post-Kantian heritage after him would—for resources to help him overcome the entrenched Platonism of the Western philosophic tradition.[50]

For Hegel, as we have seen, while tragedy is a dramatic representation of misfortune and suffering that unexpectedly befalls a person of intrinsic worth and high esteem, and that often (though not always) ends in disaster and human wreckage, it is not the spectacle of wretchedness and misery that is itself tragic and that solicits our fear and pity. Such misery, he says, may well come upon a person without their contributing to it and without their being at "fault"—merely, in other words, as a consequence of external or natural circumstances.[51] However "harrowing" such misfortune may be, it is not specifically tragic for Hegel because it has not proceeded from the agency of human *action*. Here, then, is the *epicenter* of Hegel's idea of tragic collision: action. Truly tragic suffering, Hegel says, "is only inflicted on the individual agents as a consequence of their own deed which is both legitimate and, owing to the resulting collision, blameworthy, and for which their whole self is answerable."[52] In tragedy, in other words, human action comes into conflict with other human action, and in this collision of action, particular embodied aims, passions, or interests assert themselves against particular others that obstruct or otherwise impede their satisfaction, so that action becomes mired in intractable strife. And because tragedy is centrally about deeds, and only doers do deeds, only actions can be *praiseworthy* or *blameworthy*; action for Hegel *entails* answerability and therefore responsibility. This, as I will show, is a point of considerable moral and political significance.

"Action" is a central term in the Hegelian lexicon, as important to the earlier theory of Spirit and history in the *Phenomenology* as for the mature understanding of drama in the *Aesthetics*.[53] Indeed, for Hegel dramatic poetry is a privileged domain of aesthetic practice because what we see on stage is precisely a *mimesis* of human action, and tragic drama in particular is a mimetic enactment of those actions in opposition and negation and division that are of the very essence of ethical life and of the self-movement of the dialectic of history. Here, as a number of commentators have pointed out, Hegel shows his indebtedness, however constrained, to Aristotle—not only to his famous definition in the *Poetics* of tragedy in terms of "action" as opposed to "character" (as a modern, Hegel was very interested in the role of character), but more fundamentally in his *conception* of action itself.[54] As Hegel expresses it vividly in the *Aesthetics* lectures, action is the "vehicle through which the great powers in their conflict and reconciliation" are disclosed; it is the "clearest revelation of the individual, his temperament as well as his aims; what a man is at bottom and in his inmost being comes into actuality only by his action."[55] (We will later see this understanding of action elaborated in the work of Arendt.) What Hegel is articulating here is a conception of action in which our purposes are understood to be internal to, and coterminous with, our actions and not to precede them as extrinsic, pre-existing motivations. In contrast to causal theories of action (Cartesian ones, empiricist ones) that depend on a separation between an agent's motives and the action that follows from them, on Hegel's view, our purposes (partially anyway) *constitute* our actions—that is, as Charles Taylor puts it in a well-known essay, actions are "intrinsically directed"; they are "inhabited by the purposes that direct them."[56] Purposes and actions, therefore, are *co-constitutive*. Consequently, an agent's purposes only become manifest, as it were, *retrospectively*, as they emerge from the unfolding action itself. Against the view that rational agents enjoy an incorrigible, immediate knowledge of their motives *prior* to acting, Hegel's "corrigibilist" perspective holds that our knowledge of our intentions is imperfect, our self-awareness incomplete, and therefore we do not in fact know with certainty what we do, or why we do it.[57]

Embodying the volitional propensities of will and initiative and purpose, action for Hegel comprehends not only the cognitive faculties of our reflective reason but also the register of our *pathos*, our affective capacities for, and dispositions toward, emotional states of pity or sorrow or compassion or anger or fear. Again, there is the trace of Aristotle—here the *Rhetoric*, in particular. But for Hegel, it is in the tonality or "living activity" of pathos that the distinctive shape of a "character" appears, so that what is *disclosed* in action are not only individuals in their general humanity, but individuals in their rich *individuality* and, consequently, in their *finitude*.[58]

Moreover, action for Hegel is always at once *plural* and *worldly*—plural inasmuch as a human life is never reducible to a single purpose but rather is multiple in its ends and diverse in its projects, and worldly insofar as action inhabits, not the rarefied region of the gods but the mundane and circumstantial domain of human affairs.[59] What follows from this is that action is always vulnerable to contingency, to chance, and to accidents. It is therefore easy to see that, setting in motion as it does a plurality of aims and interests, action is bound to give rise to *agonism* in human relations, and even to *collision*. Conflict, in short, is an *endemic* feature of human action in the world of affairs.

In tragic action specifically, according to Hegel, we see a collision of the "ethical powers," the essential powers or principles that claim our strongest allegiance (family, civil society, and the state are famously the powers that animated his understanding). Each of these principles or powers exerts an equally valid claim, but they sometimes serve ends that are incompatible and irreconcilable with each other, and sometimes as a result they find themselves in situations of rivalry in which (as, for example, in Sophocles's *Antigone*, Hegel's paradigmatic tragedy) the principle of family claims what the principle of state refuses.[60] "The original essence of tragedy," Hegel writes, consists "in the fact that within such a conflict each of the opposed sides, if taken by itself, has justification; while each can establish the true and positive content of its own aim and character only by denying and infringing the equally justified power of the other."[61] The reason that these competing forces develop to this point of collision is because of the "one-sidedness" of the character through whom the rival ethical claims are made. The character of the tragic hero is distinguished from that of ordinary mortals by an uncompromising *one-sidedness*, a concentration of pathos that drives them single-mindedly and with absolute determination toward their aims and sometimes, therefore, toward their doom. This one-sidedness of pathos, says Hegel, is the real ground of tragic collisions.[62]

In a world of difference, conflict is ineradicable and unavoidable, and tragic collision is at least very nearly so. Such is an invaluable Hegelian truth. Where there is active ethical life—which is to say, a life of action in the given mortal world—in which finite individuals act and interact in and through the nonidentical passions, aims, and interests that organize their distinctive ends, there is bound to be agonism and disunion. But such agonism and disunion only lead to tragic collision where they come, as they sometimes do, to be embodied in a one-sided pathos, in a determined and exclusive attachment to the singularity of *one* of the essential powers that rule and, in certain circumstances, "over-master" the human will. For Hegel, the occasion for such tragic collisions is neither an evil or criminal intention nor a mere misfortune. To the contrary, in tragedy what we see, in a compelling and fearful way, are individuals of worth and esteem acting with ethical justification and coming into opposition with other individuals who similarly are acting with ethical justification; and increasingly absorbed in the mutually exclusive pathos of their irreconcilably one-sided pursuit, they react against and eventually destroy each other in the hubris of their blind determination to carry out their own ends.

Of course, for Hegel, such conflict appears in the historical world only to be superseded or transcended by a tragic *resolution* that annuls the false one-sidedness of the exclusive claim and, by virtue of the everlasting work of "eternal justice," restores the affirmative harmony of the Absolute. This is his story of the ultimate progress of Spirit. ("The true development of the action," Hegel says, "consists solely in the cancellation of the conflicts as conflicts, in the reconciliation of the powers animating action which struggled to destroy one another in their mutual conflict."[63]) Only by this rational design, as he put it, "can our hearts be morally at peace; shattered by the fate of the heroes but reconciled fundamentally."[64] To post-Hegelians, at least, it may be a doubtful story that such tragic reconciliation can *always* be guaranteed, at least in the historical world of political actualities. In her illuminating reading, for example, Michelle Gellrich shows how, by making the negativity of conflict but a moment in a continuous dialectical process always moving progressively toward higher resolutions, Hegel is able to *tame* tragedy's association with dissolution and disorder, with division and contradiction. The dialectical mediation, in other words, is the philosophical mechanism by which Hegel is able to *render* collision a mere aspect of a larger and permanent principle of order and unity.[65] According to Gellrich's reading, therefore, it will turn out that Hegel, no less than Aristotle, is invested in the *management* and *mastery* of tragic conflict and in foreclosing—and thereby evading—the fuller moral implications of the tragic for human action.[66]

Certainly, this is one—not unfamiliar—direction from which to come at the work of Hegel's idea of unity and reconciliation in the *Phenomenology* and the *Aesthetics* lectures. From another direction, however—one I think of as exemplified in the subtle work of Theodore George—Hegel's vision of the human spirit may be said to be guided not simply by his teleological confidence in our capacity to unify our experience, but also (and more importantly) by a somber recognition of the limits of that capacity, a recognition, in other words, of our human *finitude*. This is what George sets out to demonstrate in the reading that constitutes his splendid *Tragedies of Spirit*.[67] As he puts it, "One of the questions we must ask is whether Hegel's conception of the speculative unity in the *Phenomenology* is not simply preoccupied and enriched by his uses of tragedy, but instead comes to be predominated, perhaps even transformed by them. . . . In his more tragic moments, it is one of my intentions to suggest, Hegel enables us to catch sight of a view that allows us to identify our dignity as human beings not so much with the scope of our powers, but instead with our resolve to accept, even apprize, and cherish the terms of our finitude."[68] This, for George, would be the tragic wisdom of the Hegelian dialectic: that the upward journey of Spirit, however seemingly reflectively self-aware, is never completely transparent to itself, never completely sheltered from reversals and losses, and *therefore* never completely invulnerable to tragic contingencies:

> Throughout Hegel's presentation of its experience, one of consciousness' deepest needs is to integrate and unify its experience. In one of Hegel's more poetic turns of phrase, this aspiration is consciousness' desire to recognize itself as being at home in the world. But as we have seen, in the course of consciousness' development, it is continually forced to concede that this destination of home remains beyond its reach, and, thus, it remains a stranger in its world. . . . From this standpoint, the final wisdom of tragedy would emphasize not the scope of our powers to understand and transform the conditions of existence, but, rather, the transformation we ourselves undergo as we reflect on our limits.[69]

According to this reading, then, without trying to dissolve the dialectical tension one way or the other George urges us to see how Hegel uses the resources of tragedy to elucidate the structures and operations of our finitude. If it is undeniable that Hegel is ever looking forward to the Absolute, it is at least equally undeniable that his conception of human experience points also to the intractable pervasiveness of tragedy. This aporetic reading of Hegel seems to me most helpful in keeping before us the permanent sources in human action of strife and difference, of one-sided pathos, and the fatal collisions that are often their unintended consequences.

Tragic Collision in Revolutionary Political Action

Against the background of this discussion of action and tragic collision in Hegel's thought, I return now to the tragic *mise-en-scène*, so to speak, of Grenada, October 1983, and the spectacle of the final crisis within the revolutionary party that ultimately led to violence and death and the irreparable destruction of the four-and-a-half-year-old revolution. I argue, following Hegel (and Bradley reading Hegel) that it is not so much in the suffering that attended, or that ensued from, the events of 19 October 1983, that the profound tragedy of the Grenada Revolution lies, terrible and everlasting as that suffering has been, but rather in the unyielding conflict and irreversible collision that conducted the principal actors toward the catastrophic breach that forever destroyed them and the revolution they had made. Specifically (and admittedly, leaving a good deal of the story to the side), I will redescribe the last weeks of the unfolding crisis within the NJM—between the introduction of the proposal for joint leadership of the party in mid-September 1983 and the final armed confrontation a little more than a month later on 19 October—in such a way as to highlight how a one-sided and exclusive attachment to positions or principles, not in themselves necessarily invaluable or self-evidently illegitimate, contributed to the creation of a context of misunderstanding and mistrust among a relatively close-knit group of politically committed comrades, and effectively precluded the possibility of reconciliation or resolution.

Obviously, my point here is *not* that the tragic end was the *fate* of the revolutionary actors in Grenada (whatever that might mean). My point, instead, is to emphasize the role of action in time in these political events—its pervasive contingency and ineradicable unpredictability and its susceptibility to political emotions (pathos) such as fear and anger and resentment—and to underscore thereby the Hegelian insight that tragedy inheres in the elementary fact that while we can initiate action, we cannot entirely calculate or control its final outcome. In the last section of the chapter, I will come back to some of the implications for judgment and responsibility of taking seriously the fact of the constitutively fragile character of political action.

In the course of the "extraordinary meeting" of the Central Committee of the NJM that took place between 14 September and 16 September 1983, Liam James, a ranking member of the party and, at the time, chief of intelligence and deputy minister of defense and interior in the People's Revolutionary Government, introduced a seemingly straightforward proposal to create a joint-leadership structure within the party. It is this new action, this initiative—in proximate terms, anyway—that, in triggering other actions, and others again, precipitated the collision that ended in the catastrophe of 19 October 1983. The Central Committee of the NJM, it seemed, had been in emergency meeting almost continuously for months looking for a way to resolve what the party's leader, Prime Minister Maurice Bishop, described as a "deep crisis in the party and revolution."[70] Although it was not widely known at the time outside the closely controlled and secretive Central Committee (recall Meeks's description of the NJM's post-1974 character), this apprehension that something was fundamentally amiss in the internal functioning of the party was not entirely new. In fact, the year before, in 1982, the matter had come to a head when Deputy Prime Minister and Minister of Finance Bernard Coard (effectively also the deputy leader of the party), resigned from the party's two crucial organs—the Organizing Committee and the Central Committee—in the hope that his absence would encourage internal reform. As is clear from the minutes of the Central Committee meeting convened on 12–15 October 1982 to discuss the matter and its implications for the party, Coard's decision (made, in fact, six months earlier) turned principally on what he referred to as "strain" compounded by his sense that his authority as chairman of the Organizing Committee was systematically being undermined.[71] Furthermore, Coard was reported as indicating that he was frustrated by the lack of discipline of Central Committee members, their timidity in speaking up on issues, their lack of preparation for meetings, and their unwillingness to study. As things stood, he said pointedly, if he were to deal with the situation in the manner he thought was required, it was likely to lead to "personality clashes" with the chairman of the Central Committee—namely, Bishop—and in this he was unwilling to engage. His presence in the Central Committee, he said, had now become a "fetter" on its further development, and he was therefore offering his nonnegotiable resignation.[72]

As it happened, however, Coard's resignation did not have the hoped for disciplining effect. On the contrary, the deterioration in the internal work of the main organs of the party, as well as party work among the mass of the population, continued unchecked—so much so, in fact, that one can detect less than a year after the discussions of the circumstances of Coard's resignation a creeping atmosphere of panic that the Central Committee was in a desperate state and that the party, again in Bishop's dire characterization, was "faced with the threat of disintegration."[73] Discernible now from the minutes of Central Committee meetings was the gathering momentum of an inchoate internal storm reaching for an idiom in which to articulate its malaise. Whereas hitherto, analysis and discussion of the problems within the Central Committee had turned on vaguely articulated generalities (such as the need for more informed study and better ideological preparation among members), a new sense of urgent purpose frames the watershed meeting of 14–16 September. To begin with, Bishop's agenda was sharply criticized and categorically rejected (by Liam James) as "lacking in focus," and an alternative one was proposed (by John "Chalky" Ventour) and accepted (by Bishop) that was principally concerned with the state of the revolution and the party and, in particular, the working of the Central Committee. However, after very frank discussion largely concerned with the overwhelming sense of the weaknesses of the Central Committee, Bishop could offer no more than a rehearsal of now familiar and largely ineffectual platitudes—namely, that there was a crisis in the party and the revolution; that its main contributing factor was the "malfunctioning" of the Central Committee; that this had led to the "low mood" of the masses; and that to correct this trend, improvements needed to be made in the work and in the individual and collective leadership of the Central Committee, a proper Marxist-Leninist perspective had to be developed to guide its work, and the links between the party and the masses had to be deepened.[74]

But Bishop had obviously *misjudged* the new mood of determination among his comrades. These well-worn measures would no longer suffice to assuage the worry or quell the growing disaffection within the Central Committee. In a pointed, no-holds-barred line of criticism, James bluntly asserted that the problem with the Central Committee was not merely the admittedly "low ideological level" of many of the comrades; rather, the "most fundamental problem" lay in the "quality of leadership" of the Central Committee provided by Bishop himself.[75] In James's view, Bishop's acknowledged strengths—his unerring ability to inspire, raise regional and international respect for the revolution, and translate the party's positions to the country and to the world—indispensable though they were, were inadequate for the immediate task of pulling the party and the revolution back from the brink of collapse. What was needed, James argued, was a different set of skills—namely, a "Leninist" level of organization and discipline; depth of "ideological clarity"; and "brilliance in strategy and tactics."[76] These, he maintained, were aptitudes that, while patently lacking in the comrade leader, were possessed in abundance by Bernard Coard (who, of course, was no longer a member of the Central Committee, and therefore not privy to this discussion). James went on to propose a structure of "joint leadership" that would "marry," as he put it, the complementary strengths of these two preeminent leaders of the party and revolution. Bishop, in this scenario, would be responsible for work with the masses, militia mobilization, and regional and international work, while Coard would undertake work on party organization, strategy, and tactics.[77]

James's intervention was unprecedented; it was, perhaps, the first time that anyone, besides Coard, had ventured to be so bold as to openly and directly criticize Bishop in this way. James's proposal, though, was a masterstroke in that, in a single simple design, it made visible and intelligible the structure of the problem within the party, and offered a clear, arguably self-evident solution.[78] But fatally, in doing so, it simultaneously and unknowingly gathered up within itself all of the accumulating contradictions simmering below the surface of relations within the party and brought them to an explosive, catastrophic head.

A very robust discussion followed James's proposal in which the vast majority of Central Committee members endorsed his idea and supported its rationale and justification.[79] Bishop's response, however, was markedly tentative, ambivalent, and uncertain. He seems to have been discomfited—*discomposed*—as if taken off guard, as if trying less to engage the rational, discursive content of the proposal itself (the idea of joint leadership) than to discern the possible *subtext* of the action involved in the initiative. Warmly congratulating his comrades on the evidence of their "ideological growth" and maturity, he went on to affirm, perhaps somewhat defensively, that he had no problem "sharing power"; nor did he have, as he put it, a "bad attitude to criticism" of his well-known shortcomings. Moreover, he said, coming to the more delicate issue, he had always worked well with Coard, since their schoolboy activism, and recalled how closely they had worked together on the party manifesto.[80] Alluding to the period in 1977 when Coard had successfully spearheaded the establishment of the Organizing Committee within the Central Committee and was accused of seeking to establish a rival power base within the party, Bishop reminded his comrades that he had been the first to defend Coard against his detractors.[81] He was, he went on, in favor of cooperation and agreed in principle with the breakdown of party responsibilities James proposed. However (and here we begin to glean the outline of the inchoate suspicion and fear gradually taking hold of him), besides wanting to know what Coard's view of the proposal was and what the Central Committee would decide if Coard disagreed with it, he was, he said, concerned with how the new arrangement would be operationalized and, in particular, how it would *appear* to the party and the masses. He was worried about "image of leadership, power struggle, [and the] imminent collapse of the revolution."[82]

Image, indeed, was a critical issue. For what in the proposal seems most to have unsettled Bishop was the unbidden apprehension of the complete disappearance of the old image of himself in the eyes of his comrades: flawed, yes, but unmistakably their leader, their *chief.* As he put it himself, in the emotionally laden language that came to him, the proposal seemed to indicate a "clear vote of no confidence" in his leadership—so much so, he said, that he could not imagine how he would continue to "inspire the masses" if he had to be looking over his shoulder in fear that he had lost the "full confidence of his comrades."[83] This must have been a bitter, even resented moment, indeed. Bishop now found himself in an unprecedented situation, for which he was wholly unprepared.

When the vote was eventually taken in the late afternoon of 16 September, a large majority voted in favor of joint leadership. Three people abstained (one of them being Bishop), and only one person opposed (George Louison, who had argued strenuously against the proposal).[84] The following day, 17 September, the Central Committee met to put its decision to

Coard and to invite him back into its ranks. However, while evidently encouraged by the new mood of engaged, no-nonsense decision making among the young comrades on the Central Committee, Coard's attitude toward the proposal appears to have been one of questioning caution. It is hard *not* to note in his reported speech a palpable weariness and exhaustion. He made known his concern that their meeting with him was being held in Bishop's absence, and he wanted to have a sense of what the character of the joint-leadership debate had been in the days before—whether other options had been explored and whether Bishop was understood to have agreed, at least in principle, with the proposal.[85] He was by no means keen to return to the Central Committee, he said, because he was tired of being seen as the "hatchet man" in party discussions—that is, the person responsible for criticism—and he was wary of the danger once more of giving the impression that he was seeking to undermine Bishop's authority in favor of his own. Here was tacit recognition that the question of rivalry (however imaginary in reality) was a genuinely sensitive one. Having expressed his misgivings, Coard nevertheless wanted his views put before the party as a *whole*, and this led to the historic meeting of the general membership of the NJM on 25 September 1983. By all accounts, the meeting was an overwhelming success. Again, there was both unanimous support among the general membership of the party for joint leadership and an overwhelming and moving show of love and admiration for Bishop. For his part, Bishop admitted to the party members that his response to the Central Committee's decision had been unwarranted ("petit bourgeois," he called it) and that he now accepted it in full, and agreed with the view that "joint leadership would help push the party and revolution forward."[86] At the end of the meeting, it is reported, the entire membership of the party broke out in a jubilant rendition of the Internationale and one by one filed past to embrace their two—now evidently joint—leaders, Bishop and Coard.[87]

Already, though, there was something ominously misshapen about this state of affairs. According to the view of the Central Committee and the party, a formal procedure of rational argumentation had been worked through, in good faith, to its end. Not only had the majority in the Central Committee spoken, but so had the majority in the party as a whole. In the course of this process, the Central Committee protagonists of joint leadership had managed to overcome Bishop's doubts and reluctance, it seemed, and had demonstrated that, contrary to his initial worry, his esteem was intact and his value to the Central Committee and the party was undiminished. As far as the Central Committee was concerned, therefore, the crisis had been rationally averted—a solution had been found for the larger problem of the party's malfunctioning, and the great work of the revolution could resume with renewed enthusiasm. It was, as we know, a *fatally* mistaken optimism.

Absorbed in the unimpeachable principle of procedure, as it was, the Central Committee had perhaps misjudged the aroused moral emotions—specifically, it had misrecognized Bishop's fears and unease as superficial and, as a result, miscalculated its ability to put them to rest by an exchange of reasons. Bishop was of course only too well aware of the Central Committee's concern about his personal indiscipline, his notoriously laissez-faire way of handling the party's affairs—not to mention his own. But he was also no doubt aware that his personal authority within the party and Central Committee, as well as his unrivaled stature among the population at large, made it difficult for anyone (with the single exception of Coard) to criticize him openly and seriously. After all, to many the name "Maurice Bishop" was synonymous with the Grenada Revolution. What could the party be without his leadership? What could the revolution be without his stewardship? Consequently, when his junior comrades now boldly and baldly asserted, one after another with almost one collective voice, that he was not only a dimension of the problem within the party but its *principal* source, that he lacked the qualities of leadership necessary to lead the party out of its current malaise, that what was now required was not his reform but his *supplementation*, it is easy to imagine that Bishop must have received all this as something like a body blow. His suspicions were understandably provoked. However carefully qualified the Central Committee would now be in its administrative and procedural detail, in the allocation of duties, and in reiterating its indebtedness to him, nothing could alter the simple fact that his undisputed authority in the party had been questioned and *therefore* compromised, and that, as a result, his stature could no longer be what *he* had assumed it was prior to the meeting of 14–16 September. Perhaps more than the formal matter of comradely critique of his individual failings (which, as he reiterates in the minutes, he was not uncomfortable accepting), his pride must have been mortally wounded. What Bishop had lost in a single stroke—in the proposal of joint leadership and the characterization it attached to him—was the implicit confidence, the *unquestioned* regard, of his comrades in the Central Committee. This was now gone, *vanished*, and it surely would have been obscure to him, to say the least, how it could have been restored to its former untarnished luster.

But the Central Committee, focused as it was on following procedure, seems to have been oblivious to this dimension of Bishop's ambivalent response. It might in any case have argued, and with justification, that such ambivalence was unwarranted, that after all, joint leadership had been an aspect of the structure of the NJM from its beginnings when JEWEL and MAP had merged and their two founders, Unison Whiteman and Maurice Bishop, respectively, became the joint coordinators of the new organization. But more than this, Bishop's response, his easy willingness to suspect his comrades of betrayal and subversion, might have led some to feel that he had—arrogantly—begun to conceive his role quite differently from what it had been in the early Jamesian days of the party's formation, and differently from what his comrades understood it *should* be. In other words, it might have led some to feel that a cult of leadership was emerging.[88] But whatever the case, the mutual unintelligibility—or, perhaps more accurately, mutual deafness—suggested that Bishop and the Central Committee were now set on a collision course.

As I have said, in the wake of the general meeting of the entire membership of the NJM on 25 September, there was a very widely shared sense that the crisis had been resolved, that Bishop now clearly recognized that there was in fact no conspiracy against him, and that joint leadership could only improve the overall functioning of the party. So when he left the following day on a state visit to (the now former) Eastern Europe, everyone felt that the breach had been avoided. Or anyway, *almost* everyone. Because what both sides perhaps sorely miscalculated was that the initial collision might set off other unpredictable actions. For example, it might trigger the action of those within the Central Committee whose harbored resentments might cause them to stoke Bishop's uncertainties; to urge him not to trust the Central Committee and Coard in particular; to induce him to see that his authority had in fact been irretrievably undermined; and to press him, therefore, to rescind his agreement on joint leadership. The shadowy figure of Louison looms large here, because he is alleged to have played a crucial role in misrepresenting the party's decisions to comrades abroad and in *inciting* Bishop to change his mind during the trip (for which he was later expelled from the Central Committee).[89] Fidel Castro, it is speculated, also reinforced the change of heart during Bishop's mysterious, unscheduled stopover in Cuba en route to Grenada from Europe.[90]

The fact, in any case, is that when he returned to Grenada on 10 October 1983, Bishop sought to reopen the discussion on joint leadership in order to reverse his earlier agreement. The Central Committee, however, declined to do so on a point of principle. Thus rebuffed, Bishop chose a drastic course of action that dramatically inflamed the already unstable situation and injected into the atmosphere a sinister and violent tone, propelling the conflict into a very different register: he released a wholly false rumor that Phyllis and Bernard Coard were planning to assassinate him.[91] In other words, thwarted in his attempt to reimpose his will on his Central Committee comrades, Bishop decided to appeal over their heads to the larger and more certain constituency of his unfailingly loyal supporters, the mass of the Grenadian population—and to appeal to them, moreover, in a potentially *incendiary* way.[92] In a certain sense, this was the real beginning of the end. In inviting the masses into the conflict in this way (a conflict about which they could have had only very imprecise knowledge), in drawing a line between the people on one side and the party on the other, and in personalizing the conflict by suggesting the picture of a titanic struggle between himself and Bernard Coard, Bishop irrevocably sealed the breach and opened the door to violence.

As is well known, Bishop was subsequently placed under effective house arrest. And while his supporters began to mobilize in the streets of the main towns, bringing the country's affairs to a standstill, a series of discussions began between a group representing the Central Committee and a group representing Bishop, seeking to find a workable resolution to what was now a veritable standoff (what Meeks graphically calls "gridlock").[93] Indeed, on the evening of 18 October, worried about the growing civil unrest and afraid of providing the United States with an excuse to invade (which it was known to have been preparing for), the Central Committee conceded everything to Bishop. It surrendered its one-sided demand for joint leadership and agreed to return to the status quo ante of the NJM, with the one proviso that Bishop agree to accept responsibility publicly for precipitating the crisis by going against the unanimous decision of the party. Thus, the one-sidedness of one side was obliged to capitulate almost entirely to the adamant, intransigent one-sidedness of the other. In the circumstances, perhaps, it was the *only* solution. Yet it was quite obviously *no* solution at all. The Central Committee had finally bowed to Bishop's indomitable will and to the will of the galvanized people speaking in his name. Demonstrating the full measure of his standing, Bishop had managed to secure what he wanted. But *had* he?

The following morning, when the final discussions were to take place (in which the details of the Central Committee's capitulation were to be worked out), Bishop allowed himself to be "liberated" from his house by a large demonstration waving placards threatening the Central Committee and Coard.[94] The demonstration then wended its way through St. George's in the direction of Market Square, where another large group of people was waiting to hear its leader speak. But at a certain intersection, Bishop and a contingent of the crowd changed course and headed toward Fort Rupert, the army headquarters, which they occupied, disarming the soldiers, opening the armory, and distributing arms to the civilians. It was a very grave decision to have made. What were Bishop's calculations in doing so? What motivated this *tragic* choice? Why did he break off negotiations with the Central Committee when they were on the verge of completion, and when he stood to gain virtually everything he was demanding? And then, once he had been "liberated" from his house, why did he choose an *armed* rather than a *political* solution, Fort Rupert rather than Market Square? Because overrunning Fort Rupert could only invite the People's Revolutionary Army into the standoff, transforming a political conflict into a potentially military one. One can only speculate what the answers to these questions might be. Perhaps in Bishop's view, it was already too late for politics. Perhaps events had already pushed him beyond the point at which the mere capitulation of the Central Committee could suffice to regain the ground he had lost. Perhaps something far more drastic was now required to ensure the return of his absolute authority, since after all, it would now be impossible to rule through the old NJM, let alone the erstwhile Central Committee. There are indeed many unanswered questions regarding Bishop's motives in choosing as he did at this point in the conflict (among them the calculation or miscalculation concerning a Cuban guarantee of armed support),[95] but what is certain is that the conflict was now set not merely on a path of *violence*, but even more threatening, on a decidedly *eliminationist* path. The decision to arm a popular opposition to the party and army guaranteed the irreversible doom of the revolution. It ensured that the conflict would end in catastrophic violence and death—as indeed it did.

The foregoing paragraphs redescribe in outline aspects of the unfolding conflict within the Central Committee of the NJM in such a way as to underline the Hegelian contours of a tragic collision between two one-sided positions, each claiming an exclusive legitimacy or, at least, an exclusive intelligibility. On one side was the overwhelming majority of the Central Committee (including Coard), standing, justifiably, on the recognizable principle of party procedure; on the other side was Bishop (and his close associates), standing, understandably, on the principle of loyalty to the comrade leader whose name embodied the revolution for so many. From the point of view of political judgment, what was lacking in this unfolding crisis? Better, more compelling reasons? More courage or inter-subjective imagination? What Kantian or Habermasian maxim might have saved them from each other and from themselves? As they collided with each other in adverse conditions—emotional and physical stress, threat of imminent US invasion, economic deterioration—the participants' stead-fast allegiance to their positions led to mutual suspicion and mistrust, fear and anger, that only entrenched the conflict, so that each move made by either side only deepened the dilemma and made the conflict more in-tractable, more irreconcilable, conducting it eventually to the catastrophe that destroyed their lives and destroyed the revolution. It is not important to my inquiry whether we can determine by some foolproof method the moral rightness or wrongness of one side or the other in this conflict; the moral *quality* of the individual acts is irrelevant to the collision. It is important only that what this entailed was a clash of irreconcilable powers, each demanding an absolute sway, an exclusive priority, over the other. And this denial to the other of any right or justification is what propelled both sides toward collective disaster.

In his revision of the Hegelian idiom of tragic collision, Bradley speaks eloquently of the tragic "waste" that results from "spiritual conflict" where what is at stake is of seeming *absolute* value. The more the spiritual value at stake, Bradley argued, the more tragedy in conflict and waste.[96] It is not hard, I think, to understand the catastrophic collision in Grenada in

September–October 1983 in terms such as these. For here were men and women selflessly and unequivocally committed to the same substantial ends, the same substantial hopes, but who in the pursuit of a one-sided vision of how to secure these ends and hopes found themselves in conflict with each other and, unable to compromise, were driven mercilessly to destroy almost everything they had sacrificed in the revolution to establish, including the revolution itself.

Tragedies of Freedom

Tragedy is the price of freedom. This, above all, is the lesson that I want us to take away from my description of the tragic collision that brought about the catastrophic collapse of the Grenada Revolution. Not that Marxism is bad, or that some Marxisms are worse than others; or that some men and women have vicious plans and are willing to go to extremes to achieve their ends. Rather, tragedy is the price of freedom. This is a Hegelian idea, to be sure, but one that has been given a particular shape in the thinking of Arendt in her considerations of human action in time and its distinctive relation to the human condition.[97]

Given the nature of human action in time, Arendt suggests—its boundlessness, its unpredictability, its uncertainty, its unreliability—to use one's freedom is inevitably an *invitation* to tragedy.[98] To act in freedom is to act self-disclosively among a plurality of other (only partially knowable) self-disclosive agents, themselves acting and reacting in time in relation to others in unpredictable ways and in temporally contingent circumstances. Therefore, to act in freedom is to initiate a pursuit of ends that, however reasoned, willed, or well-intentioned, are always in significant part *incalculable*. Shorn of the Hegelian metaphysic, Arendt is likely to have agreed with Bradley: that we can initiate action, but can neither fully control nor guarantee its outcome is a *tragic* fact.[99] She might only have added that it is also a fact of *freedom*. For freedom, Arendt reminds us, is not usefully thought of as a metaphysical substance; it does not belong to the realms of mind or will.[100] Freedom is the gift of human action, preeminently of *political* action; it is the consequence of our endowment with the capacity for (the temporal mode of) beginning, for the unprecedented, the improbable, even the miraculous.[101] But at the same time, given the fragility of human affairs and the frustrations to which action is ever exposed, freedom is also, and in equal measure, the *hazard* of action, and perhaps even its *curse*.

And nowhere is the risk of tragedy more present, more burdensome, and more consequential than in the upheaval of revolution, the *event* of modern political action par excellence. In undertaking to uproot the institutions and practices of the status quo, in daring to interrupt the necessity by which we are ruled and therefore to be otherwise than we have been obliged to be by the powers that have control over our lives, revolution is almost *purely* a matter of action, of intervention, of initiatives without precedent. Therefore, revolution entails a permanent exposure to risk and reversal.[102] By the same token, nowhere is the price of freedom more dearly paid than in the collapse or failure of revolution when *everything* has been risked in action—and *everything* has been lost to it. To act in freedom, as the Grenadian revolutionaries did in the pre-dawn hours of 13 March 1979 when they moved to take the army barracks at True Blue on the outskirts of St. George's, was to enact a break with the intolerable repetition of the tyranny of the Gairy regime, to refuse to be prisoners of a long colonial past and its traces in the imperialist present, and to strike out upon an uncharted road without a sure compass or any exact means of measuring the distance to be traveled or of defining—much less preventing—the certain dangers along the path. Thus, to have acted in revolutionary freedom, as these political agents did, was to have exposed themselves to such unforeseeable conflicts of interest and passion as, at a certain point, overtook them and eventually destroyed the small and fleeting spaces of freedom they had brought into being.[103]

The threat of tragedy casts a permanent shadow over political action. The point is not to suggest here that revolutionary actors (such as those who made the Grenada Revolution) are innocent or naïve—far from it. The principal difficulty of revolution (again, as James, Arendt, and Williams recognized) is less the immediate act of breaking with the old than that of institutionalizing the new, of establishing a sustainable, durable space for free political action.[104] Given the permanent vulnerability of human action to frustration, Arendt argues, there has always been a temptation to find a substitute for action, "in the hope," she says, "that the realm of human affairs may escape the haphazardness and moral irresponsibility inherent in a plurality of agents."[105] From Plato to Marx, Arendt maintains, this urge to banish uncertainty from the world of human affairs—to tame contingency and chance, to reduce the perplexities that come with the fact of human plurality, to impose on action the form of an ordered regularity—has attracted political thinkers and political leaders. Modern revolutionary movements have often sought to insulate themselves from the inherent unreliability of human action in one or both of two ways: they have sought to bind action to abstract and invariant principles or to bind action to a single personality—which is only to say, to degrade or defeat or preclude political action, properly speaking. They are, in this sense, *antipolitical*. As we have seen, the conflict that emerged within the Central Committee of the NJM might be described as a conflict between both of these mistaken ways of insulating politics from the pervasive hazards of human action: on the one hand, the abstract principle of party procedure, and on the other, the demand for the prerogatives of the commanding leader, the chief. The passionate one-sidedness with which they were respectively and exclusively adhered to ended not in a Hegelian resolution (like the aging Oedipus reconciled at last with "supreme justice"),[106] but in the tragic extinction, the tragic waste, of the revolutionary project as a whole.

Tragedy is the ineradicable risk to which we expose ourselves in the act of using our capacity for freedom. It may be that one of the moral implications of this truth is that political action, if it is to remain *free* political action and not to congeal into modes of unfreedom, ought to be guided as far as possible by the practice of certain virtues—namely, *modesty* and *responsibility*.[107] These virtues, needless to say, are not always near or dear to the volatile heroism of revolutionary actors (and I do not discredit heroism as necessarily unworthy), but, it seems to me, they are entailed by a tragic vision of political action; they are virtues that may be said to *follow* from the tragic wisdom that political action is permanently and unavoidably marked by opacities and therefore by outcomes that are not always calculable or intentional. Modesty and responsibility are expressly *moral* categories, bespeaking as they do the *ethos* of a certain attitude toward action and its aspirations. But I do not mean to offer them as *moralistic*—that is, as reflecting on the improprieties or otherwise of personal political behavior. I mean, instead, to offer them as entailments of an ethics of a properly tragic vision of political action in the sense that if you agree that such action ought indeed to be understood as I have described it, these virtues will be recognized as helping to foster a certain political morality:

on the one hand, modesty, to stay the inclination to hubristic confidence in our boundless capacity for mastery and self-mastery (our conceit, in other words, that history is merely waiting to be remade), and on the other hand, responsibility, to give reflexive pause to the tendency to see ourselves as merely determined by forces larger than ourselves and to which we are bound to surrender our capacity to act in freedom (our conceit that history is governed by abstract forces or laws). The story of modern political sensibility—particularly, modern revolutionary sensibility—has been the story of the unrelenting tension between the constructionism and necessitarianism that drives these respective orientations. A tragic vision of political action, such as the one that the Grenadian revolutionaries understandably but to their cost eschewed, perhaps in the erroneous belief that such a vision must be fatalistic or defeatist, is a vision of political action in which these virtues (modesty, responsibility) shape the imagination of the possibility of other beginnings.

TWO

STRANDED IN THE PRESENT
The Ruins of Time

> For to make sense of our lives from where we are, as it were,
> stranded in the middle, we need fictions of beginnings and fictions
> of ends, fictions which unite beginning and end and endow the
> interval between them with meaning.
> —FRANK KERMODE, *The Sense of an Ending*

In the lectures that comprise his unendingly stimulating book
The Sense of an Ending, Frank Kermode sought to draw our attention to the centrality, in lived experience, of the narrative fictions
of temporality through which we order our imagined relations
to pasts, presents, and futures. Fictions for him serve an essentially sense-making function; they are consolations of meaning.
And from where we *find* ourselves, stranded in the "middle" (Kermode's term for the discursive present in which we apprehend
our world), we have a sort of Aristotelian need to connect beginnings and ends to lend our lives a recognizable shape. Thus,
we compose fictive models of temporality, of time's passing, in
order, he says, to *humanize* cosmic time; to impose intelligible
paradigms on nature's time; to shape concords between beginnings, middles, and ends. As Kermode writes, the clock's "tick-
tock" is a model for what we call "plot"—that is, the discursive
organization that *configures* time by giving it a distinctive form,
and the "interval between 'tock' and 'tick' represents purely suc-

cessive, disorganized time of the sort we need to humanize."[1] The allure of endings, then, the way we project a fictive "sense of an ending" on time so as to produce an illusion of consonance between beginning and end, shapes the manner in which we make intelligible the fleeting interval of our lives. These fictive models of time, whether literary or historical, impart a certain reliable structure or pattern that—depending, for example, on whether they are informed by *chronos* (the idea of successive time) or by *kairos* (the idea of cyclical time)—renders the narrative passage from beginnings to endings in formally different ways, with perhaps formally different implications for the intelligibility of human experience. Memorably, Kermode was especially interested in the fictive model of "apocalyptic," the idea of the coming "end of the world," because it seemed to him crucial to our late modern notions of crisis and transition and change and redemption. Apocalyptic, and the eschatological time it embodies (the teleological time that carries us ineluctably through the Last Days toward our final End), was for him almost an archetype—a "radical instance," he called it—and one that, in its thematic concerns with progress and catastrophe, continues to shape how we make temporal sense of our moral lives and our moral world.[2]

Kermode, needless to say, has had his doubters and detractors—those, for example, who have lamented what they perceive to be an excessive abstraction, even a deliberate obscurity, and a tendency to project onto literature a metaphysical concern with time that it does not, properly speaking, possess.[3] I am not so sure that there lurks in Kermode—or, anyway, in *The Sense of an Ending*—a specious metaphysics of presence by which the assumption of a background of "pure time" guarantees his methodological reflections, or if so, what damage it does to his central insights and intimations. In any case, Kermode remains instructive to me because what he attunes us to is the *artifice* of temporality by which we arrange or order our experience. More than this, though, he orients us not only to the idea that how we live in time is not *given*, but also to the idea that how we live in the present—stranded in the "middest," as he might say—depends very much on our projection of the *ending* of our story. This strikes me as enormously important to how we think about the interconnections among pasts, presents, and futures.

Perhaps the single most sustained attempt in recent decades to think about human time or temporal experience has been Paul Ricoeur's magisterial three-volume work, *Time and Narrative*, a hermeneutic-phenomenological study of vast scope published in the 1980s.[4] In many ways inspired by Kermode (and subjected to some of the same criticism), Ricoeur takes himself to be responding to paradoxes of time raised by Augustine in the famous eleventh book of the *Confessions* and left unresolved in the work of later philosophers—Edmund Husserl's *Phenomenology of Internal Time-Consciousness*, for example, but most especially Martin Heidegger's *Being and Time*.[5] For Ricoeur, significantly, it is *narrative* (both literary and historical), not speculative thought, that best responds to the recurrent and seemingly inescapable *aporias* of temporal experience.[6] At the center of his argument (and I am being deliberately summary and schematic here) is the idea of the *reciprocal* relation between time and narrative, a constitutive circle that continuously joins together temporality and narrativity. As Ricoeur puts it right at the beginning of his study, "Time becomes human time to the extent that it is organized after the manner of a narrative; narrative, in turn, is meaningful to the extent that it portrays the features of temporal experience."[7] Human action, then, unfolds in time, and the linguistic form best suited to the intelligibility of the temporality of action is narrative. As is well known, Ricoeur constructs the problem about time and narrative by way of building a connection between Augustine's *distentio animi*, or "distention of the soul," by which the threefold present (the present of the past, the present of the present, and the present of the future) is constituted, and Aristotle's idea of mimesis and emplotment in the *Poetics* (emphasizing the priority of action over character and the exemplary place accorded to tragedy in his picture of the concordance of poetic composition).[8] The mediation between time and narrative that Ricoeur constructs in this uncertain marriage between Augustine and Aristotle is articulated through what he calls the three moments of mimesis—namely, the *prefiguring* activity grounded in a pre-understanding of the world of action; the *configuring* operation of the emplotment of action; and the *refiguring* moment that draws on the receptivity of the text by its reader. Of these, not surprisingly, it is the configuring dimension that is pivotal for the composition of temporal experience: "the dynamic of emplotment is . . . the key to the problem of the relation between time and narrative."[9]

Now, the form of narrativity that interests me in this chapter is that of fiction, the novel in particular—a form of narrativity that has an especially intimate, even originary, relationship to the problem of time. Indeed, the novel might well be the temporal literary form par excellence, a literary form designed precisely for the representation of time in its varied dimensions. As Abram Mendilow put it more than a decade before Kermode's reflections on fictive models of time, and endings in narrative time, "A novel, even at its longest must come to an end; the writer must plan his beginning and ending, and his whole work must provide within itself the reason why these should fall where they do and not elsewhere. He must exploit different devices to urge the reader's attention forward and prompt his unposed question: 'what next?'; 'what then?' He must consider how to relate or link one part to another. He will experiment with suspense and tempo, with rhythm and climax and plotting. And time is a central feature of them all."[10] Mikhail Bakhtin would undoubtedly concur. For him, one might remember, time is simply the most essential element in the novel. The whole point of his idea of the *chronotope* was to call attention to this dimension of literary forms, the generative, organizing dimension along which "the knots of narrative are tied and untied."[11] Every literary image in the novel, Bakhtin argued, is chronotopic, saturated with what he called "time-values" that lend artistic unity to a literary work's relationship to reality.

Here, then, is the conceptual focus of what interests me in this chapter: the fictive models through which temporal experience is discursively *rendered* and, in particular, the way narrative models of time connect beginnings, middles, and endings, or pasts, presents, and futures. But more exactly, I want to incline the question of time and narrative in a way that is slightly different from that of Kermode or Ricoeur or Mendilow or Bakhtin, however profoundly I will rely on them to orient me. Notably, although they are resolutely focused on time, they are not particularly interested in historicizing their preoccupations and characterizations—that is, with locating them in any specific *conjuncture*. By contrast, I am expressly interested in conjuncture—a conjuncture of temporal crisis, as I have expressed it. So I want to ask what happens to renderings of temporal experience when the conditions of an accustomed sense of an ending alter rapidly and catastrophically to such an extent as to undermine the salience of an old mode of temporal configuration, say, the salience of the temporal configuration that drove the modern longing for total revolution?[12] In other words, what happens when established fictive models of time are suddenly made obsolete? Are we then left, so to speak, *stranded* in the present?[13] In this chapter, I am concerned with the sense, in our extended historical present, of a certain ending. It is not quite an apocalyptic one, perhaps, but it is nevertheless dramatic and, in any case, seemingly *terminal*—that is, the end of the great modernist narratives of revolutionary overcoming. This end of alternative futures, I have been arguing, has precipitated a certain experience of crisis of time or, anyway, of the temporality of the present that seems so much like the ends of time.

I want to consider this conundrum of the temporal experience of being stranded in the present—a present specifically of ruined time—by contrasting two fictional accounts of the collapse of the Grenada Revolution rendered by the same novelist: Merle Collins's *Angel*, published in 1987, and *The Colour of Forgetting*, published in 1995.[14] A writer of considerable range and accomplishment, whether of the novel, the poem, the short story, or the essay, and an engaged, courageous intellectual who played an active role in the Grenadian revolutionary process, Collins has been one of the most perceptive and eloquent interpreters of the catastrophe of October 1983.[15] She is almost never not returning to it as though it were an inexhaustible source of both perplexity and learning. To read Collins's work, the fiction and the nonfiction alike, is to enter into the discomfiting spaces of an evolving argument she is conducting with herself about the uncanny persistence in the present of that haunting political past: how to remember it, how to forget it, how to render audible the wounded silence with which the collapse of the Grenada Revolution is surrounded.[16]

In a very arresting way, both *Angel* and *The Colour of Forgetting* are expressly concerned with time—specifically, as we will see, with *generations* of time. In both novels, generations constitute the principal social and institutional form through which temporal experience is fictively rendered. Generations organize and drive the social imaginaries of time at play in each novel. In my reading of *Angel* and *The Colour of Forgetting*, therefore, I pay special attention to the conceptual work of generations in shaping our apprehension of the experience of time. In doing so, I take some direction from Karl Mannheim's still cogent social-phenomenological way of thinking about generations as existential locations as much as social facts.[17] A good deal is implied even in this condensed formulation (and I return to dimensions of it in chapter 3). But for my reading of Collins's two novels, what is important to bear in mind is Mannheim's idea that the roughly integrated age cohorts that constitute successive (and overlapping) generations acquire frameworks of collective identity, as well as modes of connecting memories of the past to expectations for the future by virtue of their location in relation to *eventful* collective experience, such as wars, riots, revolutions, natural catastrophes, and the like.[18] The implosion of the Grenada Revolution has this eventful quality of a defining generational experience.

But what is also notable about *Angel* and *The Colour of Forgetting* is that, whereas they share a framework of generations, they manifestly operate contrasting *generic* models of time and thus organize temporal experience (particularly the temporal experience of catastrophic *endings*) in significantly different ways, with significantly different moral and political effects and implications. Consequently, I also pay attention in these novels to the work of *genre* and, more specifically, to the work of the *content of the form* of genre. In keeping with some recent critical work on literary modes and forms, I treat genre here as crucial to how social realities are textually constructed and interpreted. I think of genres as encoding conventions that effectively constrain how we represent experience—temporal experience, say, or temporalities of generational experience—simultaneously enabling and generating the meaning conditions of some experience, and restricting and foreclosing the meaning conditions of others.[19] From this perspective, then, texts exercise active or performative relationships to generic structures and conventions; they are not passive containers of genre.[20] Therefore, the interesting question to ask is not what genre a text somehow *is*, but how texts *use* the resources of genres and, in so doing, how they *activate* the knowledge and value structures and assumptions of genre in order to produce one or another sort of rhetorical work.

In formal terms, it will be easy to see that Collins's first novel, *Angel*, owes much to the literary tradition of the Bildungsroman, the so-called novel of formation, telling as it does the coming-of-age story of the eponymous protagonist and with it (or, better, *through* it) the making of the modern social, political, and ideological conditions that gave rise to the Grenada Revolution and its eventual demise. In *Angel*, Collins constructs a dramatic social-realist story of unfolding progressive time leading gradually to the triumph of the revolution and followed soon after by its sudden, unbidden, and violent implosion. We are reminded here of Bakhtin's observation that, in contrast to the strictly "biographical" novel in which the individual's development is set against a temporally static background, in novels of Bildung, the individual's emergence, growth, and transformation are accomplished in (a simulacrum of) real historical time—the realistic time, for example, of social revolution.[21] But the Bildungsroman is not merely the novel of historical experience; it is classically, as Franco Moretti has argued, the novel form of *modernity*, of modern historical time, and is therefore constructed around the sense of a dynamic and developmental *futurity*. Youth is its animating figure, leaving the rapidly receding past behind and leaning expectantly and radiantly into the anticipated time to come. The Bildungsroman is essentially a genre of *progressive* time, of temporality as modern historical progress precisely of the sort that Collins's protagonist, Angel, experiences.[22] Angel is imagined as a young, self-conscious militant who participates in the revolution's rise, suffers its disorienting collapse, and barely survives the violence of the US military invasion that follows. But, alas, as she emerges from the catastrophe in the novel's final pages, she finds herself at a sort of temporal *standstill*, stranded in the limbo—the pure, desolate duration—of a postrevolutionary present that has nowhere to go. In a certain sense, I argue, Angel's predicament here defines something fundamental about the temporal experience of our own shared present marked by the collapse of the normative temporal order that generated the expectation and longings of socialist revolutionary futures. A central aim of this chapter, therefore, is to describe the contours of this temporal dilemma in such a way as to draw out the assumptions about past-present-future, the sense of an ending, embedded in this particular *generic* representation of the Grenada Revolution and its catastrophic collapse.

However, that the generic form of the Bildungsroman is not the only way to think through such an experience of catastrophic ends fictively is suggested by the model that organizes the second of Collins's novels, *The Colour of Forgetting*, published less than a decade later. It seems to me that *The Colour of Forgetting* offers a striking contrast with *Angel* in its fictive rendering of a roughly similar set of thematic concerns—namely, the Grenada Revolution and its violent collapse—and in its fictive reliance on the temporal form of generations. Here, sensing, perhaps, the temporal dilemma of the first novel, the paralyzing dead end that finally imprisons her protagonist, Collins revises the fictive model of time that shapes the generic and generative labor of what nevertheless remains a profoundly historical novel. *The Colour of Forgetting*, I suggest, affiliates with allegory, a somewhat embattled generic form but one that works to destabilize some of the conceits of narrative closure that drive the fictional form of the Bildungsroman.[23] Allegories arguably are the most critically *self-reflexive* and *meta-linguistic*—and, at the same time, the most *didactic* and emphatically *moral*—of narrative genres. Long neglected as a mode of literary expression, allegory has recently emerged (or reemerged) as a genre of some prominence in literary fiction as well as in literary and cultural-historical interpretation, partly, no doubt, because of the waning of the long-held prejudice of the superiority of forms of literary naturalism and realism, and the renewed attention that has been paid to the *symbolic* rather than the referential or representational features of language.[24] For my purposes here, what is interesting about allegory is the way it draws our attention less to character and plot and their role in the evolution of the story as a whole, than to the very labor of *language* itself.[25] Indeed, many of the well-known signals of allegory follow directly from this constitutive relation to language. Take, for example, "personification," a familiar allegorical technique that plays a significant role in *The Colour of Forgetting*: a fictional figure is made to *personify* an abstract idea or an abstract moral force. Often, the figure will bear the idea as her or his proper name. By making abstract moral ideas into subjects in this way, these ideas are accorded narrative *agency* and *potency* in the symbolic action of the fiction. And in the quest or journey that Angus Fletcher says is typically the moral dynamic that propels the allegorical narrative forward, the personified idea will work out its destiny—it will carry out its task, whose will it concretizes or embodies.[26] Now, notably, while *The Colour of Forgetting* is allegorical in all these senses, what it principally allegorizes is *time* itself. However, this allegorical construction of time is governed not by a linear temporality of developmental progress but, rather, by the symbolic or metaphysical order of *repetition*. It is *kairos*, not *chronos*, that predominates in shaping the model of temporal experience in *The Colour of Forgetting*. Within its allegorical economy, the collapse of the Grenada Revolution is conceived not as the catastrophic end of a teleological history of continuous progress but, rather, as merely one significant *episode* in a larger story of generations of conflict in what is now imagined and represented as the cyclical pattern of a general history whose generative logic is catastrophic.

In a certain sense, of course, this contrast among fictive models of the temporality of the past—one seeing history as a linear, progressive sequence of events and achievements and the other, as a mythic repetition of submerged resonances and presences—is by no means unfamiliar within the literary context of the (Anglophone) Caribbean novel.[27] On the whole, the Caribbean novel belongs to what Wyndham Lewis (speaking somewhat combatively about certain modernist writers of the early twentieth century) called the "time-school of modern fiction."[28] Indeed, the Caribbean novel almost by definition has been saturated with an obsessive "quarrel" with the past, one that makes of the past a pervasively recurrent *question*; it has been saturated with an anxious sense that the past, whatever it is, cannot be taken for granted as a resource of spiritual confidence and therefore, paradoxically, with a (sometimes ambivalent) conviction that its textual framework might offer a platform on which to work out imaginatively something of a relationship with time and even with historical identity.[29] Not surprisingly, perhaps, James Joyce's well-known remark in *Ulysses* (placed in the mouth of his literary alter ego, Stephen Dedalus) that "history is a nightmare from which I am trying to awake" has held a particular fascination for Caribbean writers.[30] The reason for this might not be too hard to discern. After all, quite apart from the exemplary status of Joyce's modernist experimentations with the novel form, what these writers would have recognized in his work is the shadow of the colonial background and the distinctive distortions and prejudices of history that characterize the colonial project as an intimate experience of terror and violation. The particular dilemma of colonial history for the Caribbean writer has, of course, been shaped by the peculiar circumstances of catastrophe that brought the Caribbean into being as an arena of European empire: a constituting genocide, deracination, enslavement, and dispossession that seemed to render the Caribbean an object (or victim), rather than an *agent*, of historical consciousness. The absence of "ruins"—of the discernible trace of an unbroken, organic continuity with a distinctive identity and tradition of achievement—seemed to suggest that the Caribbean was a theater of mere artificiality and mimicry.[31] It may be altogether understandable, then, that a never-ending preoccupation with history should burden Caribbean writers and that the novel (given its own historical formation) should be a contested literary space of rival conceptions of the past's intelligibility, even for the same novelist. Think, for example, of the contrast within V. S. Reid's oeuvre between his classic realist historical novel *New Day*, which maps a linear narrative of nationalist awakening, and the later, no less historical novel *Leopards*, which allegorizes the relationship between the Caribbean and Africa.[32] Or think of the tensions within George Lamming's novels *Of Age and Innocence* and *Season of Adventure*—for example, between the directly realist representations of struggle and intrigue around the unfolding political decolonization and the mythographic narrative (in the tale of the Tribe Boys in the one and the Ceremony of the Souls in the other) through which the subaltern temporality of another past's presence is imagined.[33] There is a sense, then, that however filial the gestures of apprenticeship, Caribbean novelists have always felt an agonistic relationship with the nineteenth-century conventions of historical realism. Undoubtedly, though, it has been the fiction and critical essays of Wilson Harris, more than any other to date, that have provided the most searching challenge to the novel as a platform for the representation of the past in the present. In Harris's work, unlike in Lamming's, myth is not a device within the temporal landscape of an otherwise largely realist fiction. It is the fictive model of time itself.[34] From the early Guyana Quartet—*Palace of the Peacock*, *The Far Journey of Oudin*, *The Whole Armour*, and *The Secret Ladder*—onward, Harris's literary art offers the view that the novel is not a window onto how the past became the present but a visionary "gateway" of discordant concordances in which past is present is future, an echoing passageway that opens less onto prosaic structures of political sovereignty (important as these are) than onto new sensibilities and intuitions of time and communities of consciousness.[35]

Collins's two novels draw deeply on the heritage of this tension in Caribbean writing between fictive models of representing the past.[36] But it will be important, too, to recognize some of the ways in which both *Angel* and *The Colour of Forgetting* depart (however differently they do so) from the masculinist assumptions about politics and history embodied in the fictive art of the male writers of the so-called Caribbean literary renaissance, and engage other heritages shared by female Caribbean writers.[37] For example, at the center of Collins's novels (as is the case in fiction written by a number of other women of her generation) are communities of female characters—grandmothers, mothers, girl-children—whose intimacies and enmities, whose modes and disciplines of socialization, constitute the discursive space in which the past inhabits the present, and in which the private sphere of domesticities frames the public and political world of the state and nation. In this discursive space, the natural language of perception and communication is typically creole; the ground of social, moral, and historical knowledge is that of the little, or "folk," tradition; and the tropic sensibility of criticism (at once distance and embodiment) is that of irony.[38] We will see, then, that even though *Angel* is unquestionably a political novel—as, say, Michelle Cliff's *No Telephone to Heaven*, Grace Nichols's *Whole of a Morning Sky*, and Margaret Cezair-Thompson's *The True History of Paradise* are—it is not animated by exactly the same motifs of intellectual angst or existential despair and alienation or the pathos of resentment and recrimination that, in admittedly different ways, drive the worlds of Lamming's novels or the worlds of V. S. Naipaul's *Mimic Men* and *Guerrillas*.[39] Neither an earnest confidence in the heroic male leadership of revolutionary politics, on the one hand, nor an overwhelming sense of its fraudulence and pointlessness, on the other, shapes the poetics of experience and expectation among the women in Collins's fiction. Similarly, the allegorical fictive model in *The Colour of Forgetting* certainly subverts the mythos of conventional progressive time with its sequential principle of cause and effect—in a way, for example, that Erna Brodber's novels, especially *Myal, Louisiana*, and *The Rainmaker's Mistake*, do.[40] But even though it projects a catastrophic sensibility through the evocation of pre-slave plantation presences and works through an idea of the novel as "gateway" rather than "window," it is yet not governed by the same *topoi* of gender and community that compel the male-centered dream work of Harris's oeuvre.

The overall concern in this chapter, then, is with the moral and political implications that might be drawn from these contrasting generic models of time and catastrophic experience. Are there formal features of the Bildungsroman as they are activated by Collins's first novel of the Grenada Revolution, *Angel*, that constrain temporal experience in particular ways? Does allegory open up productive possibilities for thinking the narrativization of time generally and of catastrophic time specifically? And are these possibilities activated by Collins's second novel of the Grenada

Revolution, *The Colour of Forgetting*, and if so, how? These are the questions to which I aim to attend.

Stranded in the Present

Written in the traumatic years immediately after the collapse of the Grenada Revolution and US-led military invasion, and from the relative coping distance of London, it is not hard to see that *Angel* constitutes a deliberate act of memory—indeed, a deliberate act of political memorialization. As I have said, Collins was a partisan in the revolutionary process, and *Angel*, written alongside a nonfictional account of Grenada's modern political history that Collins submitted for her doctorate at the London School of Economics in 1990, bears witness to her commitment to reconstructing imaginatively and internally the story of the making of the historic popular revolution that transformed the Anglophone Caribbean's political idea of itself, and the moral disaster of its violent collapse that sealed the doom of the region's hope. As a realist work of historical fiction about the (then) immediate and still palpably resonant past, Collins is working with a rough fidelity to the known events (such as they are) that constitute the revolution and its downfall, but she is not by any means aiming at mere verisimilitude. The novel, in her hands, is not a "transcript of reality."[41] *Angel* is an imaginative exploration of *plausibility*, which seems to me what literary realism properly is.[42] It is, in short, a fictive *suggestion* (or, if you like, a fictive *projection*) of how best to conceive, historically, the temporal complex of moral actions that gave rise to the revolution as a horizon of expectation and that shaped the experience of its collapse as an intimation of doom. As a fictive document, therefore, of Collins's own engaged memory, mediated as it is by ambiguous forgetting and uncertain remembering, the novel lays before us an intelligible "world" through which to interpret the catastrophe of 19 October 1983.

I have suggested that *Angel* participates in many of the generic assumptions of the Bildungsroman. Its overall plot sketches a steadily rising curve of progressive, chronological time. Thus the story it tells hangs to a very large extent on the evolution of the character of the novel's protagonist, Angel—in particular, on the development of her social and political consciousness against the background of a transforming historical context. But as I have also suggested, in many ways *Angel* is a novel less about individual characters (rich as they are in Collins's dramatic portrait of them) than about generations and, specifically, the *temporality* of generations. *Angel*, I suggest, is a novel about generations and the "frameworks of memory" through which they construct the temporal relations between individual and collective pasts remembered, presents lived, and futures anticipated. This is the critical perspective on *Angel* that informs my reading of its narrativization of temporal experience, its representation of revolutionary catastrophe, and, especially, its fictive sense of an ending.

Broadly speaking, there are three generations of nonelite Grenadian women whose social interactions, memory frames, and imagined futures drive the temporal rhythm of the narrative of Collins's first novel: that of Angel; that of her mother, Doodsie; and that of her grandmother, Ma Ettie. As the novel opens on an intensely riveting scene of violent political upheaval, the burning down of an estate house, the permanent referent of their historical lives of slavery and postslavery—at once the great symbol of their suffering and disenfranchisement and the ambiguously defining source of social value and political legitimation—we are made to see them, Angel, Doodsie, and Ma Ettie, together and separately, against the backdrop of the fire-lit sky, each inhabiting her own bewilderment and anxiety, connected to one another but with contrasting attitudes toward the events unfolding before them. They all stand, in a generational chain, on an uncertain threshold, a sort of temporal border that marks the end of one form of social and political life and the beginning of another. This originary "event" with which the novel begins marks the inauguration of the political modern in Grenada and sets up the temporal matrix within which these three overlapping generations orient themselves toward past, present, and future.

Their social locations need to be sketched. Beginning with the earliest of the three generations, Ma Ettie was likely born in the last decade of the nineteenth century or in the first years of the twentieth century. Thus, she belongs to the world founded in the immediate aftermaths of slave emancipation in 1838, when sugar production was in its final decline (especially after the withdrawal of British imperial protection in 1846) and the old sugar plantations were being converted to cocoa production.[43] The rise of an independent peasantry had effectively been curbed, and former slaves and their descendants were being obliged to reconnect themselves to the estates as worker tenants with unstable and inconsistent usufruct rights.[44] In other words, a new structure of subjugation and asymmetrical obligations was emerging in which, as the historical anthropologist M. G. Smith writes, the "bond between master and slave, or employer and laborer, had become a relationship between patron and client on the one hand, and planter and peasant on the other."[45] (The distinction between those descendants of slaves who could eke out a quasi-independent existence as peasants and those who could do no better than reattach themselves to estates would be a crucial one for the Grenadian poor, and it surfaces throughout Collins's novel—for example, in the contrast between Angel's mother and father.) Accompanying these social and economic changes were constitutional and political ones, most importantly the self-abolition in 1877 of the "representative" constitution (inaugurated in the eighteenth century for propertied whites to enact such legislation as suited their interests) and its replacement by Crown Colony rule.[46] This was, in short, the beginning of a new imperial era in colonial Grenada (the Caribbean and, indeed, the wider British colonial world), defined by the emergence of an explicitly racialized and paternal colonial ideology.[47]

Ma Ettie's formative years would have been shaped by this new political-economic dispensation. Fiercely independent and proud of her peasant heritage, her imaginary is nevertheless constrained by the rigid racial-social order in which the black poor are made to accept their subjugated place and urged never to reach beyond their given civic status. Ma Ettie embodies the deep inclination of the peasantry to embrace the certainty of what she knows in a customary way.[48] She is the past in the present. But as the novel opens (in the early 1950s), Ma Ettie and her social-political world are beginning to rapidly fade from the historical scene. Thus, she is at a complete loss as to how to comprehend the nature of the political protest unfolding around her, the arrival of a new kind of agitator, "Leader" (a barely disguised Eric Gairy), or what his movement and its methods represent. "Just under the hill from the crowd, Ma Ettie sat down in her house and secured the folds of her headtie. She wrapped it tightly round her head. She looked out of the window at the bright glow in the sky. Her short, squat figure stood framed for a moment against the quiet evening. Then she closed the window again and walked restlessly with both her hands behind her back. Pacing. Pacing. Wandering" (4). She can do little more than sink to her knees in prayer: "Lord, let this tribulation pass from us. Let not our enemies triumph over these your children, Lord. Take a thought to the life and salvation of the little children in that burning house,

Lord, and to all your children of this world" (5). It is the only idiom in which she can process what is taking place. Ma Ettie belongs in this sense to the fast-approaching *end* of an era.

By contrast, there is the generation of Angel's mother, Doodsie, likely born in the early to mid-1920s and who, therefore, would have spent her formative years in a Grenada that, like the rest of the Caribbean region, was stressed by the hardships that followed the Wall Street crash of 1929, when prices for Grenadian staples—cocoa and nutmeg, principally—fell precipitously and the cost of imported food and clothing rose sharply. Even so, while other island colonies erupted in labor riots in the late 1930s— St. Kitts, Trinidad, and Barbados in 1937, and Jamaica in 1938—Grenada remained curiously tranquil.[49] The reason, Smith offers, is that the rigidly paternalistic social organization that emerged in the postemancipation years "simultaneously restricted the scope for mass action by workers, and bound planters and peasants together in solidary associations within the framework of estate-communities."[50] The forms, institutions, and ethos of this conservative paternalism shape Doodsie's self-understanding and her understanding of her world—as they did her mother's. Doodsie's, too, is the unschooled wisdom, so to speak, of popular knowledge condensed into pithy proverbs and sayings that orient social and personal conduct and help to cultivate the customary values and virtues: self-respect, hard work, and so on. (Indeed, the novel is threaded with these proverbs and sayings, which provide a resonant echo throughout the narrative of Doodsie's voice and philosophy of life.)

At the same time, however, Doodsie, unlike Ma Ettie, is by no means imprisoned by the "quasi-feudal" past of postemancipation Grenada. To use the terms I have been commending, a different generational framework of memory from her mother's constitutes her social imaginary and she therefore projects a different sense of futurity. On the one hand, Doodsie has traveled beyond Grenada. Pushed by the prolonged economic crisis during and after the Second World War, she, like many others, had left Grenada to look for work, first in Trinidad and then in the service sector that grew up around the Lago Oil Refinery in Aruba. So if she is not quite cosmopolitan in outlook, at least Doodsie's frame of reference has widened, and she is capable of taking a certain reflexive distance from her native point of departure. On the other hand, these were also years of a significant social, economic, and political modernization in the Anglophone

Caribbean prompted by the recommendations for progressive reform of the Moyne Commission, which evaluated the state of the region in the wake of the unrest of the 1930s.[51] Thus, however haphazard and uneven its scope and content, a modernizing ethos swept across the Caribbean in the 1940s and 1950s generated out of the new political technologies of colonial governmentality—namely, welfare and development. So that if, unlike her daughter, Angel, Doodsie's horizon—her sense of personal and social possibility—is not formed by modern progressive education and the worldly social and economic mobility that such education enables (in this she resembles Ma Ettie), she nevertheless is very aware of the rapid changes taking place around her and is determined to avail herself of the advantages for her children, especially for her strong-willed girl-child, Angel.

Importantly also, and partly as a consequence of her travels and the historical context of her time, Doodsie is a woman of acute social and political insight, which is often delivered with weary, sometimes bitter and resigned irony. She returned to Grenada in the early 1950s only to find herself in the middle of a time of radicalizing social and political change in the island colony, when, as Smith writes, "the structural bases of the social order were challenged and shaken rudely."[52] It is the historic moment of the rise of the charismatic Leader, recently deported from Aruba for his role in labor agitation and who was now galvanizing popular protest against the exclusionary and discriminatory political, social-racial, and economic policies of Grenada's plantocratic elite and British colonial authorities.[53] Significantly, there is nothing naïve about Doodsie. As stuck as she is obliged to be "under the nutmeg" (as she sometimes puts it), she is a woman of poignant feeling and expressive self-awareness. She is cognizant of the need for social and political change, but she has deep suspicions about the character and motivations of the newly minted Leader of whom many of her friends and family (including her brother and her husband) are now so enamored. For Doodsie had observed him closely in Aruba and has an uneasy sense that he is more flash than substance. As we hear her articulate it early in the novel in a letter to a friend who is still in Aruba:

> To tell you the truth, Ezra, the country need a shake up like this, even though I know the kine a person Leader is. I not too sure I like the way they doing things. There is a lot of violence that startin up. I even hear about people that get kill. Is a while now I didn't go down in you area,

but I hear that everybody there stout stout behind Leader. Well is what you expect? Is right there self his people come from and is like people thinking he is saviour.

If we didn't have experience of him over there [in Aruba], who know? I might even shout for him myself. Girl, I don't know. When that man dress and he stylish, you should see him. People like they going crazy about him. The other day I hear you cousin-in-law saying Oh God the boy nice. He nice he nice, all behin he head nice. If you hear them you would laugh for so. (6–7)

The sarcasm delivers a sharply precise criticism. If Ma Ettie configures the presence of the past (in Ricoeur's Augustinian language), Doodsie configures the presence of the present. But she is not, as her mother is, a static figure, a receding fount of obscure wisdom. A restless dynamism characterizes Doodsie: shaped by the past, she is nevertheless tilted determinedly toward the future. And if Angel will speak for the intellectual critique of Leader, Doodsie will articulate a certain popular intuition that his agenda is little more than a project of self-aggrandizement. This will be important for how she later judges Chief (a barely disguised Maurice Bishop) and his revolutionary moment.

This coming moment, of course, centrally belongs to another generation—that of the novel's protagonist, Angel, born in the early 1950s. Angel's lifetime will span, almost exactly, the rise and fall of Eric Gairy's long domination of the political scene in modern Grenada, and the rise and catastrophic fall of the New Jewel Movement. Unlike her parents, who come to the Age of Gairy from an earlier colonial past, Angel spends her childhood and adolescence under Gairy's shadow, and this shapes her perspective of both the past and the future. As her father repeatedly reminds her when she rails against Leader's corruption and greed, *she* does not know what Grenada was like *before* him. It is, indeed, a crucial point about generational time and the framework of temporal experience it organizes. Angel's generational time, although it overlaps with that of her parents (marked, for example, by some of the same remembered events), is nevertheless not identical with it. Her time is connected to, but simultaneously *disjunctive* with, theirs. She lives events through a different existential location. Angel has no concrete lived sense of the repressive colonial time before Leader's rise. Therefore, however abstractly right she may be about his flaws, she lacks a proper appreciation of the social-psychological demand he seems to have answered, the self-respect he helped to inspire in the black poor, and the possibility of dignity and triumph he enabled them to imagine. Still, in the scheme of things, hers is a generational perspective whose political time has come. If over the course of Angel's growing up we will witness, by turns, Leader's consolidation of power, his mastery of demagoguery and deceit, his betrayal of people's hopes, and his increasing use of intimidation and violence to repulse his enemies and retain his grip on rule, we are also made aware of an emerging popular sense of despair and even outrage at his style of political rule.

At the same time, we also pass through the stages of Angel's personal coming of age: her troubled early school years; her conflicted relationship with her parents (about religion, about politics); and her departure for university in Jamaica, where, amid the social upheavals and cultural and intellectual intensities of late 1960s and early 1970s Kingston *noir*, her political awakening begins.[54] The University of the West Indies serves as the context in which, partly through friendships, discussion groups, and theater activity, Angel begins to acquire not only a new sense of self but also, with it, a new idiom of political disenchantment that, to her surprise, bears an echo of her mother's ripe, unschooled indignation at the historical facts of social injustice in the Caribbean. When Angel returns home to Grenada after earning her degree, this inchoate political consciousness expresses itself in an edgy restlessness and flaunting irreverence toward her family. She has acquired, as her mother, Doodsie, vividly laments, a disturbing "Jezebel style" (182)—irritably vexed with the world (especially the immediate political world), godless, willfully aloof, indifferent about her appearance, and, most of all, cynical about such relationships with men as might lead to having a family. It is as though Angel, like the country, is on a path of rebellion and heading for an explosion. Her inability to abide her father's treasured photograph of Leader hanging in the living room is mirrored in the growing political opposition to him that is being organized by the new popular revolutionary movement, the portentously named Horizon (a thin disguise for the NJM).

Then the long-awaited day arrives. At 6:15 on the morning of 13 March 1979, the news crackles over the radio: "this is the voice of the free people of Grenada! The Leader government has been overthrown! I repeat . . ." (229). It is the beginning of a New Day, a new momentum of enthusiasm and participation, the real end of the colonial past. But it will not last, as Angel's dream about snakes in the bush signals (244–45). These are portents, *omens* of adversity. Collins traverses these events quickly: the time scale suddenly contracts. There are rumors about confusion in the party leadership, but the details of the internal dispute do not interest her fictively. There is barely enough interaction to support a sense of tragic doom. Chief is scarcely a figure of any distinctive presence, much less psychological complexity. The novel is very emphatically *not* about him. We are simply told that he is placed under house arrest and that, subsequently, the people, outraged, are involved in a mass demonstration of support (with some dubious elements in it) that secures his release.

As the dark, confusing doom of the revolution's turmoil and demise unfolds toward its final denouement, and the prospect of a US military invasion materializes, we witness a conflicted Angel preparing herself for a final act of sacrifice. Collins handles this moment of disaster with deft, uncluttered swiftness, leaving little room for sentimentalism. Angel suffers an eye injury in the short, intense battle against the invading forces and has been sent (perhaps paradoxically) to the United States for medical treatment. Now, as we (along with her family) watch her descend the steps of the aircraft on her return home, we—readers and characters alike—are painfully aware that we are at the end. The narrative is uncertain, no longer *called forward* by a horizon of possibility, let alone the prospect of Horizon's revolution. What is Angel returning to? The unconditional love of her family, perhaps, but not the conditional contingencies of a great political project. As the children begin to tease each other, Jessie, Doodsie's sister, remarks, "Once you hear confusion start, everyting awright again" (286). You can feel the retreat into squabbling familiarity of the private sphere. Doodsie wants Angel to marry. She has kept her family safe from predators (symbolized by the circling chicken hawks she keeps away from the vulnerable fowls in her yard). The rain suggests a modicum of peace. The temptation to engage in nostalgia is almost impossible to avoid. Angel wanders off to a secluded spot and lights a candle in remembrance.

Over the course of the novel, an arrow of ambiguous modernizing progress has propelled the drama of intergenerational time forward, from Ma Ettie through Doodsie and culminating, finally, in Angel. These characters quite clearly embody successive yet overlapping temporalities. They experience some of the same historical events but at different points in their lives and therefore in relation to different memories of the past, different evaluations of the present, and different expectations for the future.[55] If Angel embodies the coming *future* (of hope and emancipation) and Ma Ettie embodies the receding *past* (the shadow of the plantation and its varied powers of coercive subjection), then Doodsie functions as an embodied *present* transitional between them, a sort of "hinge" joining past to future. She is neither glued to the past like her mother (however formed she might be by her mother's modes of knowing) nor completely enchanted by the future like her daughter (although she is not unwilling to cultivate a certain expectation of social and political improvement). Doodsie is pure *duration*. Through her, time crosses the *threshold* of the present, coming out of the restricted past and moving eventfully toward the waiting future.

But by the closing pages, the novel, in seeking to represent the collapse of the revolution, has arrived at a curious but profound temporal conundrum—a conundrum, as I shall think of it, concerning precisely the *representability* of this experience of passing time. The revolution and its catastrophic collapse are, of course, the end toward which the novel has been *heading* all along. It is this end that has organized the "concordance" (to borrow Kermode's phrase) of the narrative's fictive model of time. The onward temporal momentum has been carried steadily forward and sustained through betrayals and setbacks by a people's longing for meaningful change, their longing to overcome the terrible shadow of the oppressive past of colonial and postcolonial authoritarianism. The political movement Horizon, as its name implies, embodies the teleological direction of the temporal rhythm of this generational longing. And the revolution it brings about on 13 March 1979 vindicates the past's faith and redeems the suffering and sacrifices of preceding generations—Ma Ettie's, Doodsie's. With Angel, we have been leaning expectantly into this coming revolutionary future, and when it arrives, we recognize in it her inheritance of a great promise. The Horizon revolution embodies the people's longed-for salvation and thus is the very fulfillment or realization of historical time.

But perhaps for this very reason, inasmuch as the revolutionary success represents the ends of time—time's triumph and terminus—and the realization of the teleological arc of the coming-of-age story (the time of

Angel's becoming), its sudden, unbidden collapse poses a serious narrative problem for temporal representation. This is so because the collapse of the 13 March 1979 revolution is not like earlier social-political dead ends or failures. This collapse seems to be about *time* itself. Within the narrative structure of the novel, there is now no larger temporal schema into which this utter catastrophe can be absorbed as a mere moment, a mere transitory event, in a more comprehensive dramatic process. For an earlier generation (Doodsie's generation), the political disaster that was Leader, the eventual betrayal of the horizon of expectation he embodied, could in the narrativization of generational temporality be superseded by a *more* authentic future of social, economic, and political change—here represented in the figure of Chief. In the retrospective teleology of the novel, in other words, Leader was but a *stage* in a progressively unfolding story of political emancipation. For Angel's generation, by contrast, the catastrophe of the Horizon revolution's self-destruction is experienced as an *absolute* ruin, the very ruin of time as a source of possibility, the absolute end of a temporal journey. It is not just the end of the fiction but the end of the book. Within the teleological structure of Bildung there seems no way for Angel—still a young woman by the novel's close—to *re-temporalize* her experience so as to imagine a horizon beyond the catastrophe, one that would give her life temporal intelligibility and thus the possibility of renewal. For her there is, so to speak, nowhere to go. *She is stranded in the present.* Angel now has to live (or perhaps more accurately, to survive) the rupture of the comfortable illusion of progressive time, the now vanished time of stable, predictable temporal succession in the direction of the realization of history's Spirit. This is the meaning and the measure of her physical and psychic wound, her trauma: an impairment of vision. She can do little more, in the given time, than mourn a loss that is larger and more fundamental than the loss (large and fundamental though it is) of the Horizon revolution itself as a form of social-political order. What she mourns, in effect, is the loss of time. It is not, in other words, that in the novel, this literary framework shaped by a realist chronological temporality breaks down (as in incoherence) so much as that it exhausts its temporal possibilities: time now suffers less from a want of intelligence than from a want of *regenerative* intelligibility.

The Repetition of Catastrophic Time

Collins's second novel, *The Colour of Forgetting*, published in 1995, offers a significant formal contrast to *Angel*. The central thematic event is still the collapse of the Grenada Revolution in October 1983, but the novel form in which the place and role of that event is organized is radically, consequentially altered. In the second novel, that psychologically rupturing political event is rendered more symbolically and figuratively than realistically, less historically than allegorically. So if *Angel* should be read as activating generic structures associated with the Bildungsroman, then *The Colour of Forgetting* should be read as activating generic structures associated with allegory.[56]

Indeed, the generic contrast between the content of the form of the novels is (almost) everything. The catastrophe of the collapse of the Grenada Revolution, as we have seen, is the temporal narrative telos of *Angel*. In terms of its mimesis of action, this is where the story is progressively headed so that, as an ending, the catastrophe frames a convergence between a historical and political dead end and the traumatic closure of the protagonist's moral development. For the narrative structure of *Angel*, in other words, the collapse of the revolution constitutes a singular, unprecedented, and therefore subjectively inassimilable disaster. By contrast, in *The Colour of Forgetting* the collapse of the Grenada Revolution is neither singular nor unprecedented in its general character as catastrophe. Rather, it is *one* disaster in a longer and deeper, interconnected catastrophic history. Its occurrence therefore does not draw history as such (history understood, say, as the temporality of social meaning) to a sudden end; it underlines, rather, a recurrent pattern—the repeatability of the logic of disaster. In *The Colour of Forgetting*, it is not only the event of the collapse of the Grenada Revolution that is catastrophic; it is Caribbean history itself that is inaugurated in catastrophe, and catastrophe (so far, anyway) is its relentless organizing principle of movement, and of intelligibility.

In short, *The Colour of Forgetting* is an allegory of time and catastrophe—or, perhaps, an allegory of *catastrophic time*. As such, it offers a reminder (much against the grain of some contemporary views) of the rich possibilities of the symbolic form of allegorical fiction. The fictional labor the novel undertakes is carried out largely through figuration and symbolism rather than (as in *Angel*) through plot, realist mimetic action, and the development of character. The allegorical heroes are more personified abstractions than fully rounded and densely portrayed individuals; they represent large, metaphysical principles or cosmic dimensions—Time, say, or Memory. They are less psychologically complex as characters, but they are more obsessed, more driven, more morally burdened by their agonic Fate and the didactic implications of their symbolic or ritual action. What matters in *The Colour of Forgetting* is the allegorical lesson that Time comes and passes, is perpetually coming and passing; that the past and the present and the future are seamlessly intertwined and sometimes interchangeable (or, at least, hard to distinguish from each other); that what happened in the Beginning leaves traces that lay upon the living a responsibility to discern and remember, because only Memory can save us from others—and from ourselves. Only a deliberate practice of collective remembering can make meaningful change possible. In this sense, obviously, the event of the collapse of the Grenada Revolution is scarcely inessential to understanding the nature of that history, but its significance lies less in the determination of the details of political ideology than in the force of the deeper pattern it repeats, and whether it will have fostered a generation that will grasp the moral of that repetition in order at last to bring the logic of catastrophe to an end.

The central allegorical figure in the novel, who poetically announces— and embodies—this logic of catastrophe is Carib, a mad or, at least, eccentric, prophetic woman who walks all over the island of Paz (Peace, thus with allegorical implications for conflicted Grenada) shouting her dire warning: "blood in the north, blood to come in the south, and the blue crying red in between" (3). There are generations of Carib, one succeeding another in an obscure and perhaps irrelevant genealogy. Their name links them, however, to the founding disaster in Caribbean history (or if you like, the disaster that founds modern Caribbean history)—namely, the arrival of the European colonizing project and the genocidal decimation of the Amerindian people it brings about. "Blood in the north" refers to the violence of the colonial powers and the desperate act of collective suicide in which the Caribs are supposed to have engaged, leaping to their deaths off the cliffs at Sauteurs in northern Grenada to escape their colonizers. This is where, in fact, we first encounter Carib, in the cemetery of the allegorical Leaper's Hill. Carib is the keeper of historical memory, the memory of those who are "forgotten and consoled. Forgotten and drownded" (3). Interestingly, Carib herself may or may not be a descendant of the historical Caribs, but she and her mother before her, and her mother, and so on, all have been called Carib because of their regular pilgrimage to this hill in memory of the terrible fate of the Amerindian people.

At the same time, while Carib personifies the memory of this inaugural catastrophe to which she constantly refers ("blood in the north"), it is the blood *to come* in the south (and therefore the temporal connection between them) that brings attention to her. She (whichever Carib belongs to the historical moment) is known principally to old people as a "warner-woman" chastising people for their indifference to the past and to the signs of the coming and calamitous land confusion. But it is not only the old who are touched by Carib. So too are the young. In fact, Carib has entered the dreams of one little boy in particular, William Janvier, nicknamed Thunder for the noise he hears like a continuous roar in his head. While Carib is an almost mythical figure whose madness or eccentricity makes her liminal, Thunder is more realistically drawn, and one can roughly locate him in historical and generational time. Carib "possesses" Thunder so that he carries a vague, dissonant apprehension of knowledge of a past to which he has no direct access. He, too, is allegorical. As Thunder's terror grows more acute, his mother, Willive (a Doodsie-like character whose name registers her personification of a determined *will* to live) is urged by her grand-aunt Mamag to take him to see Carib at her "little house in between the cocoa trees, just below the Anglican church" (11). Carib's advice for Thunder's fear invokes the therapeutic role of memory that is, in effect, the novel's resonant moral: they are to make him "walk back" through "time and story." As she tells them, "Is the younger ones to stop the blue crying red in between, but themselves looking outside. They not listening inside here self" (13). What afflicts Thunder is the result of generations of forgetting. It is therefore a forgetting that is not his alone, but he is one of the chosen whose inchoate remembering, the thunder, is "the spirits letting him hear it [the past] and it would only stop when he found a way of understanding the spirits that lived inside him" (14).

Thunder is a descendant of clashing, discordant Fates. He represents the sense in which Caribbean history is, paradoxically, both one and at odds, both interwoven and irreconcilable. He is simultaneously an offspring of the unhappy white slaveowning family, Malheureuse, and the black slave line of John Bull. The story of the fateful relation between Malheureuse and Bull is the story of epic, unspeakable violence combined with the cruel ambiguities of physical and symbolic miscegenation: "mixture in the blood of the story" (17). If the inaugural catastrophe of Caribbean history is the arrival of Europeans, the beginnings of colonization, and the decimation of the Amerindian people, this is quickly followed by the catastrophe of plantation slavery and its peculiar, intimate modes of violence and violation. The story begins with the brutal, wanton killing by Malheureuse of his slave, John Bull, in the market square of Paz City. Malheureuse kills Bull for no discernible reason other than that he has sovereign power over the life and death of his slave. But in time, as the fatal story of Caribbean history unfolds, the Malheureuse blood passes from master to slave through miscegenation, and before long there are also Malheureuses among the "John Bull nation," and it becomes difficult to tell the moral difference between the two. From here on, the catastrophe of Caribbean history comes not only from the outside but also, and perhaps most importantly and ominously, from divisions and conflicts generated from *within*. When Carib dies, some remember her as having warned, "Blood coming, yes. Blood coming in our time. With help from outside, perhaps. But is we. Who gone coming back and dividing. And the blue crying red in between" (14). It is, of course, an omen of the terrible adversity to come, the curse of inherited divisions and conflicts that will lead to the destruction of families—but also of revolutions. "Trouble inside is not new story. Is story that there from time. Nation shall rise against itself" (27).

Carib, then, personifies Memory. And Thunder is the allegorical hero whose quest for Knowledge threads the novel. But it is Mamag who is Time. It is she who renders intelligible the temporal connection between Carib's pasts and Thunder's possible futures. She is a descendant of Malheureuse, and her historical sensibility is as deep as it is cynical. There is nothing sentimental about her approach to life. Her nephew Ti-Moun and his wife, Cassandra, have been swindled out of their inherited land by one of her brothers, Son-Son, and they soon die of their blows and their grief. Mamag is obliged to look after their daughter, Willive, whom she must teach the moral lessons of life so that she will, indeed, live. Mamag teaches Willive to see the "long tail" or "riddle" in every story (71); she teaches her to trust no one but herself, especially not family and friends ("If family and friend turn out good, is a bonus. Enjoy it. But don't expect it" [70]).

History for Mamag is inescapably moral, and remembering the past's travails—indeed, being able to laugh in the face of adversity—is indispensable for future survival. But if Mamag is Time, she is time as Repetition, not time as Progress. History for her is not a linear story bringing with it new and hitherto unheard-of possibilities. Rather, history is a paradoxical and perpetual return of the past in the present. "Everything that happening today," she tells Willive, "it happen before. . . . Thing change. A lot of thing different. But, child, there is nothing new under the sun" (85). Or, as she vividly puts it later, "Yesterday is today is tomorrow" (94). Consequently, since above all it is disaster that returns, one has always to be prepared for the worst. Being caught unawares by time's contingencies or by evil is a sign not so much of naïveté as of *forgetting*. For Mamag, Willive's parents, Ti Moun and Cassandra, were not as prepared for adversity as they ought to have been. They had forgotten Carib's teaching. They had been seduced into believing that the land they so devotedly worked was securely and comfortably theirs and that nothing could come between them and what they had rightfully inherited. But they were wrong. Their own family had cynically deceived them and robbed them of that land. Not so, Mamag. With foresight, she had sold off her inherited land and bought another plot to which she had direct and incontestable title. This is Mamag's basic doctrine about time and life: remember, prepare.

It is not surprising, then, that it is Mamag who recognizes something special about Thunder—that with him, there is "something in the mortar [more] than just the pestle" (93). Thunder's fear is unusual; it points in an allegorical direction. As Mamag says presciently, "Must be something from another life that he remember" (93). Indeed, Thunder's maternal grandfather, Mamag's nephew Ti-Moun, is a descendant of the white Malheureuse who killed the black slave John Bull in the market square. But Thunder's maternal grandmother, Cassandra, is a descendant of that slave, Bull. And while Thunder's mother, Willive, is generationally an earlier embodiment of the fateful crossing of these lines of descent, it is in her son that the story comes alive to realize its promise. When Willive reminds Mamag that her mother, Cassandra, used to tell her about John Bull, Mamag unfailingly makes the link. "That is the connection," she says, "and that is where your story and the Malheureuse story cross. Is that he remembering. You know that. Lord have is mercy! One kill the other and so now Thunder have murderer and victim inside of his head. And even in we time, the story don't really change" (94). Again, note the simultaneity, the non-succession, of time. But this sound that Thunder carries as a discordant and indecipherable noise inside his head is not merely past-oriented. It has contemporary and future-oriented implications, as well. It carries a charge of moral responsibility—moral *generational* responsibility. Mamag implores Thunder to take note of what Carib is saying about the "blue crying red" and prophesying that, while there has been blood in the past, there is yet "blood to come" (96). As she says to him, "Is people like you, that know the story of the life of the land, that have to stop the red from taking over" (96).[57]

Like other allegorical heroes, Thunder is obliged to embark upon a journey (a quest) to find himself. And it is when he has come of age and is readying himself for university abroad that the revolution occurs—like that, *occurs*. Remarkably, the novel announces it matter-of-factly, without ceremony. We witness nothing we could call political preparation. There is no narrative buildup, as in *Angel*. It is, of course, not exactly a non-event, but it is not rendered—as in the earlier novel—as the *realization* of the narrative's temporal project. As an event, therefore, it is relatively featureless, characterized by an almost complete absence of dramatic action. Yet this non-sensational rendering serves only to underscore the revolution's place less as an event in modern historical time than as an occurrence in *cosmic* time, in a larger order of temporal experience in which, as time passes, such things as this *happen*. They are part of a meta-historical order of time and change. This is underlined by the deliberate sense of caution that surrounds the event, for even as the revolution takes place, Carib continues to shout and cry about blood in the south. In fact, the revolution, although relatively bloodless in itself, seems only to provoke Carib to preach with more intensity and fervor about the coming violent catastrophe (151).

Thunder's university years in England are not good ones. The gray environment drives him more into himself. Anxious to go home, he returns to Paz as people are beginning to raise questions about the revolution; there are rumors of confusion and division at the level of the leadership (154). But Thunder is a believer. As with Angel, the revolution is for him and his generation. However, this brings a degree of conflict between himself and his parents. Ned (his father) and Willive have had their eye on a small piece of mountain land during the years that Thunder was abroad. Now, with his return to a salaried job, they are hoping that he will stand security for them. But the policy of the revolution—with which Thunder is in agreement—is to discourage the sale or purchase of small parcels of land on the seemingly rational grounds that they are uneconomical. Ned and Willive are outraged both by the revolutionary government's position (which seems to fly in the face of the obvious historical relation the poor in the island have had to land) and by their son's endorsement of it. As far as they are concerned, his sympathy for the government's land policy is a sure indication that he has forgotten his history and the significance of land for his family story.

This is the beginning of the end of the revolution. Again, Collins has her eye elsewhere than on the historical details. It is a strange time. People begin to hear noises, see things, have mysterious visions and experiences (158). Carib seems more possessed than usual; she weeps as though from an impending loss. Something "is in the air," Willive thinks (159–60). People are preoccupied with the land question. The government in the meantime is talking loftily about "land reform" but quite evidently is out of touch with people's needs and, in particular, their self-understanding of those needs—namely the deep-felt memorial wounds that drive them. The government has a purely academic understanding of the "land problem." Indeed, it is this conflict over the land question that points to the disconnection between the well-meaning revolutionaries and the people (165). To address the matter, the government holds a public meeting, but tensions rise quickly, and the meeting turns violent when the government obtusely refuses to see the validity of the people's point of view. Collins does not rehearse the details of the popular upheaval; in a few quick strokes that betray nothing of her views, it is dispatched. The violence leaves several people dead, including functionaries of the revolutionary government. Then, with irony, Collins tells us that a "Great Country" intervenes to rescue people from their folly and put things on the right course once more. Subsequently, a monument is erected in gratitude for the outside help, but no monument is created in honor of the people (173). Again, the people are left without a source of memory.

So in the end, we find Carib where we first encountered her, sitting despondently among the gravestones at Leaper's Hill, her head crowded with the abject sound of screaming ghosts from the past—those "long-ago people" who jumped to their deaths to escape slavery and for whom there is no memorial by which to remember them. Like those (among them, schoolchildren) who actually leaped to their deaths from Fort Rupert to escape the shooting and mayhem on 19 October 1983, they are "forgotten and drownded" in a sea whose blue is the color of forgetting (185). We have come full circle. This is the essence of the allegory: time comes and passes, and comes and passes again (191). Thunder's generation did not learn Carib's lesson about the historical blood crying out. Maybe his daughter's will (201). Who is to know? Only time will tell.

It is sometimes said of allegories as fictive models of time that they are inherently "conservative": they resist the drive to progressive historical narrative and therefore seem to privilege timeless values and unchanging order; they depend on a hermetic structure of schematic personifications and are consequently less open-ended than literary genres that are more emplotted representations of human action; they show a tendency toward abstract generalities and so surrender the ability to capture the singularity of events, and so on. Might any or all of this be true where *The Colour of Forgetting* is concerned? Perhaps. But, then, the idea of progress is precisely what the novel is questioning.

As I have shown, *Angel* is built around a forward-oriented rhythm of narrative movement. By the artifices of Bildung, the novel projects a temporality imagined as *chronos*—that is, a developmental and progressive temporality in which the experience of personal time and that of political time are aligned. History, the novel suggests, is on the side of the protagonist, structuring an accommodating and mediating plot of interconnected action so that the circle of narrativity and temporality drive gradually toward a future that overcomes the past. The historical subject, Angel, who is immediately recognizable in the gendered humanity of her travails and her desires, leans into that coming future with the complete sense that it belongs to her and her generation. As she must be, she is impatient with her mother's cautions about the pace of change, because *she*, not her mother, is the embodiment of the future in the present. She is the child of that revolutionary longing for emancipation. The Grenada Revolution, to which she naturally attaches herself personally and politically, is the engine that will resolve the historical contradictions and finally propel her disenchanted present out of the grip of the lingering colonial and neocolonial past. Yet it is precisely this resolute conviction—the conceit of the fictive narrative's relentless and uncompromising futurity, its irreverence toward remembrance of the past's sacrifices—that will crush her, that will paralyze and traumatize her when, in the novel's *peripeteia*, the revolution veers off-course, suddenly, violently, and inexplicably collapses, and leaves her stranded in a present that has been reclaimed by the past. Collins has here to contend with the revolution's end as a limiting *fact* of history, not merely as a creative literary device. This is Ricoeur's point, I think, about the *refiguring* dimension of mimesis in which the novel's configuring sense of an ending inhabits a world of readers who already know the revolution's fate, and who therefore know in advance that Angel's finitude is final and inescapable.

By contrast, *The Colour of Forgetting* is, one might say, a Benjaminian novel in its appeal to dimensions of baroque allegory.[58] Part, at least, of what Collins is suggesting here, I think, is that the form of allegory may be suited to moments of historical crisis and political and personal loss such as the collapse of the Grenada Revolution, when the horizon of the future (in which the Bildungsroman has had such narrative confidence) is not so easily discernible from the ruins of the present. Contrary to what progressivists of one sort or another believe, so *The Colour of Forgetting* urges, the past is not a dimension of experience that we can easily leave behind, especially when what constitutes that past is in large measure a catastrophic history of un-redressed injustice. The past's leavings haunt the present, even if inchoately like the distant sound of indecipherable thunder. Moreover, and perhaps more importantly, Collins suggests that it impoverishes us morally to think that we can live without remembrance of those whose sacrifices have made us possible or of those events that have been formative in our history. It is not, of course, that such remembrance will guarantee a successful future, will keep us invulnerable to failure. Nothing will. But it will help to prepare us, as Mamag helped to prepare Willive, for the unexpected obtrusions of the past into the present. To mourn, as Carib does, those whose grief is inconsolable, whose injury no justice can repair, is not to believe that there is nothing but repetition. Instead, it is to activate a sensibility of time that is at once recursive and cumulative rather than successive and teleological, a sensibility of time that, however forgotten, is not forgetful.

PART II

MEMORY, JUSTICE

The question . . . arises as to what gives the
idea of justice its federating force with regard
to the truthful and pragmatic aims of memory
as well as to the work of memory and the work
of mourning. It is thus the relation of the duty
of memory to the idea of justice that must be
interrogated.

—PAUL RICOEUR, *Memory, History, Forgetting*

THREE

GENERATIONS OF MEMORY
The Work of Mourning

> Mourning is regularly the reaction to the loss of a loved person, or
> to the loss of some abstraction which has taken the place of one.
> —SIGMUND FREUD, "Mourning and Melancholia"

Part of the distinctive value of Freud's observations and reflections in his meta-psychological essay "Mourning and Melancholia" (1917) is the way they suggestively enable a certain (partly
speculative, of course) thinking about economies of desire and
affect that accompany and structure the experience of the catastrophic loss of *political* ideals and the futures they project.
Thus, readers will no doubt remember that in the essay, Freud is
interested not only in discerning, on the fundamental model of
dreams and neurosis, the ambiguous relationship between the
normal and the pathological or in clarifying the evolving theoretical framework of psychoanalysis (the braided conceptual labor of
"repression," "narcissism," the "unconscious," "paranoia," and so
on, that he was elaborating at the same time), but also in thinking, in some receptive measure, about the political-psychological
crisis brought on by the Great War.[1] Here, after all, was a catastrophic event of densely traumatic experience and consequence
in which abiding cultural and political ideals were irreparably lost
and new, as-yet-uncertain ones were born, and in which, even
as it unfolded with unrivaled, vivid brutality, it was clear to con-

temporaries such as Freud that European civilization would never be the same again.[2] In considerations of the work of mourning, then, the loss of *political ideals* in principle is no less important than the loss of loved people. Notably, though, beyond the cursory, almost offhand reference Freud makes to such ideals—"fatherland" and "liberty"—in his definition of mourning (quoted in the epigraph), he makes nothing more of them in the essay. The reason, perhaps, is not only that the question of political ideals is intrinsically less germane to his immediate concerns with the psychic suffering of individuals, but also that, for him, the mourning of lost people and the mourning of dead causes have an intimate—because *internal*—connection within the psychic economy of desire. People and causes can be objects of *passional* attachment. Indeed, what is crucial to notice is how, with characteristic brevity and metaphoric nuance, Freud establishes the nature of this internal connection: mourning can be a response not only to the death of a person but also to the loss of ideals that, as he says, have *taken the place* of a loved one. In other words, the attachment to such ethical-political ideals as "fatherland" or "liberty" (or "national liberation" or "socialism," for that matter, to draw closer to the issues at hand in this chapter) is, in psychoanalytic terms, a form of libidinal *displacement*, a form of substitution, in which a love object is drained of desire that is then transferred, directly or indirectly, into the realm not only of ideas but of *ideals*. In a somewhat paradoxical way, then, political ideals are *founded* on object loss. Therefore, the loss of such ideals, especially their sudden, inexplicable, and terminal loss, may set in motion an affective response that is no less intractably complex than the catastrophic loss of a loved individual—not because ideals are as tangible as individuals, but because there is always an unconscious *trace* of lost love objects in the suffering that marks the loss of ideals. One might well speculate, moreover, that the force of the sense of loss will be all the more compounded where the ideal is already *personified*, already invested in the body of an individual— a beloved leader, say—and where the loss of that ideal is at the same time the concrete death, perhaps violent elimination, of the idealized person.

Importantly for my preoccupations, the work of mourning in Freud's view is essentially an interconnected work of *time* and *memory*.[3] Mourning constitutes a psychic labor of *reparative remembering* that over the course of time enables release from an attachment that is no longer plausible or realistic to hold on to. Memory, in other words, is the *temporal* site

Difference between memory & mourning

of mourning. The grief-stricken person, Freud says, recognizing the irreversible reality of the death of the loved one (or, again, the loved ideal), the painfully simple fact that he or she no longer exists, is compelled "at great expense of time and cathectic energy" to withdraw his or her investment of desire from the lost object while "in the meantime the existence of the lost object is psychically prolonged."[4] What mourning works on, then, are, in effect, *remains*—memory traces through which the mourner both *lets go* and *internalizes* the lost object. Each such memory trace, through which the loved person or ideal is imagined with all the complex associations of hope and disappointment, is called up (in Freud's technical idiom, "hypercathected") to facilitate the withdrawal of desire and, perhaps, even the formation of new personal and political attachments.[5]

In a certain sense, it is this practice of reparative remembering that appears blocked or disabled in melancholia. In Freud's account of it, an aggressive and resolutely self-recriminatory fixation makes it impossible to let go of the lost object (or ideal), and the melancholic dwells on the past with pathological nostalgia. A hopeless sense of worthlessness and failure marks the melancholic's demeanor. The reason for this, Freud argues, is that in melancholia, the role of the unconscious and the regressive process of narcissism are particularly prominent. Unlike grief that mourns an impoverished world, in melancholia, the remains of loss or disappointment have come to be negatively identified with a part of the self: the lost object has come to be incorporated into the ego as an agency of wounding criticism. Thus, Freud writes, the loss of the object becomes "transformed into an ego-loss and the conflict between the ego and the loved person into a cleavage between the critical activity of the ego and the ego as altered by identification."[6] It is important to remember that the idea that melancholia is unsuccessful mourning is largely schematic and heuristic in the topology of Freud's early meta-psychological theory of the unconscious. Given the constitutive ambivalence of desire, its always partly narcissistic-regressive character, mourning can never be completely successful; we can never be altogether relieved of the burden of the past. (The ego, Freud later maintained, is itself built up from wounded attachments.) Therefore, the psychic conditions of melancholia, like all neuroses, are, as it were, already structured into the formation of the self.[7] Needless to say, I am not going to engage the whole internal complexity and theoretical ambition of this conception of psychological life. What is important for my purposes is the contrast between a form of catastrophic loss that seems irreparable, in which the self is paralyzed by nostalgia for the past and a loss that can be mourned in some productive form because the object relation, to begin with, is less constituted on the basis of a narcissistic identification.[8]

In this chapter, I aim to think about this contrast between mourning and melancholia in relation to generations of remembering the catastrophic loss of a political project and of the ideals and people associated with it. As I suggested in chapter 2, what interests me about generations (principally following Karl Mannheim and Maurice Halbwachs) is that, as social institutions of temporal experience, they embody successive and overlapping frameworks of remembering, successive intellectual and affective ways to assimilate or incorporate, the past in the present. In this chapter, I extend and elaborate this conception of generations of memory in relation to contrasting experiences of the catastrophic loss of a political past that, I think, can be productively thought of in terms of the contrast between melancholia and mourning. Again, the central event I explore is the collapse of the Grenada Revolution in October 1983. But my focus here is on a different generational relationship than the one that held my attention in chapter 2. There, I was primarily interested in the contrast between the frameworks of memory that shaped the experience of the revolution and its loss on the part of the generation that, more than any, embodied its hopes and disappointment (Angel's generation) and the generation that immediately preceded it, that had lived through the rise and fall of Eric Gairy's social revolution of the 1950s (Doodsie's generation). Despite their contrasting generational locations, these generations lived a direct and immediate experience of the Grenada Revolution and so have firsthand memories of its birth and death. In this chapter, however, what interests me is a contrast between the generation that lived the catastrophe of the revolution's collapse as an absolute ruin (Angel's generation) and a succeeding generation that had no direct experience of the revolution or its collapse, and whose relation to these events is therefore temporally removed and intellectually and affectively mediated.

Specifically, I turn my attention to some figurations of traumatic loss and mourning and memory in the aftermaths of the catastrophic collapse of the Grenada Revolution. This figuration of loss centers on the haunting absence of the disappeared body of Maurice Bishop, killed (along with seven others) on 19 October 1983 under circumstances that are, still, not definitively known. Bishop *embodied* the Grenada Revolution, almost literally. He was the living realization of its presence and the affirmation of its ideals and aspirations. No one else in the revolutionary leadership of the New Jewel Movement even remotely approximated his meaning and stature. He was, in psychoanalytic terms, an object of enormous cathexis and affective investment. Therefore, his seemingly inexplicable and horrifically violent death not only robbed people of the leader through whom they had projected their futures, but the disappearance of his remains has *disabled* any prospect of mourning and closure—at least for the generation that lived the expectations of the revolution and the disorienting disappointment of its downfall. For this generation, the revolution and its collapse are remembered in embittered and melancholic fixation, at best in painfully ambivalent nostalgia and at worst in a blind desire for revenge. (Indeed, I suggest in the next chapter that this desire for revenge is part of what over two-and-a-half decades fueled the relentless demand to punish—by death, if possible—those members of the revolutionary party accused of Bishop's murder and who were tried and convicted in a court of doubtful legality and unjust procedures.)

If generations are temporal institutions that successively frame and reframe the conditions of social remembering, with successive generations holding themselves differently from earlier ones in relation to formative events, might it be possible to imagine a Grenadian generation born, say, in the *wake* of October 1983 whose "standpoint" may suggest other possibilities of remembering than that of their parents, and therefore other possibilities of mourning? This is my question in this chapter. My point of entry into this discussion is the text and project of a very remarkable booklet, *Under the Cover of Darkness*, published in Grenada in 2002.[9] This slim work, a mere fifty-six pages in all, was researched and written by a group of secondary-school students (roughly fifteen years old at the time) from the prestigious Presentation Brothers College in Grenada's capital, St. George's. In a climate of considerable divisiveness, mistrust, and resentment and under the guidance of their far-sighted principal, these students embarked on a quest to find out exactly what happened to the bodies of Maurice Bishop and his seven colleagues, and why their whereabouts have been so shrouded in secrecy and mystery. It was, I believe, an unprecedented exercise, demanding courage as well as foresight. And, as we will see, it yielded rich material for understanding the circumstances of the vanished bodies. However, I mean to read *Under the Cover of Darkness* not just for the information it provides to ground its quiet claim of a plot to conceal and, in fact, to *disappear*, Bishop's remains (fascinating and important as that is in its own right) but also as an invitation to consider the *contrast* between generational communities of memory concerning the loss of the revolution. Here I am interested in the sense or senses in which these schoolboys refused to be complicit in the paralysis that characterizes their parent's generation, the abject silence that has disabled any serious coming to terms with the loss of the revolution, the betrayal of its dreams, and the humiliation of the US invasion that, in effect, rescued them from the tragic catastrophe into which they had led themselves. I will suggest that *Under the Cover of Darkness* constitutes a kind of *speech act* in that it not only says, but also *does*, something. And the linguistic action it performs, in undertaking its investigation, is that of an *intervention* in the memorial space around the catastrophe of 19 October 1983 and, in particular, the painful case of the missing bodies of the former prime minister and his colleagues. I mean to pursue the intimation that part, at least, of what the text strongly suggests is the significant contrast between the generation of the Young Leaders (as the authors are called) and that of their parents in their respective temporal dispositions toward the past and future in the present.

The Death and Disappearance of Maurice Bishop

On Tuesday, 27 May 1986, in the early months of what came to be popularly known as the "Maurice Bishop Murder Trial," the following statement—which appeared over the signature of Callistus Bernard—was read out by the prosecution in the specially constituted "court of necessity" in St. George's, Grenada.[10] It was alleged to be a true, confessed account of the "execution" of Maurice Bishop, former prime minister of the People's Revolutionary Government of Grenada, and some of his colleagues at Fort Rupert on 19 October 1983, supposedly on the orders of the Central Committee of the governing party, the NJM:[11]

> Whilst at Fort Rupert, after the crowd had dispersed, I heard Captain [Lester] Redhead say halt and I looked and I saw Maurice Bishop,

Jacqueline Creft, Unison Whiteman, and Norris Bain walking away from Fort Rupert. They halted and I went and told them to march with their hands up onto the square. . . . Maurice had his hands behind his back. I lined them up facing the wall. Major [Christopher] Stroude and Captain Redhead were behind me and we all had weapons.

Captain Redhead then told [Evelyn] Brat Bullen and [Evelyn] Maitland to go and join Maurice and the others and they went. I then told Fitzroy Bain to go and join the others on the square and he went and lined up facing the wall. Some person also sent Keith Hayling and he joined them. I told them about turn and they all turned around. Major Stroude was there with me, Captain Redhead was also there and a machine gunner who I don't know by name and another soldier who had an [AK-47 machine gun].

There were also two machine gunners on the top of the wall of the square. I told Maurice Bishop and the rest of the people with him that the Central Committee [of the NJM] had decided that they should be executed by fire. I told them about turn. I gave the command, soldiers prepare to fire and fire. On or about the time I was giving the command, Jacqueline Creft was saying comrade wait, wait, hold on. The machine gunner on the square with me and the soldier with the AK on the square with me and I all fired together. The bodies fell backward, some fell down slow and some fell down fast.

Fitzroy Bain's body was moving and after we stopped firing Officer Gabriel fired one shot in his head . . . and the body stopped moving. I then went to examine the bodies and made sure they were dead. I told Gabriel to get some blankets, wrap up the bodies and put them on a truck until further instructions. I then left the square and went to join a meeting that was in progress in the mess hall at Fort Rupert chaired by Major Stroude. About one hundred persons attended that meeting and at the end of the meeting I said, "Long live the Revolution, long live Socialism." I then left and along with the other personnel of my armoured car went back to Fort Frederick. . . .

I went back to Fort Rupert on the night of October 19, around 11:00 P.M. and the bodies were on a truck. I drove my van there and then the truck driven by a man whom I don't know and about seven soldiers on it left for Camp Fedon, Calivigny, with the bodies to be buried. . . . When they reached a road in Calivigny, the truck stuck, so I had to transport the bodies in my van. When we reached Camp Fedon, a grave was already dug, so we put in the bodies, poured gasoline, lit it and let them burn until the next day and then I covered the grave. When I covered the grave, only bones, little bits of skull, and stuff was in the grave.[12]

This is certainly the most widely held picture of Bishop's last moments, and it is, as certainly, a *contestable* picture.[13] While it seems fairly certain that Bishop and his associates were shot to death, there is in fact no un-controversial, unambiguous account of exactly what took place—the final sequence of events—in that inner square of the fort that terrible after-noon. And it is unclear (given the overwhelming context of ideologically charged intimidation and fear that surrounded the criminal investigation of the event and the subsequent trial of the accused) whether there ever will be. The alleged author of the text, Callistus Bernard (formerly known as Imam Abdullah), was one of the seventeen convicted for Bishop's mur-der (the Grenada 17)—indeed, as the text suggests, the one most closely associated with the actual killing—and one of the fourteen initially sen-tenced to death.[14] Bernard was a lieutenant in the former People's Revo-lutionary Army and part of the convoy sent to retake Fort Rupert from Bishop and his associates on 19 October. He was also a leader of the re-sistance to the US invasion forces and was captured on 8 November 1983 as Ronald Reagan's Operation Urgent Fury drew to a protracted close. In June 1986, Bernard testified in his "indicative statement" to the court that he had been beaten and tortured to extract his signature for the statement that already had been prepared by his US captors.[15] Interestingly, in his published account of the events of 1983, *They Could Only Kill Me Once*, Bernard stops short of a detailed description of what he knows of the final moments of Bishop and his colleagues.[16]

It is hardly to be wondered at that the "confession" attributed to Bernard is formulated in such a manner as to incite and circulate a particular way to imagine and remember Bishop's death and the disappearance of his body. It invites us to picture an act of premeditated violence so cold and cruel and ruthless, so brutally single-minded and unmerciful, that not even the urgent last-minute plea of the only woman among those detained (Jacque-line Creft, believed to have been pregnant with Bishop's child) could stem, much less abort, the impending death. The "confession" also offers a text of intriguing erasure, such that the preceding actions of Bishop and his supporters are neatly elided (the overrunning of the fort, the distribution of arms to civilians, the unprovoked killing of three of the soldiers in the convoy that came to retake their headquarters), as well as the chaos and fury that ensued. All we have is a neat sequence of actions leading to calculated murder. Moreover (and most important from the point of view of the trial's benefactors, a point I return to in the next chapter), the statement sets before us the performance of an execution carried out in the ideological name of the revolution and with the express authorization of the Central Committee of the revolutionary party—thus, a *political* execution. This, in fact, was the point of Bernard's "confession": it was not only to implicate himself personally in murder; it was to implicate the Central Committee of the NJM in conspiracy and, behind that, to insinuate the *diabolical* intent of former Deputy Prime Minister and Minister of Finance Bernard Coard in masterminding the overthrow and killing of Bishop.[17]

The violent deaths of Bishop and his colleagues and the vanishing of their remains from the memorial landscape of contemporary Grenada are aspects of the collapse of the Grenada Revolution that continue to haunt and afflict that island's body politic. For more than two decades, it is safe to say, the absence of these bodies, the denial to them of the dignity of a proper funeral, has been a continuous source of grief and bitterness about that past—in a personal way for the immediate families and friends of the victims, but also in a larger moral and political way for a whole generation of Grenadians who lived through the ordeal of October 1983. It is at least arguable that for this generation it is the mysterious absence of these bodies more than any other single aspect of the revolution's ending that has made it virtually impossible to bring about some closure to 19 October and its aftermath. In particular, as I have said, it is doubtlessly the absent body of Bishop that has been the most poignant reminder of the gaping wound left by the violent erasure of the revolution. Virtually identified with the revolution, he personified its hopes, its idiom, and its ambitions. In life, his body functioned metonymically; his was the personable face of the revolution's ethos, invested with all of the compulsive symbology of political desire. In death, too, his (absent) body continues to have an

evocative and protean ethical-political *afterlife*, drawing ambiguously to
its ephemeral self all of the leftover political emotions, all of the now un-
answerable questions, of an *interrupted* horizon of expectation. In death,
Bishop has become mythologized, and without his dead body, the grave
of the revolution, in a manner of speaking, stands open and empty, and
the loss of the former futures it represented remains an unburied and un-
mournable past.

Perhaps not so surprising, then, that the implosion of the revolution—
its sudden, violent, seemingly inexplicable self-destruction in the course
of a few short hours on 19 October 1983 and the US invasion that followed shortly after, on the morning of 25 October (an event experienced
by many as a hopeless mixture of violation, shame, and relief)—marked
an overwhelming, traumatic moment that has left an indelible scar on the
collective consciousness of Grenadians. Suddenly, it seemed, history had
betrayed them. Embodied in the small-island intimacy of familiar people
making the revolution, this history, once their ally and friend, had now
unaccountably turned against them; it had *robbed* them of the progressive future for which they had so long labored and brought them lurch-
ing to a bewildered—bewildering—standstill. Undoubtedly, between the
maimed and the dead, the implosion of the Grenada Revolution materi-
ally destroyed livelihoods and lives. But very profoundly (as I suggest in
chapter 2), it also ruined a generation's experience of time—that is, it destroyed the temporality constitutive of the organization of political hope
and future-oriented expectation through which a generation lived. To put
this more concretely, the experience of the collapse of the Grenada Revolution in October 1983 was not merely that of a contingent failure of political
will or political strategy, a reckless miscalculation of the environment of
local and international forces seeking to subvert its achievement (however
much some or all of these failures were felt to be causally involved in the
calamity). The collapse of the Grenada Revolution was, I think (and this,
recall, was the point of my reading of Collins's *Angel*), existentially deeper
than this, and politically more profound and long-lasting. What it signaled was a collapse of the very conditions of a generation's experience of
political time, an organization of time in which past-present-future were
connected in a chain of progressive succession so that past gave way to
present and present gave way to future in uniform and unfailing rhythms
of dialectical *overcoming*. The end of the revolution marked the collapse of

such temporal certainties. It marked the loss of futures. Now, the anticipated future could no longer be imagined as a horizon guaranteed by the memory of the past, and the present could no longer be experienced as a mere interval in the passage from remembered past to immanent future. Now the present appeared like a temporal "boundary point" of prolonged and stagnant duration. In an abrupt and surprising reversal, the future had become the past and, denuded of its old, progressive dynamic, the present could be nothing more than the endless and melancholic repetition of itself.[18]

One way to put the intimation that animates me in this chapter is the following: there is a relationship between generational memory, nostalgic temporality, and the catastrophic loss of revolutionary futures marked by the absent—or ghostly—presence of Bishop's body. This dead political body that is at once nowhere and everywhere in contemporary Grenada is one particularly concentrated cathexis point (so to call it) for a generation's palpable sense of temporal rupture, their sense that time no longer reliably bears them forward to a future already immanent in the present.[19] The intimation I mean to explore is that this generation's sense of thwarted mourning over Bishop's unburied body betokens their lingering sense of the unfinishedness of the end of the revolution, their sense that 19 October 1983 constitutes a loss that will last forever, an ending that cannot be brought to an end.

Under the Cover of Darkness

In 1999, under the mentorship of their principal, Brother Robert Fanovitch, a number of fourth-form boys entered the regional "Young Leaders" competition sponsored by the Republic Bank of Trinidad and Tobago.[20] The theme that year was "Peace." As Brother Robert remembers it, he thought it would make an interesting and worthwhile challenge to translate this urgent theme in terms of "reconciliation," a notion that had been given broad resonance as a consequence of South Africa's well-publicized and celebrated truth and reconciliation process and one that was much on the minds of thinking Grenadians.[21] Even in 1999, sixteen years after the events of 19 October 1983, there was a pervasive sense of unease and "unresolvedness" about that recent past. As Brother Robert said, there was a palpable sense of discord and enmity in the country, and talking about 1983 was made difficult by the lingering suspicions about whose side of the conflict one might have taken: former Prime Minister Maurice Bishop's or former Deputy Prime Minister Bernard Coard's.

Concretely, for Brother Robert and his students, reconciliation meant seeking to diminish the animosity felt toward members of the Grenada 17 by the families who had lost relatives and loved ones at Fort Rupert on 19 October 1983. For these family members, as in the eyes of many in Grenada and elsewhere, it is *only* the party and military leaders who were responsible for the deaths that occurred at the fort. As far as they are concerned, for example, virtually no blame is attached to Bishop's decision to abort the almost completed negotiations on joint leadership, the matter that precipitated the crisis and on which the Central Committee had abandoned its earlier stand, and no blame is attached to his provocative decision to open the armory at Fort Rupert and arm civilians, thus transforming an internal party crisis into a confrontational military matter (see chapter 1). In this context, only the Grenada 17 are understood to be blameworthy; the only debts owed are theirs—an issue I take up in the epilogue. Not surprisingly, then, when Brother Robert approached members of these families regarding what they most wanted from the Grenada 17, most people declared straightforwardly that they wanted to see them hanged, as they were originally meant to be.[22] Some, however, had other hopes. They expressed a passionate desire for information that would help them recover the remains of those they had lost on 19 October. There was an understandable—though erroneous—assumption that the seventeen people imprisoned at Richmond Hill had this information and were deliberately, callously *withholding* it. The poignant articulations of indignant loss among these family members (not least on the part of Bishop's aging mother, Alimenta Bishop), expressing the need to be able to mourn and bury their dead, turned the peace and reconciliation project in a new and wholly unexpected direction. For the students and their principal, it now became a question of how to locate the remains of Bishop and his associates and how to account for the others who died at Fort Rupert that day, many of them schoolchildren killed in the crossfire and explosions or who, trying to escape the mayhem, jumped to their deaths over the precipitous walls of the eighteenth-century fort. The fundamental insight of Brother Robert and his students was that a key to any serious prospect of reconciliation in Grenada, to providing any sustaining repair of the harms of 19 October, would be a determination of exactly what happened to Bishop's remains.[23] It was a simple but subtle recognition of the powerful symbolic role his absent dead body plays in perpetuating the general sense of anguished suspicion and despair in the country, and therefore of its importance to the possibility of a reparative mourning that might help to relieve the melancholic burden of that unresolved past. It also turned out to be a recognition that, as the students quickly found, would run them up against the unyielding silence of forces larger than their intelligence and courage alone could penetrate, much less overcome.

When the students took up their research, the question of the whereabouts of the remains of Bishop and his colleagues had long since come to a virtual dead end. Indeed, the US Armed Forces' pathology report of 12 December 1983 had officially, if sketchily and somewhat ambiguously, closed the matter.[24] In early November 1983, as Operation Urgent Fury was winding down and the United States and allied Caribbean occupying forces (Jamaicans and Barbadians principally—and infamously) had set about their interrogations, information led them to Camp Fedon in Calivigny and to the hole where the bodies of those taken from Fort Rupert had been burned and buried. According to the report, US Army Graves Registration personnel "recovered commingled remains, believed to be the Prime Minister and his Cabinet, from a shallow grave near Fort Rupert, Grenada, placed them in four body bags, and stored them in a temporary morgue facility without refrigeration." Notably, the report does not mention the date on which the actual discovery of the bodies was made. As the report continues, on 9 November 1983, the Office of the Joint Chiefs of Staff made a request, on behalf of the State Department, to the Armed Forces Institute of Pathology for assistance in identifying the remains. A team that included two forensic pathologists, two forensic doctors, and one forensic dentist left for Grenada that evening. It might have appeared from this responsiveness that a certain degree of seriousness was attached to the discovery of the bodies. Evidently, however, this was more apparent than real. The report itself states that the Graves Registration personnel made no documentation of the recovery site and that "no photographs were available."[25] The exhumed remains were subsequently taken to the anatomy laboratory at the American medical school, St. George's University, where they were forensically examined by US Army personnel, as well as by Robert Jordan of the university's Department of Anatomical Sciences. The report maintains that none of the bones exhumed at Camp Fedon were of sufficient length to be those of a man of Bishop's height. "The material available for examination and records available for comparison are insufficient to establish the identity of the Prime Minister Maurice Bishop, members of his Cabinet, or other persons who allegedly died at Fort Rupert, Grenada, on 19 October 1983," it states. "The remains are commingled, and documentation of their recovery is poor due to the hazardous conditions at the time of recovery."[26] (It is obscure what the last remark about the conditions could mean, since by this time the US Army was in complete control of the country.) Further, the report claimed that, while remnants of women's clothing were found, identifiable anatomical evidence of female remains was not found—a finding that, to these officials, ruled out the possibility that the body of Jacqueline Creft was among those buried in the hole. Both of these claims would later be disputed. However, on 12 November, everything changed. A local undertaker, Otways Funeral Home, removed the remains from the university laboratory. It is not known on whose authorization this was done, but given the fact of the occupation, it has to be presumed to have been that of the US Army command. The bodies have not been seen since.[27]

As a first line of approach to their research, the students sought clarification and elaboration from US government sources. But receiving no help whatsoever, they turned their attention in another direction: to tracking down eyewitnesses and reconstructing in more fine-grain detail the process of discovery and exhumation of the bodies. Curiously—indeed, tellingly—in the sixteen years since 1983, this seemed never to have been conscientiously done. Who was actually at Camp Fedon when the bodies were discovered? Who led the invading forces to the bodies? What might they know? What was the condition of the bodies when they were discovered? How many bodies were in the hole? Were they identifiable? And if they were identifiable, on the basis of what evidence? These were the sorts of questions that now propelled the students' investigation.

One of the important eyewitnesses the Young Leaders spoke to was the former cook at Camp Fedon, Christopher Bowen, who distinctly remembered seeing the bodies of Bishop, Creft, Whiteman, Norris Bain, and Fitzroy Bain being put into a hole on the night of 19 October—and, moreover, being put into the *same* hole. (This is an important detail because there were rumors that more than one hole might have existed and that Bishop's body in particular might even have been disposed of elsewhere—at sea, for example.) It was apparently Bowen who led the occupying forces to the site of the bodies.[28] He gave the students an account of the "slow and meticulous" recovery process and a "graphic description of the bodies, some of whom he recognized, since the parts of the bodies that were stuck in the mud had not burned."[29] Here, then, was a suggestive lead. But the discovery that provided the most crucial element in the students' research was the discovery of Earl Brown, the Jamaican soldier who had interrogated Bowen and been given the "tip-off" as to the location of the bodies. It was Brown, accompanied by the Grave Registration unit, who went to Camp Fedon to investigate the lead and subsequently found the remains in the shallow grave. (Brother Robert remembers coming across Brown's name in a newspaper article, quite by chance, and tracking him down through Catholic church connections in Jamaica.[30]) Brown, who no longer lived in Jamaica and who was no longer even a member of the Jamaica Defense Force, would eventually—and abruptly—cut off communications with Brother Robert and his students when he found out that the information he was providing was going to be published. (Such, evidently, was the murky atmosphere of intimidation and fear that prevailed so many years after the events of October 1983.) But what Brown told the students in the time he communicated with them (largely through e-mail and without knowing that they were comparing eyewitness accounts with documentary evidence) would be of fundamental importance, because it contradicted the pathology report by the US Armed Forces in a number of areas, and it furnished sufficient information to enable the students to piece together a richer and more complex story—a story, as the Young Leaders characterize it, of deliberate concealment and fabrication of the truth.

There were several discrepancies between Brown's account and the pathology report. As Brown remembered it (corroborating the story told to the students by Bowen), the exhumed bodies were only partially burned and partially decomposed, and therefore much was still identifiable to the naked eye. For example, he said, intact skulls and other body parts were in the hole, in addition to personal effects such as keys, wallets, and jewelry. Based on the reports that described the shooting at Fort Rupert and what people were said to have been wearing when they died, there was no doubt in his mind that Bishop's body was there. Nor did he doubt (based on his cursory identification of the body parts immediately visible to him) that Jacqueline Creft was among the identifiable remains. (Creft was the only woman whose body was known to have been taken from Fort Rupert to Camp Fedon on the night of 19 October 1983.) The students also quote from contemporary newspaper accounts indicating that among the scorched, decomposed bodies were skeletal remains of a woman.[31] Moreover, Jordan, the pathologist, confirmed that on his expert examination of the remains in his laboratory, there was definitely evidence of female body parts.[32] The question of the presence of female remains, as the Young Leaders argued, was of the greatest importance in light of the fact that this is precisely what the US Armed Forces' forensic report emphatically denied. And this raised the strong suspicion among the students that the United States had an interest in throwing doubt on the idea that Bishop's remains were among those found at Camp Fedon.[33]

But there is more. According to Brown (and Bowen), the remains were placed in a number of body bags, tagged as to who was in which bag, and removed from Camp Fedon. Contrary to the official report, there is photographic evidence of this. But what eventually arrived at St. George's University for examination (according to the laboratory's janitor, Christopher Belgrave) were not black body bags, as one might have expected had they been transported directly from Camp Fedon to the university, but a number of garbage bags. Those bags contained no skulls or intact bones, as Jordan reports. Indeed, according to Jordan, when he examined the remains, the ends of the bones were charred and splintered, consistent, he maintained, "with being dynamited or run over by a vehicle."[34]

Something was seriously amiss. Realistically, the students surmised that if Brown was right that Bishop and Creft were visibly among the bodies exhumed (and there was no self-evident reason to doubt the veracity of the information he gave them), someone had obviously tampered with the remains, removing skulls and other body parts and splintering the bones, as they put it, to "confuse the identification." But on whose authority? When? And by what means? Clearly something very hurried and very drastic had been done to the remains *between* their exhumation at Camp Fedon and their examination at St. George's University. Speculating that there had been a deliberate attempt to throw dust in the eyes of anyone trying to discover the truth of what took place on 19 October, the Young Leaders suggest the likelihood that the sequence of events was not as they had assumed all along. There is strong reason to believe that the remains were actually discovered on 8 November 1983, they argue, not

9 November, as previously thought; there is some newspaper evidence that the accurate date is the earlier one.[35] They were then taken that evening (since Brown remembers wrapping up the removal of the bodies from the grave late on the evening of their discovery) to an undisclosed location, where the skulls were removed and the bones were splintered by some considerable force. It was clear in the minds of the Young Leaders, at least, that "someone seems to have gone to great pains to ensure that the identity of those remains would be shrouded in uncertainty."[36] In their view, the reason this was done was not hard to discern. As they put it with disarming blandness, "One theory which seems plausible is that Maurice Bishop would have been made a martyr had his remains been discovered, and this was undesirable at the time in Grenada."[37] Indeed, this seems a quite plausible theory.

Undoubtedly, however minimal or limited its scholarship (they were schoolboys, after all), *Under the Cover of Darkness* is a remarkable investigative work of excavation and exhumation of the historical truth of the whereabouts of the remains of Bishop and his slain associates. Had they had more resources, who knows what might have been accomplished. *Under the Cover of Darkness* provides invaluable, hitherto unearthed information about what happened to the bodies once they were discovered at Calivigny by the invading forces—the sequence of unfolding events and the principals involved. The students did not succeed, in the end, in discovering the final disposition of the bodies. But this was clearly not a consequence of faulty research or want of diligence. They ran into a dead end—an instructive one, because what it revealed to these students was the unmistakable hand of political powers who had decided that the question of Bishop's remains should have no conclusive answer, should forever be a matter of perplexity and doubt. And the agency of this power was evidently not the (then still) incarcerated Grenada 17, as the relatives of the dead so wanted to believe. Whatever the motivation that led to the initial destruction and concealment of the bodies of Bishop and his associates in the early hours of 20 October 1983, thus precluding their immediate mourning and burial by their families and friends, new events and greater powers had now supervened and altered the political landscape of interests and forces. What the schoolboys learned (cautious as they were in their formulations and muted and indirect as they were in naming their suspicions) was that the effective determination seemed now to be that the tangible presence of Bishop's remains might serve as a focus and catalyst for political criticism and perhaps even political organization unfriendly to the invading powers.

Still, valuable and remarkable as this contribution is to our concern with the aftermath of the collapse of the Grenada Revolution, it is not what I want most to notice about the text and textuality of *Under the Cover of Darkness*. I want to observe something *performative* about this slender booklet, the sense in which it, in effect, intervenes in the moral space of the revolution's aftermaths by initiating a distinctive action—one of reparative mourning and remembrance, I would suggest. In other words, *Under the Cover of Darkness* can be read instructively as an initiative of generational remembering that, entering the moral and ideological field of collective memory of the revolution's downfall in contemporary Grenada, works at least to question and unsettle, if not entirely displace, the melancholic silence and paralysis that pervades an older generation's memory of that disaster. *Under the Cover of Darkness* is a kind of speech act that, in saying what it says about the disappeared bodies of Bishop and his associates, also does something to the project of collective remembering. As one discerning observer put it in his justly admiring foreword to the students' study, "As a people, we continue to wrestle with the events of October 1983. As we continue to fight to reconcile the fallout of the revolution and to heal the wounds of divisiveness, lack of trust, misunderstanding and hatred among our people, this study is a key to unlock those doors that have entrapped us for so long."[38] Notice the sense of release from an imprisoning experience. A prescient generational sensibility is at work in this warm observation, the sense of a contrast of generational experience and perspective in relation to the memory of October 1983. Not only are the wounds of that catastrophic past still open, but also, for those who lived it, its memory has been a disabling trap. As the writer of the foreword pointedly (almost self-critically) recognized, the students were not merely knowledgeable and well guided, but theirs was also a "bold and courageous attempt to address a sensitive and mysterious aspect of Grenada's history." They had intervened where others older than themselves were "afraid to venture."[39] In *Under the Cover of Darkness*, the Young Leaders appear to have little or no direct investment in a retrospective narrative of recrimination and blame. Unlike their generational predecessors, they treat Bishop's absent body less as an ideological symbol of the righteous side of the fatal party conflict that brought the revolution to its doom, the portentous symbol of Good against Evil, than as an object of a forensic investigation aimed at historical truth.

I want to underline that my intention here is not to idealize this text or celebrate its historical truth value, to make the students out as offering a sublime path to healing, as the booklet's foreword does. Indeed, we will see in a moment the text's own implication in a spurious account of the revolution's downfall, as though revising the apprehension of the remains of the bodies meant rendering unchanged the remains of the political narrative of conspiracy. My intention, rather, is to notice how *draining* Bishop's body of its surfeit of phantasmagoria and mythological longing can constitute a generational intervention of reparative mourning and remembering inasmuch as it shows one way that the catastrophic past can be remembered *without* paralyzing nostalgia and embittered divisiveness. It shows that the present can live with the past—even the not entirely resolved or resolvable past—in ways other than melancholia and in ways that potentially open the present to ethical-political intervention. Indeed, from this perspective, it is not unimportant that the publication of *Under the Cover of Darkness* led to considerable public discussion about the missing bodies (and even to a sudden, fleeting expectation that they had indeed been found in the cemetery in St. George's). And one ethical-political outcome of this renewed sense of urgency for closure was that the sitting government felt obliged to initiate—cynically and opportunistically, it turned out—a formal truth and reconciliation process.[40] I turn to this in the following chapter.

Generations of Memory and Postmemory

In contemporary, postrevolutionary Grenada, there is one imposing, public memorial to the catastrophe of October 1983. It is not, however, a monument to the lost revolution, as one might have expected, given its immense popularity. Nor is it even a monument in memory of the beloved former Prime Minister Maurice Bishop. (There is, to be sure, a small plaque on the wall at the fort against which he and the others were allegedly lined up and shot, but that is all.) Nor again is it a monument to those Grenadian patriots who died resisting the invading US Army and whose bodies lie in hastily dug, unmarked graves scattered across the battlefields of the military encounter. Curiously, the one public memorial to the catastrophe of October 1983 is, rather, a monument to the American soldiers who died in the invasion and who are remembered here as liberators. Standing just a few minutes' drive from the airport at Point Salines (a site of considerable symbolic value, since it figured prominently in the US propaganda against the Grenada Revolution), this monument consists of two intersecting arches sheltering two inscriptions.[41] The central one, atop a raised platform reads, "This plaque expresses the gratitude of the Grenadian people to the forces from the United States of America and the Caribbean, especially those who sacrificed their lives in liberating Grenada on 25 October 1983. It was dedicated by President Ronald Reagan on his visit to Grenada on 20 February 1986." The smaller plaque, erected by the US Veterans of Foreign Wars on 16 May 1995, reads, "To honor those members of the United States military who through commitment and sacrifice, returned freedom to Grenada." Here, then, looming out of the scarred and bloodied landscape of contemporary Grenada, is the lone memorial to 1983. What are we to make of this social fact? And what are we to make of the monument itself, its sheer, deliberate, even vulgar banality—its oddly remote yet willfully mocking presence? It seems to me hard not to recognize in it the embodiment of a *cynical* act of imperial power, the sneering reward empire offers to mark the defeat of a people's defiance.[42] If on one side the monument confronts us with the projection of overwhelming domination, on the other side, it registers the limp prostration of a defeated people's spirit.

As students of memorials have cogently argued for some time, the aim of such public monuments—physical inscriptions of remembrance—is to give weight and solidity, a concrete texture (literally and metaphorically), to the past they conserve in the present. Transforming a realm of "nature" (an open field, say, or the face of stone) into a locale of memory, a *lieu de mémoire*, the monument constitutes a social fact imbued with moral-political significance, with visually inscribed *referentiality*. But monuments doubtless are more than an "exteriorization" of memory, because they are never innocent of power.[43] If monuments are signifiers, *naming* a past, they are also *signatures* of relations of power, telling us not only what we are remembering, but also what we *ought* to remember. Public monuments therefore serve not only an informative semiotic function but also a laden *declarative* one. They serve to *authorize* a certain way to remember the past and, therefore, they implicitly or explicitly displace or seek to preclude other ways to remember the past. In so doing, they help to propagate the illusion of a common memory. Thus, public memorials, especially politically aggressive ones, are at once agents of remembrance and instruments of forgetting.[44] In offering a particular past to valorize, they seek simultaneously to deny or deform an alternative remembering of the past and what it stood for. This is not to say that monuments are themselves immune to time and change. Their witness need not be perpetual. They need not petrify history forever in a single image. They can be contested, destroyed.

In these terms it is easy to see the moral-political labor of memory embodied in the totem of thanks to Ronald Reagan and America that stands just beyond Grenada's airport. It is an invitation to submissive amnesia, an invitation not so much to forget the revolution of 13 March 1979 and the radical Caribbean political traditions from which it came as to *delegitimize*, and even to *criminalize*, it. (Reagan's visit to dedicate the monument to his army's sacrifice was timed to coincide with the start of the Maurice Bishop Murder Trial in February 1986, to which I turn in chapter 4.) This way to remember October 1983 is underscored by the practice of celebrating the day of the commencement of the US invasion, 25 October, as an official day of thanksgiving in Grenada's annual calendar.

There are, of course, Grenadian voices of indignation that call the monument to the dead US soldiers what it is—namely, a grotesque gesture of the "new colonialism" in the Caribbean, a warning sign that these islands are supposed to think of themselves not as sovereign states of self-determination but, rather, in the eloquent formulation of former US Secretary of State George Shultz, as lovely pieces of real estate.[45] It was an evident foretaste of the post–Cold War imperial dispensation that has rewritten the script not only of the future but also of the past. Certainly, no postrevolutionary regime in Grenada has seriously sought to challenge the memorial presence of these affirmations of the naked intimidation of American power. Thus, the monument stands there, largely ignored by the quotidian passing traffic but nevertheless unmolested, unprotested even. This very fact—the mute toleration with which it is regarded—stands as testimony to how far a formerly revolutionary generation can be reduced to shame, paralysis, and silence. For perhaps the most daunting and wounding paradox for this generation is that it was obliged to welcome its former political enemy as the agent of its salvation, as the savior whose timely arrival rescued them from themselves. This, I argue, constitutes the moral memorial space into which the Young Leaders entered with *Under the Cover of Darkness.*

As Karl Mannheim and Reinhart Koselleck suggest in different ways, it is in the succession of generations that one can discern the altering experience of the relation of past, present, and future.[46] Each succeeding generation inhabits a new experience of temporality, a new experience of the passage of social and political time.[47] Each succeeding generation constructs anew out of its inheritance and its own experience the relation to the formative events of the past that have organized the imagination of the future and how to get there. But what exactly is the relationship between the frameworks of memory of successive generations? What continuities and discontinuities mark the ways in which successive generations remember the shared past? How does each younger generation, from within the frameworks that shape their recollections, connect to—or disconnect from—the collective memories of an older generation? How do successive generations learn to remember in ways that encompass both the distinctiveness of their own generational standpoint and the difference between that standpoint and the frameworks of their elders, and do so, moreover, without being imprisoned by the authority of established memory? I suggest that *Under the Cover of Darkness* registers something of a generational succession in the experience of political time and, therefore, with the prevailing organization of the social memory of October 1983.

All of the Young Leaders were born after the catastrophic events of October 1983. They are not contemporaries of it, as participants or as witnesses. Consequently, none of them could have any firsthand memories of the politics of the period or any direct experience of the hopes and disappointments represented by the rise and fall of the NJM and its People's Revolutionary Government. This is the living past of their parents' present memories. And yet it is also, in some form, the *inheritance* of the Young Leaders; in a certain sense, they also live the traumatic *after-effects* of the catastrophe of October 1983—but they live it *belatedly,* as it were, from a generational remove. Their memories of October 1983 are somewhat akin to what Marianne Hirsch instructively calls "postmemories." These are memories, she suggests, that successive generations "have" (in the sense that they are transmitted to them, often, though not only, through family lines) of traumatic events that preceded their births but that are nonetheless deeply formative for their own present experience.[48] The memories are "post" in the now familiar sense of "coming after" some relevant past without quite leaving that past behind. For Hirsch, postmemories are not, obviously, literal memories inasmuch as they are the direct remembrances of a *previous* generation. They are therefore mediated less through recollection than through imagination. But what is important to Hirsch is that postmemories can nevertheless approximate "real" memories in their "affective force." Here, then, the principal focus of the intervention is on continuities, the way postmemories help to perpetuate the emotive cathexis of the past in the present. By contrast, the accent of my interest is more on the *discontinuities* between generations of memory; indeed, it is the *transformation* of the "affective force" of a traumatic event that concerns me, the sense in which a founding experience can be inherited in ways that allow a succeeding generation to act upon it—or with it—*differently* than their predecessors did.

Interestingly, the Young Leaders register a profound intuition of this disjuncture between their generational location and habitus and that of their parents in relation to the catastrophic events of October 1983. As they say at a certain point in the introduction to *Under the Cover of Darkness*, they found it "difficult to identify with the pain and anger" of their parents and their parents' contemporaries, a pain and anger that had plunged them into a melancholy silence.[49] (In one of her most poignant poems, "Shame Bush," Merle Collins explores the moral imagination of this burdened incapacity to speak about October 1983.[50]) Thus, the schoolboys register in an explicit way not only their proximal generational distance from the events of 1983 but also their generational *estrangement* from them. They register the generational sense in which, if 1983 is indeed their inheritance, it nevertheless belongs to them differently from how it belongs to their parents. That difference is crucial. What the schoolboys expressly do not inherit is the pain and the anger, the "affective force," of the catastrophe. October 1983 does not hang around their necks like a noose, like a paralyzing burden. This generational tension—between the relative cool-headedness of the boys' relation to the past of 1983 and the anguish and turmoil they identify in their parents' relation to it—suggests the temporal non-contemporaneity of intergenerational experience to which Mannheim refers and, more specifically, to the shift in the temporal experience of these successive Caribbean generations.

No more than fifteen or sixteen years old in 1999 when they undertook their high-school project, these boys would have been born to parents with an altogether different generational experience from theirs of the catastrophe of October 1983. They would be the children of Collins's fictive character, Angel. As we remember from chapter 2, this older generation probably was born in the early 1950s, and their social-political horizons would have been shaped by a widespread expectation of social transformation. This predecessor generation (who lived the Grenada Revolution as its own) lived through an organization—or rationality—of political temporality in which history promised the present a better future than the past. A rhythm of positive (or, if you like, dialectical) succession distributed the relation between what had been suffered and endured and what was waiting on the other side of the horizon. Or to employ the idiom of the political sociology of generations, they occupied a generational habitus in which the past (of injury, of harms) could be mobilized to underwrite the redemptive moral-political project of overcoming the present and realizing their longing for emancipation. That past was expected to converge on a present with such comprehensiveness that their longing for a world without the old sources of oppression could at last be realized. This is why its collapse—and not merely its collapse, but the unforeseen shock of the way it collapsed, the sudden, violent implosion compressed into a few hours on 19 October—brought to an end, and precipitated the traumatic loss of, something much more fundamental than the People's Revolutionary Government: something like an end, a loss, of futures. This is a profoundly traumatized and *disappointed* generation that lives the ruin of the Grenada Revolution as an absolute, irrevocable loss and a recurring, unending end. It seems to me that this is the meaning of the melancholia to which their children, the Young Leaders, point: the repeating loops of anguish, confusion, and rage that paralyze their political will and that can be channeled only through a recriminatory demand to settle old scores, finally and forever to decide who was right and who was wrong in the conflict that brought the revolution to its collapse, and who is guilty and who is innocent of the crime of 19 October. It is a generation whose loss is compounded by the ambivalence and shame of welcoming the US invasion, an ambivalence and shame that perhaps allows them to tolerate the monument to the dead US soldiers as the one commemorative gesture to the catastrophe of 1983. This is an *abandoned* generation.

By contrast, the children of this generation—and among them, of course, the Young Leaders—inhabit a different generational *habitus*, shaped by a different temporal framework for comprehending the past in the present. It is, in effect, a different community of memory. Their relation to time is not organized by the temporal structure of their parents' longings; therefore, they are not vulnerable to the exposure of these longings to the same loss and disappointment. This generation has grown up in Bandung's wake, so to speak. Born after the end of history, they are children of another era of expectation that is characterized not by the loss of the past (the collapse of the left regionally as well as globally, the end of the politics of nonalignment and the idea of the Third World it helped to establish and sustain) but by the *aftermaths* of that loss, an aftermaths defined by the active and systematic delegitimization, even criminalization, of the past. A "techtonic" shift (to use Katherine Verdery's apt phrase) has taken place so that the assumptions about temporal succession that were part of the old ethos of social and political change have lost their salience—indeed, their credibility.[51] The past, needless to say, has not gone away—this is the point about the persisting symbolic life of Bishop's body—but the cathexis that drives the search for its whereabouts is now disconnected from the temporal structure of revolutionary desire or (its sometime twin) revolutionary recrimination.

I do not mean to imply that the interruption of the narrative of vindication and recrimination I read in the generational perspective of *Under the Cover of Darkness* represents a new lease on radical politics (whatever that might mean). Nor do I mean to suggest that the account of the past of October 1983 offered by the Young Leaders is more redeeming, more critical, more truthful—indeed, more anything—than the accounts offered by their parents. To the contrary, there is much to doubt, even to reject, for example, in the story they tell about the circumstances that led up to the disaster of 19 October and, in particular, the stereotypical counter-positioning of Maurice Bishop and Bernard Coard they rely on to narrate that history.[52] What I do mean to suggest, instead, concerns the temporal organization through which this younger generation connects the present to the past and what some of the implications might be of that temporal reorganization. Let me put it in the following way: by displacing the centrality of the old structure of temporal expectation of futures-from-pasts that was organized around the longing for revolutionary overcoming, they open up a new space of remembrance that embodies the possibility of evading—sidestepping—the compulsive repetition of the familiar resentments against the past's betrayal of its promise of an indemnified future to come. They suggest (naïvely, perhaps, but still) that a sense of loss, even of catastrophic loss, that is at once personal and collective, need not be paralyzed by the hopeless returns to that crippled, crippling *mise-en-scène* embodied in the leftovers of revolutionary time, and that it need not be engaged by a willful forgetting that leaves the past behind as dead and irrelevant. They suggest, rather, that catastrophic loss can be animated by a remembrance that keeps the past alive in a fragile tension with the present in ways that allow possible modes of non-recriminatory political action. The eventual failure of the truth and reconciliation process triggered by their intervention lies not with them, of course, but precisely with the old politics of revenge that their text worked to displace.

It may be helpful in closing this chapter on the generational time of traumatic memory and political catastrophe to mark off what I have been trying to say from the idea of "left melancholia" that in recent years has received some attention. Readers of Walter Benjamin's "Left-Wing Melancholy" (1931) will remember that in his polemic against the moral-political stance of the poet Eric Kastner, he described a certain "heavy-heartedness" and "despair" of the leftist intelligentsia whose politics was little more than gestural, a hollow attitude that did not—or, anyway, did not any longer—correspond to meaningful political action.[53] Benjamin was describing, under the sign of "melancholia," an aestheticized political pose very like the ironic demeanor of the *flâneur* of those darkening European years, whose slightly affected morbidity hung around him (the figure is undoubtedly male) like bad faith and who, "from the beginning," as Benjamin put it, had no intention but to yield to a "negativistic quiet," a passive, consumption-driven *jouissance*. The leftist melancholic intellectual, according to Benjamin, engages in a kind of fetishistic literary work that amounts to no more than the "metamorphosis of political struggle" from a productive, transformative project into an object of mere fancy and frivolous pleasure.[54]

In a reading of this short, characteristically enigmatic essay, Wendy Brown has sought to make a claim about the political sensibility of the contemporary left living the loss of its historical moment.[55] Notably, Brown is animated by Stuart Hall's well-known suggestion that the "crisis of the left" primarily has to do with its failure to apprehend the distinctiveness of its time and to alter its mode of moral-political critique accordingly.[56] (Hall, memorably, was writing in the 1980s in the context of the disabling rise of the authoritarian populism of Margaret Thatcher.) Brown is interested in connecting Hall's analysis of the left's anachronism with Benjamin's polemic against leftist quietude, and the point of contact she identifies is the idea of a "left traditionalism." This is the idea of a left clinging to obsolete formulations, which operates without either a deep and radical critique of the status quo or a compelling alternative to the existing order of things. It is a left, in other words, whose structure of desire and vision of purposes is essentially conservative and backward-looking.[57]

Although I am uncertain about the conceptual warrant for reading Benjamin and Hall together in this way, I can very well see the virtue of Brown's critique of the sullen quietism of what she calls left traditionalism and can sympathize with her desire to rescue critique from such conservative habits of thinking. But I hope it is clear that this is *not* my concern here in thinking about the ruins of time and the generations of memory. I am not interested, strictly speaking, in the perversity of the erstwhile revolutionary sunk in a willfully aestheticized sense of political abjection. In my view, this preoccupation tends to underestimate the profound— perhaps uncanny—sense of temporal *rupture* and collective *disorientation* brought about by the collapse in our time of the socialist revolutionary project, of which, to me, the collapse of the Grenada Revolution is a dramatic instance. Melancholia, as Freud understood, is an aspect or a dimension of the phenomenology of an intractable temporal experience, not the outcome of a volitional attitude toward the passage of time. The ruin of time and the accompanying loss of futures cannot be redressed by the mere redoubling of our commitment to the reform or renewal of critique (as Brown seems to think), because it is precisely the temporal structure of critique that is now in question: the propositional way it organizes, in the interval of the present, the dialectical prospect of immanent futures emerging from injurious pasts.

The members of the generation who made the Grenada Revolution of 13 March 1979 and who, however hesitantly, ambivalently, and conflictedly, recognized themselves in the idiom of its hopes and longings, in the emancipationist narrative by which it connected their experience of the past to a horizon of expectations of future possibilities, have been chronically unable to get beyond the tragedy of its violent loss. Overtaken by shattering grief, rage, and shame, this generation has been paralyzed by a stupefying and aggrieved silence, locked in a melancholia in which the past only returns as nostalgia. This is why the booklet produced by the Young Leaders, *Under the Cover of Darkness*, is so fresh and so instructive in both its undertaking and its accomplishment—and so suggestive even in its limitations. The Young Leaders have only a "postmemory" of October 1983, and they tend, it is true, to rehearse the history of the collapse of the People's Revolutionary Government in a somewhat unquestioning way. They are the first postrevolutionary generation in Grenada, and for this very reason they do not inhabit the same social framework of memory, the same temporal habitus, as their parents. Consequently, they do not experience the loss of 1983 as a fundamental rupture, a disorientation of their very mode of expectation of possible futures. Nor do they experience their relation to the state in that odd mixture of defeat and shame that afflicts the generation of their parents, who were rescued by the US imperial state in their hour of darkest trial, self-doubt, and generational failure.

It is not clear whether Bishop's body will ever be found. (There are conflicting views on what the chances are.) Nor is it clear whether the larger loss of the Grenada Revolution can ever be fully resolved, personally or collectively. But the Young Leaders have offered what seems to me an example of an ethics of memory, of how our responsibility to remember the traumatic past and our moral obligations to the dead can be worked out, worked through, with fidelity, with agonistic respect, and with cautious hope.

FOUR

EVADING TRUTHS

The Rhetoric of Transitional Justice

> When the victims of disasters refuse to resign themselves to their
> misfortunes and cry out in anger, we hear the voice of the sense of
> injustice.
>
> —JUDITH SHKLAR, *Faces of Injustice*

In contemporary discussions concerning the aftermaths of political atrocities, regimes of systematic political repression, or exceptional state violence, the question of the *ends* of justice has
come to play a prominent role. Ethics, it is argued, has assumed
a new priority over politics, and justice, so it is said, is the first
of its virtues. Thus, in addressing itself to the past of sanctioned
political wrongs, the question is sometimes posed: what should
justice in "postconflict societies" demand? Is the answer to be
found in the domain of the law, narrowly conceived as punitive
justice? Are perpetrators, for example, to be punished to the full
extent of the law? And if so, which law applies? Is it the law of
the predecessor regime or that of its successor? In these discussions, a curious instability *between* law and justice has seemed
to emerge such that their former convergence can no longer be
assumed, much less guaranteed. In "settling accounts" with the
past, as the practice is now widely called, it is held that criminal
law may no longer be equal to justice or that justice may have a
wider and more profound claim than such law by itself can con-

ventionally answer. It is no longer clear, for example, that the identification of criminal culpability, the determination of individual guilt, and the assignment of proportionate punishment in a court of law are adequate to the comprehension and pursuit of justice in circumstances of violently conflicted pasts. Rather, in confronting these pasts, it is argued, there is a need to supplement or transform our very understanding and expectation of what righting wrongs entails and a need to develop new and more relevant conceptions of the ends of justice and of the institutions and techniques that will serve to bring them about. These novel ends of justice are thought of as being served by the legitimating subjection of both perpetrators and victims to the technologies of "truth and reconciliation" and, moreover, as serving the broader horizon of a political *transition* from authoritarian or illiberal rule.[1]

Here, in fact, is the central, and often obscured, issue: however much ethics may have superseded politics, what justice requires as a new norm, above all, is something decidedly *political*—namely, a "transition" away from illiberal rule in the direction of liberal democracy now understood as the single direction of an acceptable political future. Justice, so it is said, may well demand punishment for the commission of particular crimes, but that punishment will be directed less at the legally culpable individuals than at the political *regime* of which these perpetrators are deemed mere representatives. What is at stake here, from the point of view of transitional justice, is that these crimes are taken not to be arbitrary acts of illegality, but on the contrary *exemplifications* of the practice of "illiberal" politics. Transitional justice, in other words, is about evil regimes, not only about bad people.[2]

The rise of transitional justice as a mechanism for settling past state crimes is an *effect* of the post–Cold War reorganization of the constraints and possibilities, values and expectations, of the global political landscape.[3] The varied catalytic political transformations that occurred toward the end of the twentieth century—the end of communism, the implosions of Third World socialism, the collapse of military dictatorships, the demise of apartheid, and so on—seemed to many to leave liberal democracies as the only viable political options still standing. Memorably, in those fin de siècle years, an attitude of triumphalist self-congratulation marked liberalism's appraisal of its world-historical renewal, its militant sense of its *right* to a global mission. Whether articulated in the historicist idiom of

Francis Fukuyama's "end of history" or the constitutionalist formulations of Bruce Ackerman's "liberal revolution" or the proceduralist language of Samuel Huntington's "third wave of democracy," what was registered in this euphoria of vindicationism was the gathering confidence that liberal democracy had at last regained the historical ascension over its discredited ideological and political rivals, and could now survey the world with an absolute sense of *entitlement*.[4] Significantly, these late twentieth-century transformations not only destroyed the legitimacy of non-liberal democratic alternatives—especially Marxist or Marxism-inspired ones—they also *reorganized* the very social and political imaginary in terms of which liberal democracy articulated its distinctive virtue.[5] For example, it is a familiar enough story that at the beginning of the Cold War, the imaginary of liberal democracy often represented its distinctiveness in the language of Karl Popper's "open society" (where liberal democracy was rendered as an order that uniquely allowed a plurality of free individual expression).[6] At the end of the Cold War, however, a new conceptual language emerged to define liberal democracy's special, universal political claim—namely, the idiom of "human rights."[7] Or rather, so as not to suggest that these are mutually exclusive descriptions (after all, they share the fundamental Other of totalitarianism), what liberalism as an open society is now said to shelter is not merely one version of ideologically competing conventions of human well-being but indisputably universal *human* rights. If in 1948, as a participant in the drafting of the Universal Declaration of Human Rights, the Soviet Union could claim a share in the protection and promotion of human rights, now liberal democracy presents itself as the exclusive form of political regime eligible to make that claim.[8] International human rights, it is now urged, constitutes the inner core value of the global project of liberal democracy, or to put it more precisely, liberal democracy is no longer seen as one of rival or contestable political options that variously serve to protect human rights, but as itself an *absolute* human right.[9]

The rise of the transitional justice idea is best understood as a prominent chapter in this story of the re-semanticization of liberal democracy as both a background assumption of political discourse and as a political condition for the realization of international human rights. It has also to be understood as part of the rise to prominence of international law as a "gentle civilizer of nations" and therefore as part of the view that, in general, law should have a disciplining effect on politics.[10] In this sense, perhaps, the international law idea of transitional justice as the establishment of human rights regimes that underwrite the "transition to democracy" is an extension of the larger *legalism* that became dominant in Anglo-American liberalism in the last decades of the twentieth century.[11]

In the mid- to late 1980s, when "transition" was first becoming a term of art in liberal political theory (it had earlier been a concept in socialist theory in its account of the transformation from capitalism, but times were already changing), it was not explicitly linked to the ethics of a human rights agenda. Rather, it was part of a political assessment of the relative balance of forces among existing ideological options. In 1986, for example, when Guillermo O'Donnell and his colleagues at the Woodrow Wilson International Center for Scholars published their four-volume *Transitions from Authoritarian Rule*, a comparative inquiry into how liberal democratic "transitions" take shape after periods of repressive rule, their considerations were drafted in a context in which the very possibility of a post–Cold War world was only barely a horizon of expectation.[12] It was certainly not yet anything like an existing condition of political experience, much less a background evaluative norm. Understandably, therefore, their "tentative conclusions" were still animated by the Cold War worry about the conflict between (as they put it) the "instauration of a political democracy [and] the restoration of a new, and possibly more severe, form of authoritarian rule."[13] As Patricia Haynor noted, looking back at this work from the first years of the new century, as much as it helped to define the terms of "transition" discourse, the transitional justice question of "closing the books" and "settling past accounts" was not explicitly on their agenda, even as they recognized "the difficult tension between the desire to bury the past, in order to avoid provoking the ire of powerful wrongdoers, and the ethical and political demand to confront the crimes of the prior regime."[14] Less than a decade and a half after its publication, however, the stakes would seem quite different, as the controversial postdictatorship prosecution process in Argentina and the commission of inquiry report *Nunca Mas* (also published in 1986) was absorbed into the fin de siècle political landscape.[15] By the late 1990s, when Haynor was conducting her own pioneering work in the wake of the definitive dismantling of apartheid in South Africa, there no longer seemed any real worry on the part of former Cold War liberals about the return of authoritarianism (whether from the right or from the left) because the historical vector was now clear, liberal democracy having dispensed with its rivals. Corresponding with this profound political shift was a rapidly cohering language and ethos of postideological international human rights and the emergence (partly out of a series of conferences between 1988 and 1994 and partly shaped by Neil Kritz's three edited volumes, *Transitional Justice*, published in 1995) of the framework for defining the "transition to democracy" and the distinctive work of "transitional justice."[16] A whole new idiom and a whole new range of institutional strategies emerged to grapple with "postauthoritarian transitions"—idioms and strategies concerned not only with punishment, but also with establishing truth, repairing harms and damages, paying respect to victims, and, above all, pursuing reconciliation, that is, the reintegration of perpetrators and victims in a postconflict society. The reconciliation of perpetrators and victims became the *summun bonum* of transitional justice, and it was to be arrived at, as Martha Minow put it in her influential formulation, by finding a path between vengeance and forgiveness.[17]

I already suggested in the prologue that an effect of the postrevolutionary reorganization of experience is that the *temporal* grounds of moral judgment concerning past political action have altered. The way we conceive of the temporal connection between past social and political ills and injury, on the one hand, and the horizon of possible futures of social and political repair, on the other, is no longer what it was because the past is no longer imagined as a time that can be overcome. In our liberal and liberalizing time, emancipation has given way to accommodation, and reconciliation has displaced revolution as the language of social and political change where the future has been reduced to a mirror image of the present. To my mind, part, at least, of what makes the question of transitional justice so important as an aspect of contemporary political discussion is that it presents one crucial *face* of liberalism: this is a face of liberalism as it confronts a certain otherness, confronts it *armed*, and from a position of global power *regained*.[18] Not since the nineteenth century, perhaps, has liberalism been able to stand astride the world with such powers at its disposal to impose its will to liberalize "illiberal" others, and with such guaranteed impunity, and consequently with such confidence in the civilizational virtue of its moral and political project. In this sense, I believe the question of transitional justice is not a mere adjunct to deeper and more central issues in liberal debates about political and civic liberty, and just distribution and repair (as may appear from the endless numbers of books on liberal political theory). It stands at the animating center of that debate and with implications that have *global* significance.

In this last chapter of my study, I enter into a critical engagement with some aspects of the liberal—or liberalizing—project of transitional justice through an inquiry into the historical instance of the Grenada 17, who were accused of, and convicted and imprisoned for, the killing of Prime Minister Maurice Bishop and his seven associates (Fitzroy Bain, Norris Bain, Evelyn Bullen, Jacqueline Creft, Keith Hayling, Evelyn Maitland, and Unison Whiteman) at Fort Rupert on 19 October 1983. The Grenada 17 are Hudson Austin, Dave Bartholomew, Callistus Bernard, Bernard Coard, Phyllis Coard, Leon Cornwall, Liam James, Vincent Joseph, Ewart Layne, Colville McBarnette, Andy Mitchell, Cecil Prime, Lester Redhead, Cosmos Richardson, Selwyn Strachan, Christopher Stroude, and John Ventour.[19] They have always maintained their innocence of the criminal charges brought against them and the fundamental unfairness, irregularity, and political motivation of the judicial process to which they were subjected. Over many years, they waged a legal battle to have their convictions overturned. They take themselves to be victims of a fundamental miscarriage of justice. Their case thus offers an opportunity to raise some doubts about certain models of justice that, as Judith Shklar suggests, may be morally deaf to some experiences of injustice—less because these models are in principle uncharitable than because what injustice discloses may include, but also *exceed*, the simple denial of justice.[20] The Grenada 17 have now all been released from prison. On 2 December 2006, Vincent Joseph, Andy Mitchell, and Cosmos Richardson, the soldiers accused of being directly involved in the killing, were freed after their sentences were reduced for good behavior. On 7 February 2007, however, a significant dimension of the Grenada 17's struggle to vindicate themselves was realized when the Judicial Committee of the Privy Council in the United Kingdom impugned the constitutional validity of the original death sentences of the thirteen appellants named in the appeal and advised that they be resentenced by the Eastern Caribbean Supreme Court.[21] As their Lordships pointedly observed, "For obvious reasons, the question of the appellants' fate is so politically charged that it is hardly reasonable to expect any Government of

Grenada, even 23 years after the tragic events of October 1983, to take an objective view of the matter. In their Lordships' opinion that makes it all the more important that the determination of the appropriate sentence for the appellants, taking into account such progress as they have made in prison, should be the subject of a judicial determination."[22] Although the Privy Council did not directly take up the question of the *criminal* charges laid against the appellants, its judgment led to the release of the political prisoners. At the resentencing hearing on 27 June 2007, Prime, Redhead, and Stroude were ordered released, followed on 18 December 2008 by Austin, McBarnette, and Ventour. Finally, on 4 September 2009, after more than twenty-five years at Richmond Hill Prison, the last members of the Grenada 17—Bartholomew, Bernard, Coard, Cornwall, James, Layne, and Strachan—were released.

Although it has not generally been discussed in these terms (insofar as it has been seriously discussed at all), it seems to me that one illuminating way to think about the case of the Grenada 17 is precisely in relation to the domain of "transitional justice." Their trial, and the truth and reconciliation process of which they were the absent center, form part and parcel of the *aftermaths* not only of the particular history of the collapse of the Grenada Revolution but also of the larger world-historical end of socialist revolution in the Third World, with which it roughly coincides. True, the discursive and institutional domain of transitional justice was practically nonexistent at the time of the collapse of the Grenada Revolution in 1983, but it is certainly the idiom that, during the long course of the political, legal, and personal ordeal of the Grenada 17 (spanning the last decades of the twentieth century and the first decade of the twenty-first century), became the normative framework for cases such as theirs, involving what transition scholars call "liberalizing political transitions." Indeed, though ignored in the now considerable literature on transitional justice, Grenada is arguably one of the earliest instances of that political engineering experiment, beginning as the Cold War was winding down, of turning "illiberal" regimes into "liberal" ones. After all, the whole point of the US military intervention to topple the Revolutionary Military Council, which had taken over the state after the implosion of the People's Revolutionary Government, was to reverse the course of the Marxist-led revolution and return Grenada to the fold of obedient Caribbean client states. Grenada, as I have said, was an early—and relatively easy—target for the neoconservative Reagan doctrine of rolling back communism rather than coexisting with it.[23] Therefore, thinking about the predicament of the Grenada 17 in the context of the last years of the Cold War and the emerging imperial dominance of the United States helps to illuminate the ideological character of the rhetoric of transitional justice, particularly the normative consensus about liberal democracy and human rights on which it thrives.

Successor trials and truth commissions are often taken to be paradigmatic dimensions of transitional justice, weaving possible paths, as Minow would have it, between vengeance and forgiveness in responding to political atrocities. In the aftermaths of the collapse of the Grenada Revolution and the subsequent US invasion and occupation, both processes were instituted. Whether they fulfilled such hopes as Minow and others invest in "postconflict" transitional justice institutions is to me a matter of doubt, and it is this doubt that I explore in what follows. First, I consider some aspects of the work of Ruti Teitel, one of the most thoughtful—indeed, provocative—scholars working in this field and evidently one of the founders of the term "transitional justice" itself.[24] What makes her elegant and straightforwardly titled *Transitional Justice* worth critically engaging and challenging, at least for my purposes, is not only the authoritative comprehensiveness of its interpretive project of a political theory of liberalizing transitions (the ambition is a meta-theory of transitional justice that has implications beyond periods of political flux), but also its theoretical self-consciousness of some of the defining tensions—between universalism and historical particularism, for example, or realism and idealism, or determinism and constructivism—in contemporary debates about politics, law, and justice.[25] *Transitional Justice* is an example of the legalism prominent in contemporary liberalism, and in considering this work, I am especially interested in how this theoretical self-consciousness serves to normalize the direction of liberal democratic change and to rationalize the legal powers deemed necessary to bring it about. Second, against the background of this critical appraisal of Teitel's framing of the problem of transitional justice, I take up the trial of the Grenada 17—the so-called Maurice Bishop Murder Trial—and consider the systematic legal irregularities and open display of hostility and prejudice against the accused that characterized it. This was perhaps the highest-profile trial in modern Caribbean political history, involving as it did the alleged implication of ministers of government in the killing of the sitting prime minister.[26] I will suggest that, far from being the sort of occasion that transitional justice theorists extol, this successor trial constituted a process that can only be described as a "show" trial, a politically motivated exercise aimed not at impartially investigating the truth of the killings but, rather, at sending an unambiguous warning to Grenada and the wider Caribbean about the consequences of the pursuit of revolutionary self-determination. Third, and finally, I take up the truth and reconciliation process that followed the trial by a decade and a half, while the Grenada 17 were still incarcerated. Unlike the trial, notably, the truth and reconciliation process passed without notice in the region, and almost without interest in Grenada itself. I will suggest that this exercise was not only an implicit acknowledgment of the failure of the prior trial to determine the truth of the events of October 1983 and to bring closure to that historical period, but was itself little more than an exercise in politically motivated *evasion*. It certainly served the purpose neither of the disclosure of a full and truthful account of what took place on that fateful day and why, nor of the just reconciliation of an admittedly conflicted society.

My overall aim here, I should caution at the outset, is not to offer an exhaustive historical account of the trial of the Grenada 17 or of the later truth commission process. As with other aspects of this terrible political catastrophe, a comprehensive history is waiting to be written. Nor is it my intention to argue the innocence of the Grenada 17 of the crime with which they were charged. Undoubtedly, in the course of my research, I have formed my own impressions. But my principal concern lies in using the case of the Grenada 17 to cast some doubt on the ideological self-understanding of transitional justice and its relation to the circumstances of a liberalizing global order.

The Liberal Rhetoric of Transitional Justice

Ruti Teitel is an erudite protagonist of the contemporary idea of transitional justice and, more broadly, of the special role of law in directing liberalizing political change. As she puts it in the stage-setting opening of her influential *Transitional Justice*, societies all over the world—in Latin America, Eastern Europe, the former Soviet Union, and Africa—have overthrown military dictatorships and totalitarian regimes for freedom and democracy.[27] In these "transitions" from "illiberal" rule, she asserts, there is one recurrent question: how are states and societies to deal with past political evil? In particular, she asks, What legal acts have transformative effects? What is the relation between a state's response to its repressive past and its prospects for creating a liberal order?[28] What, in short, is law's potential for ushering in liberalization? Note the implicit teleological form of these questions, the normative political horizon of a liberal future they presume and seek to rationalize. Note, too, the *legalist* framing of the problem of liberalism or, rather, of *liberalizing* change, that it is, above all, the technologies of law—not the agonistic give and take of politics—that is to be charged with defining the sought-after transformation.

At the center of Teitel's concerns, then, is the question of the conception of justice that prevails—or *should* prevail—in periods of political transition, and law's role in formulating—indeed, securing—it. Writing at the end of the 1990s, she could say that this was a question that legal and political theory had not yet fully addressed. In her sketch of the debate about the relation of law and justice to the process of liberalization, she outlines two rival positions—realism and idealism—that in her view are both shaping and constraining. For realists (who constitute, perhaps, the dominant position in the debate), political change is thought to precede the establishment of rule of law, whereas for idealists, the reverse is the case inasmuch as there are legal prerequisites for political transition. Realists believe that existing political and institutional conditions determine a state's transitional response to the past and prospects for the future. Law here is seen as largely a byproduct of political change; justice is epiphenomenal—that is, contingent on the prevailing balance of power. Against this view, Teitel makes the familiar criticism that realists too easily conflate "descriptive" with "normative" concerns. By contrast, she says, the idealist account frames the question of transition in terms of a purely universalist conception of justice that is understood as a necessary precondition for any change in a liberal direction. Against the idealists, Teitel argues that such abstractions cannot account for the concrete historical circumstances in which law has to be connected to political change. Thus, holding both conventional positions inadequate, Teitel urges what she calls a *constructivist* view that sees law in circumstances of transition as simultaneously constituted *by* and constitutive *of* political change. Like the realists, Teitel acknowledges that context matters, especially in such distinctive circumstances; but like the idealists, she argues for a strong constituting role for law in guiding transition so as to ensure the institution of liberal principles.

Teitel is well aware that her characterization of "transition" is, to some extent, question begging: that while it is declarative concerning what transition is a change *from*, what it is a change *to* seems less clear. At one level, the answer is simple: the direction is that of liberal democracy. As in the cases of Haynor and Minow, this is unambiguous. But Teitel wants to distance herself somewhat from what she calls "proceduralist" and "teleological" conceptions of liberal democratic change because they seem to her to privilege a picture of an already constituted end point—namely, a normal, rule-of-law functioning liberal democratic state. Whether her argument can in fact be said to avoid either teleology or proceduralism remains to me a matter of doubt. But Teitel aims to picture transition not only as a liberalizing *direction* that cannot be foreclosed, but also as a distinctive historical-political moment that is neither the prior state of illiberal rule nor the future state of a settled rule-of-law liberal democracy. Transitions, Teitel says, constitute *upheavals* in the prevailing paradigms of justice. They are "extraordinary" periods of "threshold" in which law is caught "between the past and the future." In transitions, consequently, law's function comes to be "deeply paradoxical": where in its "ordinary" social role, law provides for order and stability, in the "extraordinary" periods of political transition, "law maintains order even as it enables transformation. Accordingly, in transition, the ordinary intuitions and predicates about law simply do not apply. In dynamic periods of political flux, legal responses generate a sui generis paradigm of transformative law."[29] Teitel's thesis, then, is that in such periods of political transition, the conception of justice is both "extraordinary" *and* "constructivist." It is "alternately constituted by, and constitutive of, the transition." It is at once "contextualized and partial." Or, as she puts it in a startling and revealing formulation, "What is deemed just is contingent and informed by prior injustice."[30] Law is shaped by political circumstance but is not a mere product or instrument of political transition. Rather, law helps to constitute and structure transitions in the desired direction.

Teitel's argument works through one principal meta-distinction—namely, between "illiberal" and "liberal" regimes. The former category is a catchall for a disparate array of political orders, among them communist ones such as the Soviet Union and the former Eastern bloc states, fascist military dictatorships such as Chile under Augusto Pinochet, and racist authoritarian states such as apartheid South Africa (to give the usual list). Indeed, all non-liberal regimes are now deemed to be *illiberal*. But what exactly do these different regimes have in common? And what makes it possible and so seemingly plausible to collect them together in this binary opposition with liberalism? Teitel does not explain any of this, presumably because, for her, such explanation is unnecessary. Evidently, however, these regimes are simply paradigm instances of forms of political rule that deny or repress or are intolerant of essential liberal virtues. Rhetorically, the distinction between "illiberal" and "liberal" regimes appears at once ideologically neutral and completely self-evident. But this seeming neutrality and self-evidence are mere sleights of hand because they depend precisely on the powers that have installed a new global ideological norm—defined by the "end of history" or the "end of ideology"—in the wake of liberalism's world-historical defeat of its principal Cold War political adversaries, and its subsequent revision of its self-image as a vindicated universal ideal. On this basis, liberalism now represents itself not as one competing form of the state among others but as the obvious *conclusion* of the historical march of political civilization. This is why liberals like Teitel feel no need to specifically *argue* out liberal virtues, but instead simply stipulate them in ways that presume their essential and incontestable status.

Teitel's distinction works rhetorically by occluding not only distinctions among so-called illiberal regimes but also potentially important distinctions among liberalisms or liberal self-understandings. It occludes, for example, that whereas some forms of liberalism hold themselves up as the single and universal political ideal because they shelter the *only* legitimate form of ethical-political life, there may be other forms of liberalism that are more open to the plurality of historical forms of life in the world, and more concerned about sheltering peaceful coexistence than about subverting or undermining it. Teitel clearly holds to the former, not the latter, view of liberalism—a view underwritten by the Enlightenment's confidence in rationalist principle and the legalist conceit that justice is purely a matter of the application of a transcendent law rather than the political negotiation of accommodations among conflicting goods, or visions of the good. Therefore, and hardly surprisingly, whether and to what extent certain militantly liberal democratic regimes—such as the United States—are themselves illiberal based on their fundamentalist intolerance of political pluralism (or, indeed, in consequence of their systematic infliction of universal evils such as genocide, torture, and humiliation on others), and consequently should be valid targets for the sorts of transitional justice interventions she commends, does not appear among the possible directions of discussion for Teitel. Liberal regimes are simply *exempt* from transitional justice criticism.

Liberalisms like Teitel's, moreover, understand themselves not only to be prescriptions for a universal ideal and to be, in consequence, morally superior to all other forms of political life, but also to be entitled, as a civilizational obligation, to actively remake illiberal—or non-liberal—worlds, if not entirely in their image, then at least in their *self-interest*. This inclination—or, rather, empowered *will*—is what lends an ominously *imperial* cast to Teitel's idea that in transitions, what is just is partly contingent on what is necessary to move illiberal regimes in a liberal or liberalizing direction. There is a disquieting sense in which the ghost of John Stuart Mill haunts this liberal doctrine of civilizational entitlement.[31] Mill was no legalist like Teitel, but inhabiting historical moments of extraordinary and expansionary liberal self-assurance, they are both protagonists of the view that the world can cleanly be divided between liberals and non-liberals; that the progressive *telos* of history is toward liberalism; and that liberals have a moral duty and a political right to impose special *reforming* circumstances on non-liberals in order to oblige—and, where necessary, to *compel*—them to transition in the approved direction. Famously, despite his celebrated commitments to diversity, Mill held that the *best* life for all could be lived only in a liberal regime understood as a rational and universal ideal. In consonance with Teitel's contemporary view, Mill's nineteenth-century doctrine about illiberal or non-liberal colonial states held that justice is *contextual* and *conditional* on how far along states are on their path to a liberal civilization.[32] For him, as for Teitel, a liberal form of state is the exclusive, stipulated end of human progress. In this view, liberalism has a moral pedagogic duty to guide such regimes in reforming themselves in the approved direction. For both Teitel and Mill, only in liberal regimes can law have a "settled" function. In the extraordinary circumstances of transition, by contrast, liberal law is obliged to have a somewhat arbitrary and constructive (because contingent and contextual) set of powers at its disposal so as to carry out the moral labor of disciplining the old ways and bringing them within the purview of the rule of law. In many respects, then, Teitel's liberalism is the contemporary mirror of Mill's.

A Late–Cold War Show Trial

In the face of political atrocities and state-sanctioned violence, Teitel and others argue, a crucial question has been whether to punish those responsible—that is, whether successor regimes have a duty to prosecute the violations perpetrated by their predecessors.[33] Thus, the question of punishment, central in many ways to liberal political theorizing about responsibility and accountability, plays a prominent role in understandings of transitional justice. Teitel maintains, for example, that successor trials should be taken as "foundational" in the transition from an "illiberal" to a "liberal" political order. In her view, nothing draws so *bright* a line between the old and the new dispensations, marking out in an indelible way the "normative" transformation from illegitimacy to legitimacy.[34] In conditions of transition, it is contended, punishment has "forward-looking" and "consequentialist" implications: it contributes to the social good by laying the basis for a new liberal order. But, Teitel underscores, the implications of punishment are not all about the extent to which it will move society beyond the "lawlessness" of the past. An even more consequential consideration turns on the implications of *not* punishing. To what extent does *neglecting* to bring perpetrators to book harm prospects for liberalizing change by sending the wrong message about principles and commitments? Thus, in transitions, punishment functions to delegitimize the values, institutions, and practices of the predecessor order. The trial of former political leaders, Teitel writes, is "used to construct the very meaning of state injustice" and to foreground the new regime's liberal democratic identity and commitment to rule of law. It is meant as a self-conscious "ritual" through which the ideology embodied by the predecessor regime can be publicly repudiated—and, indeed, *criminalized.*[35]

To be sure, Teitel admits that dangers are involved in the use of criminal justice to punish the leaders of illiberal regimes. But these cautions turn on purely contingent considerations rather than on a worry about the framing assumptions that govern transitional justice. As she says, in order for such trials to realize their potential, they must be prosecuted in a manner in keeping with the "full legality associated with working democracies in ordinary times, and when they are not conducted in a visibly fair way, the very same trials can backfire, risking the wrong message of political justice and threatening a fledgling liberal state."[36] But since criminal justice in transitional periods is conceptualized and adjudicated as "extraordinary" and "contextual," it may be less than clear just how it could simultaneously be guided by the settled, ordinary norms of rule of law in established democracies. Teitel cannot have it both ways. As Mill understood in his own way, extraordinary means are sometimes needed to establish the ends of ordinary liberal norms. In any case, as we shall see, the trial of the Grenada 17 raises hard questions for the ideological self-image of transitional justice, for here was a successor trial that was not just riven with systematic unfairness and prejudice but was also framed from beginning to end (as well as funded at certain points) by an imperial project confident in the impunity with which it could coercively carry out its liberalizing agenda.

The Grenada 17 have always maintained that their trial for the murder of Maurice Bishop and his associates on 19 October 1983 was a politically motivated and systematically unfair process, that it was a "show" trial aimed to appease US ideological interests and the vengeance of a traumatized and deliberately misled Grenadian population. As Richard Hart observes, it was a "travesty of justice" carried out with remarkable consistency and evident disregard for world opinion.[37] In October 2003, the human rights organization Amnesty International published a detailed report on the predicament of the Grenada 17 (to that date), effectively substantiating that longstanding claim about the trial. Significantly, the report was titled, "The Grenada 17: The Last of the Cold War Prisoners?"[38] Amnesty International had been monitoring the situation of the accused since the beginning of their trial process in 1984 and had expressed its concern on various occasions. However, the report, issued as the twentieth anniversary of the detention of the Grenada 17 approached and when it was palpably clear that nothing was going to be done by the political and judicial authorities in Grenada to remedy their predicament, was the organization's most comprehensive as well as its most indicting. The report painted a remarkable picture of judicial conduct that was in plain and gross violation of internationally recognized human rights law and standards. Moreover, Amnesty International understood, as it registered in the title of the report, that the case of the Grenada 17 could not be properly appreciated outside the geopolitical context of the Cold War and its impact on the Caribbean. Indeed, the question mark in the title is poignantly instructive. That the Grenada 17 may well have been not just Cold War prisoners, but among the *last* of them, underscores Amnesty International's sense of the passing of a geopolitical moment and the almost anachronistic situation in which the Grenada 17 appeared trapped, as though they were *leftovers* from a former political epoch.

Perhaps not surprisingly, given the pervasiveness of a certain way of telling the story, the Amnesty International report itself sketches a not-unbiased account of the course of events that led up to the shooting deaths of Maurice Bishop and the others. In particular, it reproduces, rather un-critically, the idea of a "plot" led by Deputy Prime Minister and Finance Minister Bernard Coard to overthrow Bishop. Amnesty International speaks of a "Coard faction" that decided, at a certain point, to "force Bishop out of government."[39] In the immediate wake of the events of 19 October 1983, this was certainly the story that shaped the dominant picture of the background context of the catastrophe, a story authorized not only by the US occupation forces but also by the region's most famous Marxist revolutionary, Fidel Castro.[40] That there was no such plot or conspiracy could have been gleaned by the most cursory reading of the inner party conflict recorded in the party documents seized by the US forces and later issued by the US State Department as *Grenada Documents: An Overview and Selection*.[41] Similarly, the idea that when crowds of supporters released Bishop from "house arrest" on the morning of 19 October 1983, he and his followers went to Fort Rupert to "regroup and gauge the situation" is, on the face of it, highly unlikely.[42] Why choose Fort Rupert to "regroup and gauge the situation" when preparations for a mass demonstration were being made in the nearby market square, and where Bishop was clearly expected by large numbers of people? Is it not *more* likely that Bishop and his associates chose Fort Rupert because it was the army's headquarters and the site of the armory and, consequently a more plausible place to hold out until help arrived? After all, it is well known that the armory was opened and arms were distributed to civilians, and there is now strong evidence that a call was indeed made to Castro for military assistance (see chapter 1).[43] Again, Amnesty International's story that after Fort Rupert was brought back under the army's control, "Bishop, Fitzroy Bain, Norris Bain, Jacqueline Creft, Vincent Noel, and Unison Whiteman, were singled out, detained, and summarily executed in the Fort's courtyard" is a highly tendentious account.[44] First of all, Noel was shot during the early exchange of fire with the soldiers and so was not part of the group taken to the inner courtyard of the fort.[45] But more important, the notion that those detained were "summarily executed" places the events under a certain—and obviously *prejudicial*—description: it plays into the now endlessly rehearsed story that the killing was politically calculated and premeditatedly carried out under orders. Yet as Amnesty International is well aware, no credible evidence has emerged to date that this was in fact the case. Indeed, aside from the doubtful testimony and forced statements put before the court at the trial, no uncontroversial and authoritative account of exactly what took place in that inner courtyard during those undoubtedly horrible moments exists. (That Amnesty International itself is not unaware of the doubt surrounding these events is signaled by the fact that elsewhere in the report, it refers to the shooting as an "execution-style" killing.[46]) But all of this perhaps only demonstrates once again how powerfully the story of the internal political decision to liquidate Bishop has shaped the popular and scholarly imagination of what took place on 19 October 1983.

Still, what is most important about the Amnesty International report is its recognition (one that few other individuals or organizations have publicly expressed) that the US military invasion and occupation, the illegal overthrow of the government in power, the capture of the political and army leadership, and the court trial that followed have to be framed by the geopolitical order in which they unfolded. In this context, Amnesty International found the "ostensible" reasons offered by the Reagan administration for the invasion of 25 October 1983—namely, to "resolve a condition of anarchy caused by a breakdown of government institutions"—unpersuasive and even cynically motivated.[47] But not only was the invasion a contravention of international law and the norms of international conduct, according to the Amnesty International report, so too were the detention and interrogation of the political prisoners that took place shortly after the cessation of hostilities, announced by the United States on 2 November 1983. The seventeen who were eventually charged (as well as others) were initially held incommunicado aboard US Navy vessels and in packing crates at the airport, in conditions that Amnesty International describes as constituting "cruel, inhuman, and degrading treatment in contravention of international law and standards." Once they were placed under arrest, the report further notes, credible evidence suggests that they were subjected to torture during interrogations (in which none had legal counsel present) in order to extract "confessions" that implicated themselves in the murder of Maurice Bishop.[48]

The most egregious legal irregularities, however, pertained to the constitution of the court and the conduct of the trial process by which the accused were found guilty of murder. To begin with, the trial of the Grenada 17, which ran from 3 March to 4 December 1986, was conducted in a court that the accused argued was unconstitutional. This was a *central* claim of theirs throughout the trial and subsequent appeal. When it became clear that the Grenada 17 were going to be tried for murder, the issue of which legal system would try them became crucially important because of the ambiguity of the legal situation attendant on the collapse of the revolution. On the one hand, there was the Organization of Eastern Caribbean States (OECS) Supreme Court (which was the court under Grenada's independence constitution of 1973), and on the other, there was the Grenada High Court, the court established by the People's Revolutionary Government (under People's Laws 4 and 14 [1979]) as a consequence of the withdrawal of the OECS court shortly after the revolution. With the cessation of hostilities, Governor General Paul Scoon assumed formal executive powers of state in the name of the independence constitution (by invoking Section 57[2] of the Grenada Constitution Order 1973), suggesting thereby that it was *still* in force.[49] However, the promulgation of the Constitution of Grenada Order 1984 that in effect set out the continued authority of the constitution of 1973 made an exception for the Courts Order that provided for the return of the OECS court. This exception sent a message that the new—transitional—powers were determined to try the Grenada 17 in the court of the revolution. By contrast, the Grenada 17 wished to be tried by the court of the constitution because that system allowed for a final appeal before the Privy Council. They were convinced, understandably, that given the prevailing hostile propaganda, they could be assured of justice only in a court that was completely independent of local and regional manipulation and of US interference. Not surprisingly, this was resisted by the transitional regime largely in the name of political expediency.[50] The Grenada 17 appealed the decision to try them under the revolutionary court. However, the Court of Appeal denied their application on the grounds that the Grenada High Court, while technically unconstitutional, as the appellants argued, was nevertheless, in the circumstances, a "court of necessity." Amnesty International fundamentally disagreed with this judgment, arguing that "no such procedure is recognized within either international or Grenadian law" and that "a tribunal deemed unconstitutional cannot be considered a lawful court of law."[51]

Compounding the questionable independence and constitutionality of the court in which the Grenada 17 were to be tried was the openly prejudicial process by which the jury was selected. As the Amnesty International report asserts, although it is not explicitly protected by international human rights law, the "right to a jury trial is established in most common law systems, including Grenada's, and entails several due process protections and procedures."[52] Among these, importantly, is the right of defendants to participate in jury selection on an equal footing with the prosecution. Understandably, given the pervasive and openly hostile character of the propaganda against them over the more than two years between their detention and the start of the trial, the Grenada 17 were doubtful whether an impartial jury could be empanelled. They were not mistaken in their suspicions. In Grenadian law, the Registrar of the Court draws up the array of prospective jurors who constitute the pool from which a final panel is selected. However, at the very start of the trial, after what appeared to be mischievous complaints by the prosecution, the trial judge not only dismissed the array of jurors drawn up by the registrar but abruptly removed the longstanding registrar himself and brazenly appointed to his position a woman who, to that point, had been a member of the prosecution team. Thus, the jury was largely handpicked "without probe for prejudice" and without the presence of any defendant or defense counsel. The jury so selected very quickly and very effectively made its prejudices known. From the beginning and throughout the course of the trial, the members of the jury clapped and cheered in support of the judge and prosecution, and made hostile and threatening remarks and gestures toward the defendants (calling them murderers and criminals), as well as toward the defense team.[53]

In the end, the defendants decided that under the circumstances, it would be impossible to receive a fair trial. On 11 April 1986, they instructed their legal team to withdraw.[54] In consequence, the Grenada 17 were not represented by legal counsel at their trial and subsequently were often denied access to their lawyers, as well as to materials relevant to their case.

During the trial itself, the accused protested the unfairness of the proceedings by acting disruptively—chanting, stomping their feet, and so on—and were often barred from the courtroom, which in effect excluded them from participating in their own trial and even from hearing the prosecution's case against them. According to Amnesty International's account, this was yet another breach of appropriate procedure, another instance of a politically motivated denial of the right of the accused to a fair trial. "Whatever the defendants behaviour," Amnesty writes, "it in no way relieves the State of its duty to ensure that the defendants were legally represented at all times. The appropriate course of action would have been to appoint legal counsel to represent the defendants; leaving the 17 unrepresented in court when their very lives were at stake should not have been an option."[55] According to the United Nations Human Rights Committee, justice requires that when an offense is punishable by death, a trial should not proceed if there is no legal counsel to represent the accused.[56] Of course, what justice requires was not what Cold War politics and judicial revenge demanded. The Amnesty International report was notably damning in its overall assessment of the trial procedure. "In light of such violations of fundamental principles of the right to a fair trial," it stated, "it is clear that the trial of the Grenada 17 fell short of a fair process. As such protections are crucial to ensure a process by which the truth emerges, the lack of a proper and lawfully protected defense alone indicates the trial was manifestly and fundamentally unfair."[57]

The case for the prosecution in the trial of the Grenada 17 was that the death of Maurice Bishop on 19 October 1983 was the result of a conspiratorial decision to liquidate him taken by members of the Central Committee of the New Jewel Movement (NJM), specifically the so-called Coard faction within it. This is what it needed to *prove*, because the principal objective of the Maurice Bishop Murder Trial was not the determination of liability for a capital crime but the ideological destruction of a political project. Or to put it slightly differently, the objective of the trial was the *criminalization* of the politics of the NJM (the identification of a political movement with criminal intent), and this required the conviction of its political leadership for murder. The groundwork for achieving this objective was already being laid by the attempt to establish a widespread convergence on the view that the split in the party was *ideological* rather than merely procedural, and that Bishop represented a more moderate, and therefore more palatable and accommodating, orientation than Coard. (This was the work of the US Psychological Operations team.) But drawing this background picture to suggest the context of conspiracy was not the same as demonstrating, on the basis of some judicially acceptable threshold of evidence, the existence of a plot and its relation to the actual commission of a crime. Certainly, the prosecution seemed unable to cull any material evidence of such a conspiracy from the tons of documentation carted away by the US occupation forces. And clearly, the confessions extracted from the accused—such as the one signed by Colville McBarnette to the effect that the Central Committee had met and decided to eliminate Bishop—were deemed insufficient to secure the needed verdicts.

What the prosecution needed, then, in the absence of incriminating documentary evidence, was to be able to place an eyewitness at the scene of this proposed conspiracy. That eyewitness—it will be recalled from the prologue—would be Cletus St. Paul, Bishop's former chief bodyguard. St. Paul would be the prosecution's star witness, and it would be almost entirely on his "questionable testimony" (as Amnesty International euphemistically called it) that the idea of conspiracy was determined.[58] Indeed, to be sure they did not miss its vital significance to the credibility of the case for the prosecution, the trial judge made a point of underlining it to the jury, suggesting to them that without it there could be no convictions.[59] St. Paul, who had been arrested on 12 October 1983 in connection with his role in spreading the rumor that Phyllis and Bernard Coard were planning to assassinate Bishop, had given a number of conflicting statements (to the police, at the preliminary inquiry, and at the trial itself) concerning what was supposed to have taken place among the Central Committee members at Fort Frederick. In the last of these statements, he maintained that after he arrived at the fort, he saw members of the Central Committee arrive—among them Liam James and Bernard and Phyllis Coard—and immediately begin to converse with one another. While he could not hear them, he said, he could see them nodding and gesticulating in a suggestive way. Then he saw the Central Committee member Leon Cornwall tell a group of assembled soldiers that, because of a "vicious rumor" spread by Bishop, counterrevolutionary and "big business" elements had used the opportunity to make trouble and had freed Bishop from house arrest; and consequently, these elements "must be liquidated." (As Richard Hart has observed, what is most remarkable about St. Paul's evidence is that, despite all the coaching that he must have received on what to say so as to implicate the Central Committee in conspiracy to commit murder, he did not actually say that anyone ordered the killing of Bishop. Those to be "liquidated" were, instead, the "big business" elements causing trouble.[60]) Everything depended on this testimony of St. Paul's, even though it was contradicted by most other eyewitnesses—most importantly, by Errol George, who was a witness for the prosecution at the preliminary inquiry. George had also been part of the prime minister's security detail; it was he who had reported Bishop as the source of the rumor, and he had been detained with St. Paul and arrived at Fort Frederick with him. In his testimony, he said categorically that he at no time had heard members of the Central Committee giving any instructions to soldiers. Understandably, the prosecution quickly determined that George would be of no use—indeed, would be potentially damaging—to their case and he therefore was not called to testify at the trial.[61]

In any event, it was on the basis of St. Paul's dubious evidence, supported by the confessions extracted from certain defendants, that the already prejudiced jury was invited to make a judgment regarding the guilt or innocence of the accused. On 4 December 1986, at the conclusion of a trial shot through with blatant partiality and systematic legal irregularities and in an atmosphere of ideological coercion in which the accused were vilified, the main defendants (Hudson Austin, Dave Bartholomew, Callistus Bernard, Bernard Coard, Phyllis Coard, Leon Cornwall, Liam James, Ewart Layne, Colville McBarnette, Cecil Prime, Lester Redhead, Selwyn Strachan, Christopher Stroude, and John Ventour) were found guilty of multiple counts of murder and sentenced to hang. Three rank-and-file soldiers, alleged to have fired the fatal shots (Vincent Joseph, Andy Mitchell, and Cosmos Richardson), were convicted of multiple counts of manslaughter and sentenced to fifteen years of imprisonment for each count, with certain of the sentences to be served consecutively.

If, as Teitel has argued, successor trials are meant to draw a "bright line" between the "illiberal" past and the "liberalizing" present, to ritually and publicly delegitimize, even criminalize, the values and institutions of the old regime and at the same time affirm the transparent virtues of the new order, how are we to understand the trial of the Grenada 17? How might it illuminate the project of transitional justice? Again, notably, transitional justice scholars such as Teitel do not believe that law in such "postconflict" situations is beyond or above politics. For them, law *can* only have—and *does* only have—this function in so-called settled liberal democracies where the rule of law can be taken for granted. On the contrary, in transitional situations, law is deliberately "extraordinary," as Teitel likes to say—that is, it is "constructivist" and "contextual." This, I take it, means that law has, or ought to have, a generatively transformative and normative role in establishing the conditions for a virtuous politics—namely, the rule of liberal democracy. The fact that what the transition was *from* might not have been a systematically "illiberal" regime (however non-liberal its politics), but one in which a sovereign people were pursuing a path of self-determination outside of the sphere of US influence; or that the "liberal democracy" being urged might be no more than the name of a rationality of power and of rule in which the governed are to be subject once more to the engine of neoliberal globalization and a new imperialism—these possibilities form no part of Teitel's considerations. To her credit, she admits that in successor trials, abuses may indeed occur, and when such abuses are likely trials should not proceed. But it is unclear (to say the least) who, in Teitel's view, would authorize such a decision, and because this problem is invisible to her, she fails to recognize that such abuses may not simply be contingent on bad people but *constitutive* of the self-interested functioning of liberal imperialism in a post–Cold War age.

The trial of the Grenada 17 drew an unmistakably bright line between the revolutionary past and the postrevolutionary present. It sent a clear, undiluted ideological message aimed not merely at the accused (whose fate, in any case, was self-evident) but at a wider public that included the Grenadian and, more broadly, Caribbean people. This message concerned the costs of self-determination, the consequences of political disobedience. It aimed to destroy any affirmative appreciation of the revolutionary past and the political traditions out of which it came. In this, arguably, it succeeded. From the foregoing description, drawn largely from the report by Amnesty International and the exemplary work by Richard Hart, it is hard not to conclude that the trial of the Grenada 17 was anything but a "travesty of justice." As a kind of show trial paid for in part by the US government, it was not only patently unconcerned with the truth of what had occurred in October 1983 but openly willing to distort the judicial process to ensure the sought-after guilty verdicts. For what is disturbingly odd about the proceedings of the trial is not so much the abuses themselves (which might have been comical if they had not so catastrophically destroyed the lives of seventeen people) as the sense of absolute impunity with which they were enacted, the open contempt for any minimal liberal principle of fairness, let alone any international standard of human rights; the flagrant disregard not simply for justice but even for the merest *perception* that justice was done. The trial of the Grenada 17, in other words, was a cynical act of pure vengeance carried out with the complicity of a people made vulnerable by the still fresh trauma of 19 October and the still indecipherable evolution of events that, consequently, seemed to suggest the work of political evil. In this instance, the judicial vengeance was enacted at the behest of imperial power with an impunity guaranteed both by a collapsing Cold War and a supine Caribbean political community. But however much it may have satisfied the bloodlust of US imperial power and the misguided revenge of significant sections of the Grenadian people, what the Maurice Bishop Murder Trial manifestly did *not* do was bring any closure to the festering conflict over the sources and meaning of October 1983.

Commissioned Evasions

For scholars such as Martha Minow, Priscilla Haynor, and Ruti Teitel, the failure of the trial of the Grenada 17 to resolve the matter of the criminal responsibility for the murder of Maurice Bishop and his colleagues, much less shed light on the true reasons for the collapse of the Grenada Revolution, may in the end be merely grist for the mill of their larger argument about what transitional justice requires. For them, even in the most favorable conditions, the adversarial litigation and crime-centered focus that by and large characterizes criminal trials may not provide the most suitable arena for arriving at truth.[62] And truth—historical truth; the truth of what happened in the past—is what is now argued to count for justice. Indeed, in this view, historical truth *is* justice in a certain respect inasmuch as it is the basis of the moral accountability that prepares the ground for *reconciliation*, the ultimate goal of transitional justice. Therefore, it is argued, what such unresolved and unreconciled situations demand is precisely a truth commission—that is, a legally instituted platform for an authorized public historical inquiry. These institutions, which began appearing in the 1970s and arose with increasing frequency in the 1980s, are fundamentally different in intent and conception from trial courts.[63] They do not carry out the functions of the prosecutorial process; nor are they invested, as legally instituted courts are, with the powers of compulsion and punishment. Nevertheless, with the South African case held up as exemplary, truth commissions have become paradigmatic sites for the enactment of transitional justice.

Theorists of transitional justice argue that historical inquiries are necessary to the reconstruction of social and political order in postconflict societies. The normative claim is that they enable a transition to a more liberal order; they help, in other words, to generate a liberalizing turn. In this view, "history itself is universalizing and redemptive," and "historical truth in and of itself is justice."[64] At the same time, while appreciating the impulse of this approach to law and transitions, Teitel maintains that it presupposes a positivist idea of the identity or convergence of history and truth; it "evinces a belief in the possibility of an autonomous objective history of the past belying the significance of the present political context in shaping the historical inquiry."[65] Against this view, Teitel urges a more social-constructionist approach that takes into account the "interpretive turn" in historical knowledge. Now, she says, "there is no simple, clear, and determinate understanding or 'lesson' to draw from the past but, instead, recognition of the degree to which historical understanding depends on political and social contingency."[66] Here, once again, it seems, context matters. For her, "transitional histories" have a peculiar, "interested," character, given their normative role in *advancing* a liberalizing transformation. Transitions, as she suggests, are not settled conditions of historical truth making but, rather, "vivid instances of conscious historical production" in a context driven by specific political purposes—namely, the creation of liberal democratic states out of illiberal ones. Aligning herself with what she sees as Nietzschean and Foucauldian critiques regarding the present-centeredness and will to power of discursive orders, Teitel acknowledges that "all regimes are associated with and constructed by a 'truth' regime."[67] In this view, then, collective memory is always a process of constructing the past in light of the present. However, in periods of transition, the historical reconstruction process takes a special form, for here, the relation of the construction of collective memory to politics is at once "discontinuous and intertwined." The construction of transitional history is predicated on drawing a clear line of discontinuity at the same time that it adheres to some sense of historical and political continuity.

The intention to establish a truth and reconciliation commission in Grenada was announced in early 2000 by Prime Minister Keith Mitchell amid mounting public discontent that some of the fundamental questions surrounding *what* had happened on 19 October 1983, and *why*, remained unanswered.[68] Nearly a decade and a half had passed since the end of the Maurice Bishop Murder Trial that found the Grenada 17 guilty as charged, but the events that led to the downfall of the Grenada Revolution and the violent deaths of Prime Minister Maurice Bishop and his associates were as shrouded in mystery as ever. As discussed in chapter 3, there was the painful question of the whereabouts of the remains of Bishop and the others killed at Fort Rupert. The research carried out by the students at Presentation Brothers College and published in *Under the Cover of Darkness* had done much to focus public attention on the longstanding issue. The subsequent announcement that bodies had been found in St. George's Cemetery (even though they were later determined not to be the remains in question) only added urgency to the suspicion that the whole truth about what happened in 1983 had yet to be satisfactorily unearthed.[69] This, needless to say, led back to the Grenada 17, who, given the nature of their trial, had not yet had an opportunity to tell their side of the story in full. In the years after the commutation of their death sentences in August 1991, when they were no longer simply fighting for their lives, the Grenada 17 had sought to give an account of themselves and, in the course of doing so, to issue apologies for their role in the catastrophe of 1983. These apologies, it is important to note, did not amount to an *unqualified* acceptance of responsibility for what had taken place. The Grenada 17 were careful to distinguish between what they fully accepted (namely, partial moral and political responsibility for the conditions that had led to the disaster), and what they rejected (namely, criminal liability for the deaths that occurred on 19 October 1983).[70] Moreover, a number of prominent citizens, including former detainees of the People's Revolutionary Government, such as the distinguished journalist Leslie Pierre (editor of the *Grenadian Voice*, who had attended the trial), had been making public their view that there might be much *more* to the story of 19 October 1983 than was generally assumed, and that it was time for those in prison to be given the opportunity to have their say about what took place, and their role in it.[71] Consequently, there was perhaps a degree of pressure on the government to act (or, at least, to be *seen* to act) in response to the growing public demand for an inquiry of some sort to bring closure to the open wound of the past. Thus, in consultation with some former participants in the establishment of the famed South African Truth and Reconciliation Commission, principally Abdullah Mohamed Omar (better known as Dullah Omar), the former minister of justice in Nelson Mandela's government, the Grenadian prime minister announced that a similar body would be established in Grenada.[72]

After much delay, the Grenada Truth and Reconciliation Commission (TRC) was constituted in September 2001 (pursuant to the provisions of the Commissions of Inquiry Act of 1990). It consisted of three persons: the chairman, the Honorable Donald Trotman, former judge of the Supreme Court of Guyana; the Right Reverend Bishop Sehon Goodridge, Anglican Bishop of the Diocese of the Windward Islands; and the Reverend Father Mark Haynes, administrator of the Roman Catholic Cathedral in St. George's, Grenada. Its terms of reference mandated it to "inquire into and record certain political events" that occurred in Grenada between January 1976 and December 1991, with special reference to the period of the Grenada Revolution.[73] Central to its mandate, therefore, was an investigation of the events that led up to the overthrow of Eric Gairy's regime by the NJM on 13 March 1979; the political conduct of the People's Revolutionary Government while in power (its attitude toward political dissent, in particular); and the events that led up to that government's demise on 19 October 1983, including the shooting deaths of Bishop and his associates at Fort Rupert. In this respect, also, the Grenada TRC was to concern itself with the lingering question of the disposal of the remains of those who were killed at the fort that day. The commissioners were charged with reporting their findings and making their recommendations within a period of six months of the commission's first formal sitting. To this end, they began taking evidence in October 2001, and the last witness appeared before them in August 2002.[74]

The aim of the Grenada TRC was to "uncover the truth" underlying the political events in question and to provide a "proper and comprehensive understanding" of what had taken place "so that any mistakes made in the past may not be repeated."[75] And of course the objective of this truth telling was to provide the nation with "an opportunity to become genuinely reconciled and permanently healed."[76] The title of the commissioners' report, *Redeeming the Past: A Time for Healing*, gave point to their intention to provide a platform for such truth telling as would "create opportunities for forgiveness and reconciliation among relevant parties affected by [the events under investigation]; and that could help to heal wounds so that they do not fester in the future."[77] Clearly, then, the Grenada TRC meant to wrap itself in the familiar humanitarian rhetoric (drawn largely from the South African case) of the virtues of such institutions—namely, that the public discovery of the truth of the past would enable a conflicted society such as Grenada, a society burdened by the silences surrounding an unspeakable historical event, to gain some perspective and so enable it to release itself from its imprisonment and face the future free and reconciled.[78]

Truth commissions traffic in history because historical justice requires historical truth. Thus, the Grenada TRC's report divided the historical past under its purview into three discrete, successive periods—the prerevolutionary period (1976–79); the revolutionary period (1979–83); and the postrevolutionary period (1983–91)—and offered condensed portraits of each of them. Needless to say, it is its description of the revolutionary period that is of most interest. Given the thick cloak of prejudice that has so resolutely shaped the perception of this past, how did the commissioners understand it? What new light were they able to shed on 1983? What story of this past would enable Grenadians to be reconciled for the future?

The answers—if that is what they should be called—are disappointing. The commissioners start off by describing the Grenada Revolution in the most startlingly dramatic terms, as a "cataclysmic" event that "engendered a socio-political eruption of volcanic intensity and consequences." They continue, "Never before or since, in the life of the Grenadian people, was there anything so shattering of the national and political structure of Grenada. . . . From then to the demise of the Revolution in October 1983, the whole fabric of Grenadian society was to be shredded and to undergo an almost total reweaving." The revolution, we are told, brought with it a "complex pattern of good and evil." There were, for example, positive social and economic changes (such as opportunities for education and employment, the establishment of cooperatives and small industries, improvements in health care, and the development of social programs) that benefited the mass of the population. But these changes were overshadowed by the "desecration of democracy," the stifling of freedom and denial of political expression, so that on the whole, "when weighed in the balance, the goodness of the revolutionary gains [was] found wanting." By 1982, according to the commissioners, "the cookie was clearly crumbling." The "socialist fervor among the initially enthused and indoctrinated [supporters] began to cool and the revolutionary experiment began to go against the inherent democratic grain of the Grenadian people." The revolution, in short, was in a state of terminal disintegration. As the party lost the undivided loyalty of the masses, "there appeared to be growing evidence or apprehension" that Bernard Coard and his clique were "plotting to remove and overthrow Maurice Bishop, the maximum leader," on the grounds that he was a "weak leader, a moderate socialist" who was disposed to construct political relations with both Cuba and the United States. Moreover, the commissioners conclude, the Coard faction "resented [Bishop's] failure to comply with its request for joint leadership of the party and government. Consequently Bishop was placed under house arrest, later freed by some of his supporters whom he led to the Fort Rupert where he and some of his ministerial colleagues were executed."[79]

This in large part is the commissioners' story of the revolutionary period, 1979–83, from the moment the revolutionaries took power to the moment of their government's violent collapse. It is not an especially erudite account, but it is nevertheless notable for the nonchalant anticommunist biases and assumptions that frame it and the misinformed (at best) or deliberately misleading (at worst) story it tells. The Grenada Revolution was a destructive, almost demonic intrusion into a supposedly settled way of life, a force that perverted the natural political instincts of the Grenadian people. It may have generated some social and economic good, but this was far outweighed by the illiberal, even evil political character of the regime. And as the scales of indoctrination began to fall from the eyes of the people, deceived but now recovering their inherent democratic inclinations, this incipient political evil showed itself in the vicious plot to forcibly remove Bishop, the moderate leader, because he was friendly to Cuba and the United States and had failed to "comply" with the party's "request" for joint leadership. This is clearly a version of the popular story.

But it might have been imagined that the commissioners, given their remit and the potential materials they had at their disposal, would have been able to construct a more complete and complex picture of the events of September and October 1983. (I return in a moment to what some directions of investigation might have been.)

Needless to say, readers of the report would have been particularly keen to see what the commissioners had to say about the Grenada 17. After all, one can scarcely deny that the terrible events of 19 October 1983 lie at the heart of what stands in need of truth telling—and the reconciliation that it would enable. In view of this, it might have seemed self-evident to many that the participation of the Grenada 17 in the TRC would have been crucial to the process and that their testimony would have been essential to a full understanding of what took place on that October morning and afternoon, as well as of the actions and decisions that led to the catastrophe. Astonishingly, however, the commissioners did not once meet with any of the members of the Grenada 17. As far as the commissioners were concerned, they "were at all material times available to meet 'the 17' and [were] satisfied that the failure of the several reasonable efforts it made to do so, was not of [the TRC's] own making."[80] In their account, it was the Grenada 17 who were uncooperative, not *they*, the commissioners, who were gravely neglectful of their public duty to vigorously seek after the truth. However, a cursory glance at the relevant materials collected in the second volume of their report leads one to suspect that the commissioners' account may be disingenuous, if not downright misleading. It appears that from the outset, the Grenada 17 welcomed the TRC. In a letter dated 5 February 2000 submitted to the committee responsible for organizing the commission, they wrote, "We wish to state that we stand willing and ready to fully participate in the proceeding of a 'Truth and Reconciliation Commission,' including giving evidence and facing cross-examination once it is clear that truth and reconciliation are indeed the objectives of the exercise."[81] Evidently, then, the Grenada 17 were not confident that "truth and reconciliation" were the real objectives of the exercise.[82]

Indeed, in the report the commissioners' lack of sympathy for the Grenada 17 is hard to miss. They showed not only disdain for them but also little interest in the trial that had sent them to prison. According to the commissioners' brief account, after being captured by the US forces, the detainees were handed over to Grenadian authorities, who charged them on 22 February 1984 for murder and conspiracy to commit murder. In reference to the trial, they note simply that the Grenada 17 "claimed inter alia, at various times and in several submissions at the trial, and in motions and appeals, that the Court in which they were tried and convicted was unconstitutional; that the trial was unfair, that the Court of Appeal hearing was flawed and no written decision of it delivered; that they have been unjustly denied access to the normal legal processes available to other Grenadians, particularly as regards their being prevented from accessing the Judicial Committee of the Privy Council."[83] But the commissioners were not interested in how we might understand, much less evaluate, this claim. At a certain point, in reference to the various appeals submitted by the Grenada 17, the commissioners write with obvious impatience and blatant partiality that "their steadfast assertions of innocence and unfairness of their trial contrived to create waves of upheaval among the otherwise now stable Grenadian society."[84] Now, quite apart from the bias explicit in this remark, the commissioners surely would have to concede that, had Grenadian society really been "stable," as they assert, there would have been no need for their commission in the first place. Still, the commissioners felt obliged to allow that it would be wrong to be "dismissive and disregarding" of the representations eventually made to them by the legal counsel of the Grenada 17 and, in particular, "their persuasive complaint that their guilt and conviction were determined on the basis of an unfair trial."[85] Even so, the commissioners seemed to feel no need to inquire minimally into these complaints.

In respect to truth, then, what could the commissioners say for their endeavor? Their objective, as I have indicated, was historical truth in the moral service of reconciliation; and truth was needed because it seemed, justifiably, that almost two decades after that fateful October morning and afternoon, little was known about what had happened and why. But the report offers precious few substantial truths by which to guide the hoped-for reconciliation. In fact, in the report, the commissioners are compelled to admit that *nothing* they found adds anything new to the existing stock of knowledge about 19 October 1983. "The Commission [would] be less than frank," they write with unabashed sincerity and straightforward brevity, "if it did not confess that during its extensive and intensive inquiry, it unearthed little more knowledge of the truth of facts and events pertaining to the periods under inquiry, than that which was already known."[86] This is, of course, an astonishing admission. The commissioners even console themselves by saying that "what is important is that the Commission considered all this information, old and new correlatively, and reached its conclusions in accordance with its own deliberate and independent judgment."[87] But deliberate and independent judgment surely was only the least that should have been expected from a commission such as theirs. How can it be the grounds on which they solicit appreciation for their work? To be fair, it seems clear from what the commissioners say (in somewhat oblique and guarded language) that the Grenadian government, while duly constituting the commission and providing it with its terms of reference, had very little interest in seeing to it that it was able to carry out the investigation that was—and undoubtedly still is—warranted. The commissioners maintain, "Throughout much of its work, the Commission suffered from several setbacks occasioned by the administration; inadequate logistical accommodation; and some unwilling and uncooperative official personnel."[88] However unsurprising this may be, it only underlines the sense that many people in Grenada had that a good deal of cynicism went into the process and that the case of October 1983 was opened *only* to be deliberately evaded and foreclosed.

And yet, that there were at least the *conditions* for a very different story to emerge from the TRC process is clearly evident from the materials supplied to the commission by the Grenada 17, and which are assembled as appendices in the second volume of the report. Even as it became clear to them that the TRC process was not going to take the shape that they had urged, the political prisoners provided the commission with various documents, hoping, no doubt, in some small way to have their predicament taken seriously.[89]

One of the manuscripts enclosed was the essay titled "October 1983: The Missing Link," written in 1988–89 by John "Chalky" Ventour, a former general secretary of the Grenada Commercial and Industrial Workers Union, a former member of the Central Committee of the NJM, and one of the Grenada 17.[90] The essay concerns the question of the role—not known to many—of Cuban political authorities in precipitating the final crisis in October 1983. Among the already known variables that contributed to the crisis, such as the internal handling of the joint leadership decision, economic and political pressure from the United States, fatigue, and so on, something seemed to be missing from the story that would explain in particular the turn toward a *military* solution to the crippling political standoff between Bishop and the party. As Ventour suggests, there are a number of unanswered questions that *point* in the direction of Cuba. To begin with, what made Bishop decide to return to Grenada *by way of* Cuba instead of the United Kingdom following his state visit to Hungary and the former Czechoslovakia? It is well enough known that while on this trip, which took place in the immediate aftermath of the historic general meeting of the NJM on 25 September 1983 when Bishop agreed to joint leadership and acknowledged that there was no conspiracy against him, a number of people (principally George Louison) prevailed upon Bishop to change his mind.[91] In Cuba, Bishop spent a day (7 October) in closed talks with Castro who, as again is common knowledge, was a mentor to Bishop and treated him, many said, like a son or like a brother. Is it plausible to believe (especially given the detour) that the trip to Cuba was not for the express purpose of consulting with Castro on the Grenada crisis?[92] And why would Cuban Ambassador Julian Rizo, who conveniently was in Cuba at the same time and returned to Grenada on the same flight as Bishop (on 8 October), immediately move his residence to the Cuban Embassy and surround himself with Cuban security personnel? Might he have expected military danger? Or again, what made Bishop precipitate the popular revolt against the party by spreading the rumor (on 12 October) of a plot to assassinate him by Phyllis and Bernard Coard? And most important, what made him decide to seize the army's headquarters after his supporters took him from his house at Mount Wheldale (on 19 October)? Ventour suggests that this decision in particular was uncharacteristic of Bishop and one that he was not likely to have made in the absence of such guaranteed support as would enable him to defeat the People's Revolutionary Army. So was a plan already afoot? In 1981, Ventour writes, the Cuban authorities signed an agreement with Grenada that made a small battalion of Cuban soldiers available to supplement the People's Revolutionary Army in the event of an invasion. What was not widely known, however, was that this battalion would respond to a request for military assistance *only* from Bishop himself. As Ventour observes, the significance of this did not become evident until after the events at Fort Rupert on 19 October.[93] Moreover, he concludes, the suspicions of the Grenada 17 that

Bishop had tried to contact Castro from Fort Rupert to trigger the use of these troops seemed to be confirmed by remarks Castro made in 1985. In an interview with US Congressman Mervyn Dymally and academic Jeffrey Elliot, Castro revealed that when the "people's uprising took place, and Bishop was taken out of prison [*sic*], one of Bishop's comrades went to the embassy to seek our support. A wire was sent to Havana saying that Bishop was asking for support from the armed Cuban personnel in the construction brigade. The wire was accompanied by public reports on the repression, the people's demonstration, and Bishop's assassination."[94]

Was this suspicion of the Cuban connection a direction of inquiry worth exploration by the TRC? Did the commissioners not have an obligation at least to determine whether any part of it could be corroborated? Might it not have altered significantly the general perception of the course of events that led to the violence at Fort Rupert on 19 October 1983? Might it have offered a different view of what took place and of *who* might have been conspiring against whom? Indeed, might its very plausibility, even taken as a self-interested account, require us at least to entertain a different picture of Bishop from the one the commissioners stood ready to accept?

Another essay included in the materials supplied to the commissioners was "A Travesty of Justice: How 10 NJM Leaders of the Grenada Revolution Were Convicted by One Lie," written by Ewart Layne, a former lieutenant-colonel and day-to-day commander of the People's Revolutionary Army, and one of the Grenada 17. It was Layne, twenty-five years old at the time, who on 19 October 1983, in the midst of the paralysis of the revolution's political leadership, took the fateful decision to send troops to regain control of Fort Rupert after it had been overrun by Bishop and his supporters. "A Travesty of Justice" is concerned with just *one* crucial detail of the prosecution's case against the Grenada 17 that, Layne argues, "has been buried under a mountain of propaganda."[95] This is the discrepancy about time in the testimony of the prosecution's key witness, Cletus St. Paul. Recall that the trial judge had underlined to the jury that the entire case for the prosecution rested on St. Paul's testimony. Therefore, Layne reasons, if St. Paul's evidence was flawed, the convictions were flawed and, as a matter of law, should be thrown out.[96] Layne maintains that there was considerable consistency among all the witnesses at the trial regarding the time of certain important events—with the exception of St. Paul. These witnesses, located in various positions around St. George's on 19 October, all agreed that the crowd overran Fort Rupert at around 11 AM and that the armored personnel carriers arrived there from Fort Frederick at about 1 PM—a lapse of two hours. St. Paul's story had a different timeline. As Layne records it, St. Paul testified that he was standing near the entrance of Fort Frederick when Bernard Coard and other Central Committee members arrived in a state of urgency. They immediately huddled together, gesticulating with their hands and heads, after which Leon Cornwall delivered his famous "liquidation" speech to the assembled soldiers. Subsequently, Layne spoke to a number of army commanders, and after this, the armored vehicles left Fort Frederick to carry out their mission. Then, according to St. Paul, ten to fifteen minutes later he heard shooting from the direction of Fort Rupert. Thus, according to this version, no more than fifteen to twenty minutes could have elapsed between the seizure of Fort Rupert and the arrival of the armored vehicles from Fort Frederick. Since the rest of the prosecution's evidence places the former at roughly 11 AM and the latter at roughly 1 PM, two hours are missing in St. Paul's testimony. According to Layne, St. Paul is simply lying. The truth, he maintains, is that St. Paul (who, remember, was under detention) could not have witnessed the arrival of any Central Committee member at Fort Frederick because at the time they were arriving, St. Paul was still being held at Camp Fedon in Calivigny. According to Layne's account, the time of St. Paul's arrival and the departure of the troops is not only known to the many soldiers who would have witnessed it but were too terrified to testify at the trial but, more pertinently, can be corroborated by the duty officer's diary, which recorded all movements into and out of Fort Frederick and which was seized by the United States and never returned.

Again, would this not have been a text worth the commissioners' time and consideration? Might it not have suggested that something was terribly wrong with the substance and conduct of the trial? Layne's account poses a challenge that goes to the very heart of the prosecution's case against the Grenada 17—namely, the credibility of St. Paul's testimony. The commissioners would certainly have known, after all, that at the appeal the president of the court, Justice Haynes, had had grave misgivings about the number of different statements St. Paul had made and was on the point of calling him to account for them when he died. One might have expected the commission to make it its business, as a matter of the truth seeking with which it was duly charged and as a matter of resolving an evident controversy, to summon St. Paul themselves—as was in their power to do—to appear before them.[97] But alas, here again the commissioners decided to forgo an opportunity to pursue the historical truth of 19 October 1983.

Together, these two testimonials by members of the Grenada 17 offer a picture of the events that led to the collapse of the Grenada Revolution that is radically different from the one typically rehearsed in popular, official, and scholarly accounts. Indeed, had the commissioners taken these documents seriously (along with the others sent or suggested to them by the Grenada 17), it would not have been possible for them to conclude, as they did, that the knowledge that they had at the end of their inquiry of what led to the terrible violence at Fort Rupert on 19 October 1983 was essentially the same as what they had at the beginning.

Truth commissions, many transitional justice scholars maintain, are meant to traffic in history; they aim to set the record straight, because only the full and undistorted disclosure of what happened in the past can serve as the basis for reconciliation. As victims and perpetrators unburden themselves, it is argued, the revealed truth of the past will enable individual and national reconciliation and lay the foundation for a shared and peaceful future. Commissioned remembering is the basis for collective repair. In Teitel's view, though, it is a mistake to think that such historical truths can be merely disinterested. On the contrary, truths are always worldly, and the truths of transitional histories ought to be *self-interested*, because they serve the purpose of advancing a liberalizing transformation. Of course, Teitel can hold this view only because she believes that such transitions are essentially virtuous. Non-liberal and illiberal pasts hold truths about themselves that are really distortions, and the horizon of the liberal future is the standard against which those distortions can be recognized, judged, and corrected—cost it what it may. In this view, then, the commissioners of the Grenada TRC were only right to console themselves that while they had not learned anything new about the terrible events of 19 October 1983—nothing about the intransigent positions staked out in the party, nothing about the stoking of Bishop's anxieties, nothing about

the decision to go to Fort Rupert and the possible role of the Cubans, nothing about the testimony that sent the Grenada 17 to prison—such truths
as they retailed in their report were all that were contextually useful for
advancing the forgetting of the revolutionary past and the transition to a
liberal future.

It is arguable, of course, that the process and outcomes of the Maurice
Bishop Murder Trial and the Grenada TRC only prove that state-sanctioned
power can sometimes be cynically manipulative where justice and truth
are concerned. It does not prove that the principle of transitional justice
itself should be suspected of so base a motivation. But, then, it is not cynicism as such that has been the burden of my concern in this chapter so
much as the global political-ideological conditions—essentially, the empowered entrenchment of an intolerant and fundamentalist version of
liberalism—that make cynicism an acceptable, if not always necessary,
part of so-called transitions from illiberal rule. For Teitel and others, the
whole point of the construction of transitional justice regimes is to mark
a clear distance between predecessor (that is, illiberal) and successor (that
is, liberal) regimes. In the reductive formulation that has come to define
the transitional industry, illiberal political regimes rely on repression and
the distortion of truth, whereas liberal regimes are characterized by rule
of law and the transparency of truth. In the period between these two
political statuses, when transitional powers are actively seeking to reveal
the illegitimacy of the old and establish the legitimacy of a new direction,
there is need, it is said, to attach ideal liberal norms more deliberately,
more closely, and more vigorously to the emerging order. This is why, as
Teitel says, transitional truth is not disinterested or neutral but, rather,
draws the fund of its normative legitimacy from the fact that it has virtue
on its side, for it serves the self-evidently greater good of transforming
an illiberal state into a liberal one. The burden of my argument here is to
suggest that liberal cynicism may be only *one* expression of liberalism's
arrogance of entitlement to global power, the swaggering self-confidence
it displays of a *right*—even a moral duty—to impose on others its civilizational truth. The story of the Grenada 17 and the political-legal aftermaths
of the collapse of the Grenada Revolution is not merely a minor episode in

the history of a geopolitically insignificant part of the world; it is a chapter inseparable from the larger story of the emergence of a world in which the socialist past can appear in the present *only* as a criminal one and in which liberal democracy parades as the single—and, if need be, militarily enforceable—direction of a worldwide political order.

THE TEMPORALITY OF FORGIVING

> The possible redemption from the predicament of irreversibility—
> of not being able to undo what has been done though one did not,
> and could not, have known what he was doing—is the faculty of
> forgiving.
> —HANNAH ARENDT, *The Human Condition*

Forgiveness, on Arendt's account, is one of the moral implications of the temporal nature of action—namely, its *irreversibility*.[1] Action unfolds in one temporal direction only, out of the
present and into the coming future, so that what is set in motion by action cannot be undone or reversed. It can only be suffered, interpreted, embraced, judged, remembered, forgiven. We
act with intention and knowledge, but we cannot foresee or entirely control the effects or consequences of what we have done.
We are vulnerable to the time of contingency. In this sense, as in
others, we are constrained by our *finitude*. And because this is
so, Arendt argues, we need a way to be *released* from the consequences of what we have *unwittingly* done—that is, from the *unintended* consequences of our actions, even our political actions.
Were we bereft of this power, she says, we would forever remain
victims of the reverberating consequences of some single deed,
forever trapped by the past. This power of release is that of *forgiving*. As we can see, forgiveness is connected to *freedom* and
therefore to *futurity*. Without forgiveness, our freedom to act—to

act afresh into the coming future—would be constrained, curtailed, even canceled. "Only through this constant mutual release from what they do can men remain free agents," Arendt writes. "Only by constant willingness to change their minds and start again can they be trusted with so great a power as that to begin something new."[2] The present, which is always the time of action, has to be released from the burden of past deeds in order to make new futures possible.

Unlike the moral code derived from a Platonic notion of rule as exception and time as eternity, the morality inferred from a practice of forgiving is based on the temporal co-presence of others—the time it takes to act with others. We need forgiving powers because action takes place in a plural, temporal world of other actions and actors whose intentions and responses cannot exactly be known in advance or entirely assimilated in their aftermath. Our actions have consequences for others with whom we act in the public realm. It is these others who have the power to release us, knowing that their own misfired actions will soon enough require forgiving from us. Forgiving, then, is an *ordinary* power, an ordinary moral duty—not a transcendent one. It grows immanently out of the very fabric and character of the temporality of mundane action itself. But it is meant to apply, note, first and foremost to *unintended* consequences. It does not apply, Arendt firmly argues, to what she calls "willed evil," and undoubtedly it does not apply to "radical evil."[3] Forgiveness presupposes that punishment is a possible alternative, for what cannot be punished, as she famously said, cannot be forgiven.[4]

In contemporary discussions of what justice entails in the context of political catastrophe, forgiveness has become something of a leitmotif.[5] But the conception of forgiveness that is prominent here departs from Arendt's focus on the unintended consequences that derive from the irreversibility of action—even as they often share the same Christian root and route as her idea. Take, for example, the views of Jeffrie Murphy, whose work has focused on the "retributive emotions"—anger, resentment, and hatred—directed at wrongdoers especially by their victims.[6] These emotions are crucial, Murphy argues, because they help to defend certain values of the self, that of *self-respect* in particular. Not to resent moral injury, he says, is nearly always to be wanting in a proper elementary regard for the self's integrity. Yet such retributive emotions can also be debilitating, disabling the restoration of otherwise valued relationships or dimensions of relationships, which are important for self-respect. Forgiveness seeks to forswear or overcome resentments—it is, Murphy says (following Bishop Butler), the "resolute overcoming of the anger and hatred that are naturally directed toward a person who has done one an unjustified and non-excused moral injury."[7] Notably, then, one can forgive only what it is appropriate to resent. They form a pair. And resentment and forgiveness, in this view, are directed principally at "responsible wrongdoing," or the wrongdoing that remains intact as transgression (that cannot be erased by justification, for example, or mitigated by mercy). However, Murphy maintains, the forswearing of resentment in forgiveness is not always a virtue. A too hasty readiness to forgive can show both a lack of self-respect and a lack of respect for others who have been equally injured. Forgiveness, in this view, is only a virtue when it is consistent with self-respect and respect for others, and it can be consistent in this way only if there are good moral reasons for exercising the powers of forgiving. In the list of such reasons, Murphy names as examples sincere repentance (a genuine change of heart) and sufficient or redemptive suffering (like the broken Oedipus in Sophocles's finale, *Oedipus at Colonus*).[8] Forgiving for reasons such as these is deemed consistent with self-respect and respect for others.

Note the contrast here between Arendt's and Murphy's conceptual concerns, the one focused primarily on *unwilled* harms and the other on *willed* harms; the one derived from the temporality of action itself and the other governed by an external moral logic of respect. What is the question about forgiveness, we might ask, as we close this book, in the case of the Grenada 17? Much—perhaps *everything*—depends on the description under which their fateful actions are viewed. Was the catastrophe of 19 October 1983 the unintended consequence of the tragic collision of actions? Or was it the result of the willful intention to commit murder?

In a New Year's message delivered in January 2008, Nadia Bishop, daughter of the slain Prime Minister Maurice Bishop, urged forgiveness of the Grenada 17.[9] In very humane and moving language, redolent of Murphy's ethos and idiom, she described her long, difficult struggle with retributive emotions—her hatred and resentment—toward those who were accused and convicted of the killing of her father, and her decision finally to try to overcome these emotions and forgive. She was ready at last to release the debt she felt was owed to her and to forswear resentment. She described her meeting in December 2007 at Richmond Hill Prison with Dave Bartholomew, Callistus Bernard, Bernard Coard, Leon Cornwall, Liam James, Ewart Layne, Colville McBarnette, Selwyn Strachan, and John Ventour. It was, she said, the first time she had met them since her father's death and their incarceration. She spoke of the meeting in the transcendent language of joy and grace. She was aware, as Murphy would have wished, that she could only forgive on her own behalf, and she was cognizant that where a deed of the magnitude of political murder is concerned, the self-respect of others (as much as her own) is at stake. Indeed, she willingly acknowledged that many felt, and told her explicitly, that if there was to be any forgiveness, it should only be "conditional"—first, on the Grenada 17's acceptance of full responsibility for what had taken place on 19 October 1983; and second, on their own explicitly expressed desire for atonement and forgiveness. Interestingly, and clearly with long-considered deliberation and respect, Bishop rejected this view and urged instead that any forgiveness ought now to be *unconditional*. It was as if she had posed the question with which Derrida lately became associated: "must one not maintain that an act of forgiveness worthy of its name, if there ever is such a thing, must forgive the unforgivable, and without condition?"[10] For Bishop, it would seem, dampening her passion for retribution and releasing the past was crucial to repairing valued relationships that had been broken for decades. Forgiveness could only be a "gracious gift, without exchange."[11]

It was a deeply felt and powerful message, enjoining closure of the traumatic past and renewal of the sense of a common future, the resolute overcoming of resentment and the transformation of pain into collective purpose. But however well intentioned, Bishop's message is also notable for what it *neglects* to mention and for the assumptions it makes about the nature of the events of October 1983, including who bears responsibility—of what kind and for what—and therefore *who* has moral standing to offer or withhold forgiveness. After all, the prerogative to forgive, as Murphy and Derrida variously suggest, can sometimes be misappropriated, can sometimes be the arrogation of a misplaced sovereignty.[12] Bishop's message passes over the public fact (which I have already mentioned) that the members of the Grenada 17 more than once have apologized and sought forgiveness for their role in the catastrophic events of 19 October 1983.[13] Therefore, the "conditions" for forgiveness to which she refers (that is, acceptance of responsibility and repentance) are in fact *not* such as to be weighed and generously set aside but *moot* to begin with, preempted by the initiative of the condemned themselves. The more interesting question, however, may be why the published apologies of the Grenada 17 are so easily and persistently overlooked. And the answer may be that to accept those apologies (with the careful qualification they make regarding the *moral*, as opposed to the criminal, liability of the former Central Committee members of the NJM and the implication that a field of political responsibility that is wider than theirs alone must be taken into account) would require revising our understanding of the *whole* of the events of October 1983 and, in particular, the vital role Maurice Bishop himself played in precipitating the political disaster and transforming it into a violent catastrophe. It might mean undoing the demonization of Bernard Coard and the deification of Maurice Bishop, twin sources of the relentless narrative of evil conspiracy and sanctified death. This revision Nadia Bishop's message is understandably unwilling or unable to make, and by not referring to the well-established doubts about the trial that convicted them, it makes the familiar assumption about the criminal guilt of the Central Committee members of the Grenada 17, centering, as usual, on the supposed mastermind, Bernard Coard. Therefore, the message, without hesitation or question, presumes the moral innocence of Maurice Bishop and his colleagues. *They* bear no responsibility whatsoever for the catastrophe. Suffering as they did their terrible, irreversible deaths, they remain *immune* to moral implication, protected against culpability in the plurality of clashing actions that ultimately conducted them to their doom.

But let us say, for the sake of the argument, and against the background of the questionable legal process and the all but irrelevant and ineffectual truth commission, that there was no conspiracy on the part of the members of the Central Committee of the NJM to murder Maurice Bishop and his colleagues. Let us assume, in other words, that there was no "responsible wrongdoing" on their part, no "willed evil." Let us say that what transpired was a sequence of political actions (including Bishop's) each giving rise to and compounding the others in an increasingly blind, divisive, and emotionally escalating and eventually violent collision. Let us say it was a *tragedy*. Let us grant, of course, that there were soldiers who fired the fatal shots—acknowledging, however, that this fact has never been the fundamental issue of the case against the Grenada 17 and that the exact circumstances in which the soldiers fired the shots have not been incontrovertibly established. Allowing this to be the case, and further taking into account the evidence of torture and the length of incarceration to which those alleged to have committed premeditated murder were subjected, with whom might the moral debt—and the moral credit—rest? Who might harbor a *just* resentment against whom? Who might owe an apology (or more) to whom? Who has standing—and who does not—to forgive? With whom lies the prerogative to release the burdensome past?[14]

On Friday, 4 September 2009, more than a year and a half after Nadia Bishop's message of forgiveness, the minister of government responsible for the Advisory Committee on the Prerogative of Mercy under the Constitution of Grenada advised the governor general to effect the release from Richmond Hill Prison of (among others) the last members of the Grenada 17: Dave Bartholomew, Callistus Bernard, Bernard Coard, Leon Cornwall, Liam James, Ewart Layne, and Selwyn Strachan. They had been in prison for more than a quarter of a century for their alleged role in the deaths of Maurice Bishop and his colleagues at Fort Rupert on 19 October 1983. As the seven men emerged from the now automated gates of the nineteenth-century prison nestled in the hills above St. George's, local and regional journalists were keen to know from them—and especially from Coard—what *they* had learned from their ordeal of near-execution and long incarceration. Had it changed their perception of their actions in 1983? Did they now have a different account to make of the terrible events that had unexpectedly brought them to this point in their personal and political lives? Were they sorry, repentant? Did they think their suffering had redeemed them in any way? And so on.[15] How are we to understand the nature of this sort of inquiry? Was it innocence or presumption that prompted it? Was it the familiar elision and disavowal that so marks and mars modern Caribbean politics? The real question, it seems to me, is what *we*—Caribbeans as a whole—have learned in all the years since the collapse of the Grenada Revolution and the US invasion that followed in its wake. How have we changed? Are we in a better position today, with the blurring and weakening of the lines of cleavage and antagonism that characterized the Cold War, to appreciate what moral and political demand was answered by *our* desire to convict and punish the Grenada 17 on the clearly doubtful evidence produced by the prosecution at their trial? Are we in a better position today to gauge in retrospect what regional anxiety, what wounded fantasy of sovereignty, was assuaged by so egregious a travesty of justice? Are we in a better position today to acknowledge the senses in which the Grenada 17 might really have been hostages to our own political hypocrisy and shallow opportunism—scapegoats, in effect, on whom we projected the rage and resentment of our fatally compromised revolutionary will to power? These are not easy-to-answer questions. But they are pertinent ones.

The collapse of the Grenada Revolution is one of the most traumatic events in recent Caribbean political history. Who knows just how irreparable the scars are? It may be obscure how or whether Grenadians—and other Caribbeans—will ever recover completely from its effects. But it is unlikely that any repair is possible unless we recast our assumptions about that past—and, indeed, about past action in general. The virtue of Arendt's account of the power of forgiving is that it pays attention to the vulnerabilities that constitute the temporality of action—not least, revolutionary action. To the extent that action unfolds in one direction in time (a fact of our finitude), to that extent it is irreversible and open to blindness, to error, to pathos, to collision, to *tragedy*. And since no one is immune to its conduct or its effects, tragic action relies on forgiving to preserve the possibility—the freedom—of new action. This is why, in Arendt's account of it, forgiving is linked to another (to her, *more* political) faculty: *promising*—that is, the faculty that performs the prospect that something of futurity can endure in the fragile passage of time.

ACKNOWLEDGMENTS

This book has taken a long time to think and to write, and its shape has more than once altered over the years of thinking and writing—but not its central object. The book began as a doubt that gathered and grew to haunt and perplex me—namely, a doubt about the inherited story of the catastrophic collapse of the Grenada Revolution and its meaning for our time, especially the story of the crisis within the revolutionary party and of the events that led to the terrible death of Maurice Bishop, then the prime minister, and the story of the trial of those accused of his murder, the so-called Grenada 17. The Grenada Revolution, after all, was the revolution of my Caribbean generation: however brief its existence, it defined the prospect of a more authentic decolonization than had emerged with formal political independence, the prospect of a more vernacular politics of self-determination. Now virtually forgotten (*repressed* is perhaps more diagnostically accurate) by many in the Caribbean region and beyond, these events remain, in Grenada, unresolved, a deep, unrelenting, and unhealing wound. As I reflected on this catastrophe in the context of reflecting on the shifting contours of our world-historical present (contours shaped in many ways by the end of the Cold War and its ideological complexes and by the reengineering of empire, with its distinctive self-congratulatory discourse of transitional justice and human rights), the collapse of the Grenada Revolution and its aftermaths gradually came to acquire for me a larger significance than solely the story of revolutionary failure. It came to signal to me an instance, a tragic but perhaps paradigmatic one, of the ambiguous temporality of the postcolonial present experienced as a kind of prolonged ending, experienced as a kind of living on in postrevolutionary aftermaths, among the confusing ruins of socialist futures past.

Many, many people have helped me in varied ways with the realization of this project. I mention here the most prominent among them. To begin with, I thank Phyllis Coard, who, in trying circumstances, was willing to hear and respond to my questions of fact and interpretation. I also offer my thanks to Bernard Coard (with whom I spoke on several occasions before his release from prison) for his invaluable insights into his decisions and actions during the course of the revolution, the arc of his relationship with Maurice Bishop, and, in particular, his perspective on the last fateful days of the political crisis that led to the downfall of the revolution. I very much hope that our more formal conversation will soon be published. No one, it seems to me, can properly engage the historical problem of the Grenada Revolution without passing through the work of Merle Collins. A writer of profound poetic sensibility and political integrity, she has humanized the landscape of postrevolutionary Grenada as no one else has. I am enormously grateful to her for the time she took to talk to me, and for entrusting me with her story. Occasionally, in projects such as this one, one meets people whose dedication and generosity is at once direct and unencumbered: acts of moral plenitude. One such person is Brother Robert Fanovitch, former head of Presentation Brothers College, St. George's. Over several conversations, he helped me form an idea of the state of mind in Grenada when his students, under his guidance, commenced their landmark intervention to try to discover the whereabouts of the bodies of Maurice Bishop and his colleagues. I am forever indebted to him. I am also indebted to the late Alister Hughes, known to be a journalist of formidable authority, who, when I rang him up out of the blue one Sunday morning, was willing to share with me not only a very agreeable brandy, but also his fiercely held views about the revolution, its collapse, and the trial of the Grenada 17. A story is waiting to be written about Hughes and the end of the Grenada Revolution that will undoubtedly surprise many people. His friend Leslie Pierre, founder and editor of the *Grenadian Voice*, may be the man to write this story—or not. But in the conversations I had with him in the crowded offices of his newspaper I found a man of rare and distinctive courage, a man who, despite his treatment by the revolutionaries, was willing to speak out against the inhumanity of their continued incarceration. I learned a great deal, too, from the late George Brizan, teacher, writer, and politician, whose grace and hospitality and good humor I will never forget. When at last I tracked down the controversial writer Maurice Paterson (now alas, also deceased), our meeting was as brief as it was (for me) riveting. He passed scorching judgment on everything and everyone, including me. But I learned some vital truths from his dissenting disposition and his curious modes of realist fiction (or, if you like, fictional documentation). Father Sean Dogget of St. Patrick's Missionary Society, St. George's, was forthcoming and generous, as everyone told me he would be. Michael DeGale, the late poet and playwright, bestowed on me his very stern, unflattering opinions of the revolutionary period and, to my surprise, his sense that much about Eric Gairy had been misunderstood. I very much thank Susan Meltzer for introducing me to him—and, indeed, for sharing her own thoughts on the politics of Grenadian literary culture. The sociologist Oliver Benoit, himself a scholar of Gairy, doubtless would disagree with DeGale, and I learned a lot from his always pointed skepticism. The trade unionist André Lewis is a man of singular discretion. I could not have conducted my work in Grenada without his quiet help and unassuming commitment to social justice. To the attorney Ruggles Ferguson, a distinguished member of the bar in Grenada and the Caribbean (and a member of the defense team for the Grenada 17), I owe a debt of thanks for helping me to understand the nature of the legal case against those accused of conspiring to murder Maurice Bishop. Finally, I thank Meg Conlon and Erik Johnson for the many memorable evenings spent in their company on my various visits to Grenada. On the whole, I doubt that among any of these generous and committed people, any will endorse all of what I have written here.

As is true of others of my books, I have written this one while in an ongoing conversation with Talal Asad and Stuart Hall. Although neither, obviously, is responsible for the line of investigation I have adopted here, my discussions with them nevertheless frame my way of thinking about thinking, about the form and purpose of intellectual work.

I presented two of the chapters in progress to academic audiences. An earlier version of chapter 3 was read at a conference at Brown University in March 2009 around the theme of "postcolonial melancholia." I am grateful to Elliott Colla and Nauman Naqvi for the invitation to what proved a very stimulating conference. An earlier version of chapter 1 was read at a seminar at Yale University in November 2009 organized by Hazel Carby. I thank her for extending me this invitation, and I thank those in the audience who offered critical comments and suggestions. Subsequently, in January 2010, a slightly revised version of the same chapter was read as the Bernice Nugent Lecture at Queens University, Kingston, Ontario. My thanks to Ishita Pande for inviting me and for being such an engaging host. If in the years that followed I withdrew the chapters from public view, it is because I needed to work up an idea of the whole arc of the book, to see it as the curve of one interconnected argument. I do not know whether I have succeeded. But for her critical assessment of that whole I am grateful to Ritty Lukose for not withholding her judgment.

NOTES

Prologue

Epigraph: Saint Augustine, *Confessions*, trans. Henry Chadwick (New York: Oxford University Press, 1992), 243.

1. See, e.g., Norbert Elias, *Time: An Essay*, trans. Edmund Jephcott (Oxford: Blackwell, 1992); Genevieve Lloyd, *Being in Time: Selves and Narrators in Philosophy and Literature* (New York: Routledge, 1993); Irwin C. Lieb, *Past, Present, and Future: A Philosophical Essay about Time* (Chicago: University of Illinois Press, 1991); Peter Osborne, *The Politics of Time: Modernity and Avant-Garde* (London: Verso, 1995); Syliane Agacinski, *Time Passing: Modernity and Nostalgia*, Jody Gladding, trans. (New York: Columbia University Press, 2003); Mark S. Muldoon, *Tricks of Time: Bergson, Merleau-Ponty, and Ricoeur in Search of Time, Self, and Meaning* (Pittsburgh: Duquesne University Press, 2006); David Couzens Hoy, *The Time of Our Lives: A Critical History of Temporality* (Cambridge: MIT Press, 2009).

2. Augustine, *Confessions*, book 11 ("Time and Eternity"). For a discussion, see Lloyd, *Being in Time*, chap. 1.

3. Augustine, *Confessions*, 243.

4. David Scott, *Conscripts of Modernity: The Tragedy of Colonial Enlightenment* (Durham, NC: Duke University Press, 2004). I borrow the phrase "longing for total revolution" from Bernard Yack, *The Longing for Total Revolution: Philosophic Sources of Discontent from Rousseau and Marx to Nietzsche* (Princeton, NJ: Princeton University Press, 1986).

5. See, e.g., Hayden White, *Metahistory: The Historical Imagination of Nineteenth Century Europe* (Baltimore: Johns Hopkins University Press, 1973). For an instructive engagement with White's work, see Frank Ankersmit, Ewa Domanska, and Hans Kellner, eds., *Re-Figuring Hayden White* (Stanford, Calif.: Stanford University Press, 2009).

6. C. L. R. James, *The Black Jacobins: Toussaint Louverture and the San Domingo Revolution* (London: Secker and Warburg, 1938), viii.

7. Hannah Arendt, *On Revolution* (New York: Viking, 1963), 21.

8. See Perry Mars, *Ideology and Change: The Transformation of the Caribbean Left* (Detroit: Wayne State University Press, 1998).

9. See David Scott, *Refashioning Futures: Criticism after Postcoloniality* (Princeton, NJ: Princeton University Press, 1998).

10. See ibid., coda.

11. Strictly speaking the Grenada 17 consisted of fourteen who were part of the leadership of the NJM, the People's Revolutionary Army, and the People's Revolutionary Government, and three who were rank and file soldiers. As we will see, the former were accused of a conspiracy to commit murder, while the latter were accused of actually firing the fatal shots. In a certain sense, then, their cases are separable, but throughout their political and legal and personal ordeal they represented themselves as the "Grenada 17."

12. For an instructive exploration of the general sense of aftermaths, see Gerhard Richter, *Afterness: Figures of Following in Modern Thought and Aesthetics* (New York: Columbia University Press, 2011).

13. Walter Benjamin, "Theses on the Philosophy of History," in *Illuminations: Essays and Reflections* (New York: Schocken, 1968), 253–64. One of the most instructive discussions of Benjamin's thinking on time is elaborated in Stéphane Mosès, *The Angel of History: Rosensweig, Benjamin, Scholem*, trans. Barbara Harshav (Stanford, Calif.: Stanford University Press, 2009). Mosès writes that Benjamin's central preoccupation was history. This is obviously true, but it seems to me more precise to say that Benjamin's urgent preoccupation was the temporality of futurity. For other striking discussions of time in Benjamin, see Peter Fenves, *The Messianic Reduction: Walter Benjamin and the Shape of Time* (Stanford, Calif.: Stanford University Press, 2010); Eli Friedlander, *Walter Benjamin: A Philosophical Portrait* (Cambridge. Mass.: Harvard University Press, 2012), chapter 3.

14. Giorgio Agamben, "Time and History: Critique of the Instant and the Continuum," in *Infancy and History: On the Destruction of Experience*, trans. Liz Heron (New York: Verso, 1993), 97–116. To be sure, since this early work—his third book—Agamben has developed a sustained preoccupation with temporality and the possible categories of futurity: the contrast between the instant and the continuum; the contrast between "chronos" and "kairos"; the idea of a "coming" community; the idea of a time that remains; and, of course, his central idea of potentiality. These are all concepts of temporality: see Giorgio Agamben, *The Coming Community*, trans. Michael Hardt (Minneapolis: University of Minnesota Press, 1993); Giorgio Agamben, *Potentialities: Collected Essays*, ed. and trans. Daniel Heller-Roazen (Stanford, Calif.: Stanford University Press, 2000); Giorgio Agamben, *The Time That Remains: A Commentary on the Let-*

ter to the Romans, trans. Patricia Dailey (Stanford, Calif.: Stanford University Press, 2005). For a wonderful discussion of Agamben's thought as a whole and his thought on time and Benjamin in particular, see Leland de la Durantaye, *Giorgio Agamben: A Critical Introduction* (Stanford, Calif.: Stanford University Press, 2009).

15. Agamben, "Time and History," 99.

16. Ibid.

17. Ibid.

18. Paul Ricoeur, *Time and Narrative*, 3 vols., trans. Kathleen McLaughlin and David Pellauer (Chicago: University of Chicago Press, 1984–85).

19. Agamben, "Time and History," 110.

20. Ibid., 111.

21. See esp. Agamben, *The Time That Remains*, 67–69.

22. Agamben, "Time and History," 113. Agamben writes that the "originality of *Sein und Zeit* is that the foundation of historicity takes place in tandem with an analysis of temporality which elucidates a different and more authentic experience of time. At the heart of this experience there is no longer the precise, fleeting *instant* throughout linear time, but the *moment* of the authentic decision in which *Dasein* experiences its own finiteness, which at every moment extends from birth to death" (italics in original). See Martin Heidegger, *Being and Time*, trans. John Macquarrie and Edward Robinson (New York: Harper and Row, 1962), especially chapters 5 and 6 of Division Two, 424–88. See also the reconstructed text of the lecture *The Concept of Time* (Oxford: Blackwell, 1992), originally delivered in 1924, in which Heidegger forecasts the themes of the essential temporality of Dasein, "concern" as absorption in the present (the "concernful present"), the future as what "the present cultivates for itself," and of time as what runs "through the present." He writes: "Everything that occurs rolls out of an infinite future and into an irretrievable past" (18E).

23. See helpfully, de la Durantaye, *Giorgio Agamben*, 97–103.

24. Within the terms that I am using here, one might wonder whether part of the reason Agamben does not ask this particular question has to do with the nature of his own problem-space, specifically its pre-1989 formation. Notably, this work, *Infancy and History*, originally published in 1978, is concerned with a general sense of the modern destruction of authentic "experience" rather than with a specific sense of the conjuncture of communism's demise.

25. Jacques Derrida, *Specters of Marx: The State of the Debt, the Work of Mourning, and the New International*, trans. Peggy Kamuf (New York: Routledge, 1994); Jacques Derrida, "Marx & Sons," in *Ghostly Demarcations: A Symposium on Jacques Derrida's Specters of Marx*, ed. Michael Sprinker (London: Verso, 1999), 213–69. See also Jacques Derrida, "The Time Is Out of Joint," in *Deconstruction Is/in America: A New Sense of the Political*, ed. Anselm Haverkamp (New York: New York University Press, 1995), 14–38.

26. The immediate occasion for the text of "Specters of Marx" was the conference "Wither Marxism? Global Crisis in International Perspective," organized in late April 1993 at the University of California, Riverside. Famously, Derrida had issued a promise to engage Marx in some future: see Jacques Derrida, *Positions* (Chicago: University of Chicago Press, 1982), 63.

27. See especially Fredric Jameson, "Marx's Purloined Letter" in Sprinker, *Ghostly Demarcations*, 26–67. And see Ernesto Laclau, "The Time Is Out of Joint," *Diacritics* 25, no. 2 (Summer 1995): 86–96.

28. Derrida, *Specters of Marx*, chap. 4.

29. Derrida, "Marx & Sons," 248.

30. Ibid., 249.

31. On Derrida's uses of Benjamin, see Jameson, "Marx's Purloined Letter," 26, 33. For a discussion of the contrasts in their uses of messianism, see Owen Ware, "Dialectic of the Past/Disjuncture of the Future: Derrida and Benjamin on the Concept of Messianism," *Journal for Cultural and Religious Theory* 5, no. 2 (April 2004): 99–114. For an especially helpful engagement with Derrida and Benjamin in relation to Marx, see Matthias Fritsch, *The Promise of Memory: History and Politics in Marx, Benjamin, and Derrida* (Albany: State University of New York Press, 2005).

32. Derrida, "Marx & Sons," 251.

33. Ibid., 254.

34. See the strenuous effort made to refute Fukuyama in Derrida, *Specters of Marx*, 14–15, 56–57, 66–75.

35. For a meditation of some dimensions of Derrida's ends, see Jacques Derrida, *Learning to Live Finally: An Interview with Jean Birnbaum*, trans. Pascale-Anne Brault and Michael Naas (Hoboken, NJ: Melville House, 2007).

36. The literature is much too large to name in anything like its entirety, but see Cathy Caruth, *Unclaimed Experience* (Baltimore: Johns Hopkins University Press, 1996); Ruth Leys, *Trauma: A Genealogy* (Chicago: University of Chicago Press, 2000); Andreas Huyssen, *Present Pasts: Urban Palimpsests and the Politics of Memory* (Stanford: Stanford University Press, 2003); Dominick LaCapra, *Writing History, Writing Trauma* (Baltimore: Johns Hopkins University Press, 2000); Jeffrey Alexander, *Trauma: A Social Theory* (Cambridge: Polity Press, 2012); Jeffrey Alexander, Ron Eyerman, Bernard Giesen, Neil Smelser, and Piotr Sztompka, *Cultural Trauma and Collective Identity* (Berkeley: University of California Press, 2004).

37. See, e.g., Charles Maier, "A Surfeit of Memory? Reflections on History, Melancholy and Denial," *History and Memory* 5, no. 2 (Fall–Winter 1993): 136–52.

38. Again, the literature is a large—and growing—one, but see Martha Minow, *Between Vengeance and Forgiveness: Facing History after Genocide and Mass Violence* (Boston: Beacon, 1999); Priscilla Hayner, *Unspeakable Truths: Transitional Justice and the Challenge of Truth Commissions* (New York: Routledge, 2001).

For one account of human rights as the consoling vindication of good over evil, see Michael Ignatieff, *The Rights Revolution* (Toronto: House of Anansi, 2000). See also Michael Ignatieff, *Human Rights as Politics and Idolatry*, ed. Amy Gutmann (Princeton, NJ: Princeton University Press, 2001). For a critical account, see Robert Meister, *After Evil: A Politics of Human Rights* (New York: Columbia University Press, 2010).

39. See Ruti Teitel, *Transitional Justice* (New York: Oxford University Press, 2002).

40. A full account of the rise of "social constructionism" in the humanities and social sciences, initially as a radical gesture and subsequently as a conformist one, has yet to be made. For one expression of doubt about what "social constructionism" does, see Ian Hacking, *The Social Construction of What?* (Cambridge, Mass.: Harvard University Press, 2000). For some of my own reflections see David Scott, "The Social Construction of Postcolonial Studies," in *Postcolonial Studies and Beyond*, ed. Ania Loomba, Suvir Kaul, Matti Bunzel, Antoinette Burton, and Jed Esty (Durham, NC: Duke University Press, 2005), 385–400.

41. The best account of Gairy, his style, and his context, remains A. W. Singham, *The Hero and the Crowd in a Colonial Polity* (New Haven, Conn.: Yale University Press, 1967). But see also Pedro Noguera, "The Limits of Charisma: Grenada's Eric Gairy (1922–97) and Maurice Bishop (1944–83): Intellectual and Political Biographies," in *Caribbean Charisma: Legitimacy and Leadership in the Era of Independence*, ed. Anton Allahar (Kingston: Ian Randle, 2001), 72–91.

42. In December 1949, Gairy returned to Grenada from Aruba. In July 1950, Gairy registered the Grenada Manual and Mental Workers' Union, which was instrumental in the island-wide strike of February 1951. By then he had also begun to organize the Grenada Political Party, which eventually became the Grenada United Labour Party, through which he entered electoral politics under the new constitution that allowed for universal adult suffrage: see Singham, *The Hero and the Crowd in a Colonial Polity*, 153–56. See also Brian Meeks, "Grenada: The Pitfalls of 'Popular' Revolution from Above," in *Caribbean Revolutions and Revolutionary Theory: An Assessment of Cuba, Nicaragua, and Grenada* (London: Macmillan, 1993), 135–42.

43. On the infamous Mongoose Gangs, see Meeks, "Grenada," 142.

44. Famously, Gairy was away in New York addressing the United Nations on the subject of UFOs when the revolutionaries made their move in the early hours of 13 March. It is said that Gairy had left instructions with his security forces that the leadership of the NJM should be eliminated.

45. See, e.g., Richard Hart, "Introduction," in *In Nobody's Backyard: Maurice Bishop's Speeches, 1979–1983—A Memorial Volume*, ed. Chris Searle (London: Zed, 1984), xvii; Meeks, "Grenada," 157–65.

46. Sadly, to date there is no work on Bishop comparable to Singham's work on Gairy, but see Noguera, "The Limits of Charisma," and the fascinating account in Omowale David Franklyn, *Bridging the Two Grenadas: Gairy's and Bishop's*

(St. George's: Talented House, 1999). Franklyn seeks to reduce the gap between these two leaders of Grenada.

47. See Maurice Bishop, "In Nobody's Backyard," in Searle, *In Nobody's Backyard*, 14. This was a national broadcast on Radio Free Grenada, 13 April 1979, and Bishop in part was responding to remarks made by US Ambassador Frank Ortiz shortly after the revolution to the effect that the US government would strongly frown on any attempt made by the People's Revolutionary Government to cultivate friendly relations with Cuba.

48. It was known that the United States was carrying out mock invasion exercises. As early as 1981, for example, the North Atlantic Treaty Organization forces landed on Vieques Island, Puerto Rico, to conduct exercises involving training to occupy an imaginary Caribbean island state called "Amber and the Amberines" (a thin disguise for Grenada and the Grenadines), rescue US citizens, and replace its hostile government with one friendly to the US government: see Hart, "Introduction," xxi. In speeches on 10 March and 23 March 1983, Reagan had asserted that Grenada was a threat to US national security: see Richard Hart, *The Grenada Revolution: Setting the Record Straight* (London: Caribbean Labour Solidarity/Socialist History Society, 2005). This is Hart's response to the misrepresentation of the revolution in the account of the former governor-general, Paul Scoon (*Survival for Service* [London: Macmillan, 2003]). More generally, see also Wendell Bell, "False Prophecy and the American Invasion of Grenada"; Robert Pastor, "The Invasion of Grenada: A Pre- and Post-Mortem"; and Timothy Ashby, "The Reagan Years," all in *The Caribbean after Grenada: Revolution, Conflict, and Democracy*, ed. Scott B. MacDonald, Harold M. Sandstorm, and Paul B. Goodwin Jr. (New York: Praeger, 1988), 69–86, 87–105, 269–78.

49. For Margaret Thatcher's disagreement with Reagan, see *The Downing Street Years* (New York: HarperCollins, 1993), 330–32.

50. There are now many accounts of the US military operation. For some of the flavor, see Mark Adkin, *Urgent Fury: The Battle for Grenada* (New York: Lexington Books, 1989).

51. For a description of the capture and initial treatment of the party and army leadership, see Callistus Bernard, *They Could Only Kill Me Once* (London: Hibiscus, 2006), chap. 1.

52. On the "psychological warfare" waged against the Grenadian people, see Hart, "Introduction," xxxix.

53. For a description of the torture, see Bernard, *They Could Only Kill Me Once*, chap. 2.

54. Richard Hart, *The Grenada Trial: A Travesty of Justice* (Kingston: Foundation for Phyllis Coard, 1996), 5.

55. The fourteen originally condemned to death, except Phyllis Coard, who had been granted leave in 2000 to seek medical treatment in Jamaica. On the resen-

tencing judgment, see http://www.spiceislandertalkshop.com/cgi-bin/talkrec
.cgi?submit=lt&fid=f1&msg_num=686323 (accessed 22 May 2012).

56. Over the years, I have been engaged in a project that explores the intellectual
and political lives of this generation: see David Scott, "The Archaeology of Black
Memory: An Interview with Robert A. Hill," *Small Axe* no. 5 (March 1999):
81–151; David Scott, "The Dialectic of Defeat: An Interview with Rupert Lewis,"
Small Axe, no. 10 (September 2001): 85–177; David Scott, "Counting Women's
Caring Work: An Interview with Andaiye," *Small Axe*, no. 15 (March 2004):
123–217; David Scott, "The Paradox of Freedom: An Interview with Orlando
Patterson," *Small Axe*, no. 40 (March 2013): 96–242.

Chapter One. Revolution's Tragic Ends

Part epigraph: Simone Weil, *Lectures on Philosophy*, trans. Hugh Price, introduction
Peter Winch (Cambridge: Cambridge University Press, 1978), 197. *Chapter epigraph*:
A. C. Bradley, *Shakespearean Tragedy: Lectures on Hamlet, Othello, King Lear and
Macbeth* (New York: Penguin, 1991 [1904]), 31.

1. Bradley, *Shakespearean Tragedy*. For a positive consideration of Bradley's work
(though without a serious engagement with his specific ideas about tragedy), see
Katherine Cooke, *A. C. Bradley and His Influence in Twentieth-Century Shakespeare Criticism* (Oxford: Oxford University Press, 1972).

2. See Max Weber, "Politics as a Vocation," in Max Weber, *The Vocation Lectures*,
ed. David Owen and Tracy B. Strong (Indianapolis: Hackett, 2004), 78.

3. I am, of course, thinking of Hannah Arendt, *On Revolution* (New York: Penguin,
1963), and C. L. R. James, *The Black Jacobins: Toussaint Louverture and the San
Domingo Revolution* (London: Secker and Warburg, 1938). For a helpful discus-
sion of Arendt's thinking about revolution, see Margaret Canovan, *Hannah
Arendt: A Reinterpretation of Her Political Thought* (Cambridge: Cambridge
University Press, 1992); Elisabeth Young-Bruehl, *Why Arendt Matters* (New
Haven, Conn.: Yale University Press, 2006). I have explored aspects of James's
thinking about revolution and tragedy in David Scott, *Conscripts of Modernity:
The Tragedy of Colonial Enlightenment* (Durham, NC: Duke University Press,
2004).

4. Weber, "Politics as a Vocation," 74–79. Memorably, Weber was responding in
this lecture to his own revolutionary conjuncture. The lecture was delivered
on 28 January 1919, in the wake both of the Russian Revolution and Germany's
surrender in the 1914–18 war—but also, perhaps crucially, in the immediate
aftermath of the assassination (on 15 January 1919) of the Spartacist leaders Karl
Liebknect and Rosa Luxemburg: see David Owen and Tracy B. Strong, "Introduction: Max Weber's Calling to Knowledge and Action," in Weber, *The Vocation Lectures*, xxxiv–xxxvii.

5. See Karl Jaspers, *Tragedy Is Not Enough*, trans. Harold A. T. Reiche, Harry T.
Moore, and Karl W. Deutsch (London: Victor Gollancz, 1953), 49. There is un-

doubtedly a connection among the tragic sensibilities of Weber, Jaspers, and Arendt.

6. Raymond Williams, *Modern Tragedy* (London: Chatto and Windus, 1966), 83. Williams had earlier published "A Dialogue on Tragedy," *New Left Review* 13–14 (January–April 1962): 22–35. For an insightful review of *Modern Tragedy*, see Stuart Hampshire, "Unhappy Families," *New Statesman* (29 July 1966): 169–70. Hampshire writes in conclusion: "I think he is trying to imagine the kinds of writing that would reflect and strengthen an active community of free men, in contemporary conditions. One may respect the vision, even if one believes that an interest in tragedy is an interest in an altogether different kind of freedom": Hampshire, "Unhappy Families," 170. One might wonder whether Hampshire understands some of his own work to point in the direction of the connection between tragedy and a "different kind of freedom."

7. George Steiner, *The Death of Tragedy* (New Haven, Conn.: Yale University Press, 1996 [1961]). Williams wrote a review of Steiner's book in which one can hardly detect any serious objections: see Raymond Williams, "The Meaning of Tragedy," *The Guardian*, 10 November 1961, 7. On *Modern Tragedy* as a response to *The Death of Tragedy*, see Terry Eagleton, ed., *Raymond Williams: Critical Perspectives* (Boston: Northeastern University Press, 1989), 2; Fred Inglis, *Raymond Williams* (New York: Routledge, 1995), 188, 193–94. It seems to me, however, that Steiner's book is much more complicated than some of his critics make it appear. Terry Eagleton, *Sweet Violence: The Idea of the Tragic* (Oxford: Blackwell, 2002), for example, simply dismisses Steiner as a "traditionalist" and "conservative." Not the least of the complexity of *The Death of Tragedy* stems from the unexpected evocation in its final pages of revolution (specifically, the Chinese Revolution) as a possible venue for authentic tragedy. Steiner writes, referring to a documentary film showing a ceremony in an agricultural commune in rural China that ends with a recital of the heroic death of one of the founders of the local Communist Party who was killed by the Japanese and is buried nearby: "Is it not, I wonder, in some comparable rite of defiance and honor to the dead that tragedy began, three thousand years ago, on the plains of Argos?": Steiner, *The Death of Tragedy*, 354–55. For a discussion of the importance of tragedy to Steiner's work, see Ruth Padel, "George Steiner and the Greekness of Tragedy," in *Reading George Steiner*, ed. Nathan A. Scott Jr. and Ronald A. Sharp (Baltimore: Johns Hopkins University Press, 1994), 99–133.

8. One can read *Modern Tragedy* as a sequel to Raymond Williams, *The Long Revolution* (London: Chatto and Windus, 1961), which, of course, is a sequel to Raymond Williams, *Culture and Society, 1780–1950* (London: Chatto and Windus, 1958).

9. On "liberal tragedy," see Williams, *Modern Tragedy*, 87–105. Perhaps paradigmatically, Williams has in mind the work of Henrik Ibsen and Arthur Miller.

10. Williams, *Modern Tragedy*, 76. For Williams, Marx's vision of revolution is "in-

escapably tragic" inasmuch as it is "born in an experience of evil made the more intolerable by the conviction that it is not inevitable, but the result of particular actions and choices" (ibid., 77). Steiner writes, "Marxism is characteristically Jewish in its insistence on justice and reason, and Marx repudiated the entire concept of tragedy": Steiner, *The Death of Tragedy*, 4. It is well to remember, though, that Steiner had also written feelingly and perceptively about Georg Lukacs: see, e.g., "Marxism and the Literary Critic" [1958] and "Georg Lukacs and the Devil's Pact" [1960], both in George Steiner, *George Steiner: A Reader* (New York: Oxford University Press, 1984).

11. The tragedy, "Koba," was published as the third part of the first edition of Williams, *Modern Tragedy*, 207–82. It seems not to have met with favorable reviews. His colleague at Cambridge, Frank Kermode, for example, panned it, writing, "Unfortunately it is disastrously bad": Frank Kermode, "Tragedy and Revolution," *Encounter* 27, no. 2 [August 1966]: 83–85.

12. Williams, *Modern Tragedy*, 82. I have benefited from Kenneth Surin's insightful essay "Raymond Williams on Tragedy and Revolution," in *Cultural Materialism: On Raymond Williams*, ed. Christopher Prendergast (Minneapolis: University of Minnesota Press, 1995), 143–72.

13. Despite the fact that there were already such terrible omens as the killing of Patrice Lumumba on 17 January 1961. One might remember that in the same year Williams published *Modern Tragedy*, Aimé Césaire published *Une saison au Congo* (Paris: Editions du Seuil, 1966), a meditation on Lumumba and the tragic circumstances of the postcolonial project.

14. Jaspers remarks that "breakdown and failure reveal the true nature of things. In failure, life's reality is not lost; on the contrary, here it makes itself wholly and decisively felt": Jaspers, *Tragedy Is Not Enough*, 41.

15. I am thinking especially of "The Revolutionary Tradition and Its Lost Treasure," the last chapter in Arendt, *On Revolution*, 215–81.

16. See Hannah Arendt, *The Human Condition* (Chicago: University of Chicago Press, 1958), chap. 5. I borrow the phrase "tragedy-inflected" from Robert Pirro, whose superb *Hannah Arendt and the Politics of Tragedy* (DeKalb: Northern Illinois University Press, 2001) is the most sustained reflection on Arendt as a theorist of tragedy. Of course, like many contemporary political theorists, Pirro reads Arendt's concern with Greek tragedy (and storytelling generally) as a concern with "fostering an adequately critical spirit compatible with membership in a viable democratic community": ibid., 17. He may or may not be right that this was Arendt's normative political objective, but I am less interested in whether this was her purpose (perhaps partly because I hold no particular stake in the disciplinary competition over Arendt). What interests me more is the way in which she foregrounds a tragic conception of action—that is, a conception of action fully alert to human finitude.

17. Brian Meeks, "Grenada: The Pitfalls of 'Popular' Revolution from Above," in

Caribbean Revolutions and Revolutionary Theory: An Assessment of Cuba, Nicaragua and Grenada (London: Macmillan, 1993).

18. This resonant phrase is from Judith Shklar, "Rethinking the Past," in *Political Thought and Political Thinkers*, ed. Stanley Hoffman (Chicago: University of Chicago Press, 1998), 360. The essay originally appeared in *Social Research* 44 (1977): 80–90. It is also quoted in Pirro, *Hannah Arendt and the Politics of Tragedy*, 24.

19. See Allen Speight, "Arendt and Hegel on the Tragic Nature of Action," *Philosophy and Social Criticism* 28, no. 5 (2002): 523–36. I am grateful to Karuna Mantena for drawing my attention to this essay.

20. See, e.g., Hugh O'Shaughnessy, *Grenada: Revolution, Invasion, and Aftermath* (London: Sphere Books, 1984); Gregory Sandford and Richard Vigilante, *Grenada: The Untold Story* (Lanham, Md.: Madison Books, 1984).

21. See, e.g., Jay Mandle, *Big Revolution, Small Country: The Rise and Fall of the Grenada Revolution* (Maryland: North South Books, 1985); Tony Thorndike, *Grenada: Politics, Economics, and Society* (London: Francis Pinter, 1985); Gordon K. Lewis, *Grenada: The Jewel Despoiled* (Baltimore: Johns Hopkins University Press, 1987).

22. Even as sophisticated an account as Lewis's *Grenada* is marred by this inclination.

23. Meeks, "Grenada," 132.

24. See also Lewis, *Grenada*, "Introduction: A Caribbean Tragedy," 1–3; George Lamming, "Maurice Bishop Lives," in *In Nobody's Backyard: Maurice Bishop's Speeches, 1979–1983: A Memorial Volume*, ed. Chris Searle (London: Zed Books, 1984), 1–6; Omowale David Franklyn, *Bridging the Two Grenadas: Gairy's and Bishop's* (St. George's: Talented House, 1999), 82. In an unpublished interview with Bernard Coard (recorded in December 2005), he also makes use of the image of Greek tragedy to describe the revolution's collapse.

25. Meeks, "Grenada," 132. In *Big Revolution, Small Country*, 53–54, Mandle had referred to "paternalistic socialism," with which Meeks ("Grenada," 157) does not entirely disagree.

26. Meeks, "Grenada," 146. It is not clear that the Grenadian revolutionaries used the term "Jamesian" to describe themselves, but many of them would have known James in London in the 1960s.

27. That Gairy's regime was willing to go to extremes is evident in the events of 18 November 1973, known as "Bloody Sunday," when Maurice Bishop, Hudson Austin, Unison Whiteman, Selwyn Strachan, and Kendrick Radix were set upon and severely beaten by Gairy's security forces (led by an infamous police inspector) while on their way to Grenville (see ibid., 148).

28. Ibid., 151. On how this discussion emerges in relation to the left in Jamaica, see David Scott, "The Dialectic of Defeat: An Interview with Rupert Lewis," *Small Axe*, no. 10 (September 2001): 117. Of course, the idea that it was the *success* of

the Bolsheviks that defined the appeal of Leninism haunted the left in the twentieth century. My interview with Lewis, a ranking member of the Workers Party of Jamaica, was partly inspired by Russell Jacoby, *Dialectic of Defeat: Contours of Western Marxism* (New York: Cambridge University Press, 2002).

29. Meeks, "Grenada," 151.

30. Ibid., 152.

31. Ibid.

32. Ibid.

33. Ibid., 153.

34. It is sometimes forgotten that it was Coard who urged the NJM's leadership to join this party alliance: see ibid.

35. Ibid., 154.

36. Ibid., 166.

37. Ibid.

38. Ibid., 166–67.

39. Ibid., 179.

40. See David Scott, "Political Rationalities of the Jamaican Modern," *Small Axe*, no. 14 (September 2003): 1–22.

41. See Giorgio Agamben, "Time and History: Critique of the Instant and the Continuum," in *Infancy and History: On the Destruction of Experience*, trans. Liz Heron (New York: Verso, 1993), 99.

42. See Arendt, *The Human Condition*, chap. 4. See also Young-Bruehl, *Why Arendt Matters*, 81–89.

43. On the moral and political emotions, see Marlene Sokolon, *Political Emotions: Aristotle and the Symphony of Reason and Emotion* (DeKalb: Northern Illinois University Press, 2006). Curiously, Sokolon does not investigate the specific role of political emotions in tragedy, although this was, of course, one of Aristotle's interests.

44. See esp. Peter Szondi, *An Essay on the Tragic*, trans. Paul Fleming (Stanford, Calif.: Stanford University Press, 2002), 1; James Gordon Finlayson, "Conflict and Reconciliation in Hegel's Theory of the Tragic," *Journal of the History of Philosophy* 37, no. 3 (July 1999): 493–520; Theodore George, *Tragedies of Spirit: Tracing Finitude in Hegel's "Phenomenology"* (Albany: State University of New York Press, 2006), 1.

45. For a helpful discussion, see Mark Roche, "An Introduction to Hegel's Theory of Tragedy," *PhaenEx* 1, no. 2 (Fall–Winter 2006): 11–20; Mark Roche, "The Greatness and Limits of Hegel's Theory of Tragedy," in *A Companion to Tragedy*, ed. Rebecca Bushnell (Oxford: Blackwell, 2005), 51–67; Mark Roche, *Tragedy and Comedy: A Systematic Study and a Critique of Hegel* (Albany: State University of New York Press, 1998). On Hegel's consideration of art, see Donald Phillip Verne, *Hegel's Recollection: A Study of Images in the "Phenomenology of Spirit"* (Albany: State University of New York Press, 1985); Robert Wicks, "Hegel's Aes-

thetics: An Overview," in *The Cambridge Companion to Hegel*, ed. Frederick C. Beiser (New York: Cambridge University Press, 1993), 348–77; George, *Tragedies of Spirit*, 8–15.

46. On the French Revolution as one context of Hegel's preoccupation with tragedy, see George, *Tragedies of Spirit*, 10. Although it is not directly connected to the tragedy question, there has been much debate about the possible place of the Haitian Revolution in Hegel's developing thought, especially in the *Phenomenology of Spirit*, particularly in the wake of Susan Buck-Morss's contention that it was a decisive framing influence on his Master–Slave dialectic and his idea of universal history (see Susan Buck-Morss, *Hegel, Haiti, and Universal History* [Pittsburgh: University of Pittsburgh Press, 2009]). I do not entirely agree. See my response to this in David Scott, "Antinomies of Slavery, Enlightenment, and Universal History," *Small Axe*, no. 33 (November 2010): 152–62.

47. See Michelle Gellrich, *Tragedy and Theory: The Problem of Conflict since Aristotle* (Princeton, NJ: Princeton University Press, 1988), ix. See also George, *Tragedies of Spirit*, 6–8. On Schelling and Hölderlin, see Szondi, *An Essay on the Tragic*, 7–14; Jason Wirth, *The Conspiracy of Life: Meditations on Schelling and His Time* (Albany: State University of New York Press, 2003). For a helpful discussion of the broader context of German philhellenic discussions of tragedy, see Simon Richter, "German Classical Tragedy: Lessing, Goethe, Schiller, Kleist, and Büchner," in Bushnell, *A Companion to Tragedy*, 435–51.

48. Gellrich, *Tragedy and Theory*, chap. 2. Gellrich's genealogy admirably demonstrates the conceptual conditions of emergence of Hegel's idea of conflict in tragedy and the break that it brings about (in at least this regard) with the tradition of thinking about tragedy derived from Aristotle.

49. Szondi, *An Essay on the Tragic*, 16, 18. See also Philippe Lacoue-Labarthe, *Typography: Mimesis, Philosophy, Politics*, trans. Christopher Fynsk (Stanford, Calif.: Stanford University Press, 1998), 208.

50. Of course, it is in many ways Friedrich Nietzsche's *The Birth of Tragedy* (New York: Penguin, 1994 [1872]) that has defined much contemporary discussion of tragedy. For a helpful discussion of this text, see James Porter, *The Invention of Dionysus: An Essay on* The Birth of Tragedy (Stanford, Calif.: Stanford University Press, 2000). For the post-Nietzsche heritage, see Paul Gordon, *Tragedy after Nietzsche: Rapturous Superabundance* (Urbana: University of Illinois Press, 2001).

51. Georg W. F. Hegel, *Aesthetics: Lectures on Fine Art*, trans. T. M. Knox, 2 vols. (Oxford: Clarendon Press, 1975), 2:1198. See also Roche, *Tragedy and Comedy*.

52. Ibid. See also Jaspers, *Tragedy Is Not Enough*, 42.

53. The "truth of intention," Hegel remarks, "is only the act itself": Georg W. F. Hegel, *The Phenomenology of Spirit*, trans. A. V. Miller (New York: Oxford University Press, 1977), 98.

54. For Aristotle's definition of tragedy as a "mimesis of action" see *Poetics* (New

York: Penguin, 1996), 10. On Hegel's debt to Aristotle, see Finlayson, "Conflict and Reconciliation in Hegel's Theory of the Tragic," 497–500.

55. Hegel, *Aesthetics*, 1:219.

56. See Charles Taylor, "Hegel and the Philosophy of Action," in *Hegel's Philosophy of Action*, ed. Lawrence S. Stepelvich and David Lamb (Atlantic Highlands, NJ: Humanities Press, 1983), 2. Taylor writes further that, on this view, "the purpose is not ontologically separable from the action and this means something like: it can only exist in animating this action; or its only articulation as a purpose is in animating this action; or perhaps, a fundamental articulation of this purpose, on which all others depend, lies in action (ibid., 3). In his reading of Hegel's tragic theory, George (*Tragedies of Spirit*, 78–79) draws on Taylor. For a more recent consideration of Hegel and action, see Michael Quante and Dean Moyar, *Hegel's Concept of Action* (Cambridge: Cambridge University Press, 2007).

57. For an excellent discussion of the question of corrigibility and the retrospective character of understanding action, see Allen Speight, *Hegel, Literature, and the Problem of Agency* (New York: Cambridge University Press, 2001), chaps. 1–2.

58. Hegel, *Aesthetics*, 2:1236.

59. Ibid., 2:1196.

60. As Bradley puts it, "The competing forces are both in themselves rightful, and so far the claim of each is equally justified; but the right of each is pushed into a wrong, because it ignores the right of the other, and demands that absolute sway which belongs to neither alone, but to the whole of which each is but a part": A. C. Bradley, "Hegel's Theory of Tragedy," in *Oxford Lectures on Poetry* (London: Macmillan, 1909), 72.

61. Hegel, *Aesthetics*, 2:1196.

62. Ibid., 2:1217. "It is the nature of the tragic hero," says Bradley, "at once his greatness and his doom, that he knows no shrinking or half-heartedness, but identifies himself wholly with the power that moves him, and will admit the justification of no other power": Bradley, "Hegel's Theory of Tragedy," 72.

63. Hegel, *Aesthetics*, 2:1215.

64. Ibid.

65. Gellrich, *Tragedy and Theory*, 38–42.

66. While I think I share much in Gellrich's strategy, I find myself, in the end, skeptical of the usefulness of Gellrich's counter-positioning of the "literary" and the "philosophical," in which the truth of tragedy can be found only in the irreducible dramatic action of the plays themselves.

67. George, *Tragedies of Spirit*.

68. Ibid., 4.

69. Ibid., 119.

70. See US Departments of State and Defense, *Grenada Documents: An Overview and Selection*, ed. Michael Ledeen and Herbert Romerstein (Washington, DC: US Government Printing Office, 1984), doc. 112-13.

71. Ibid., doc. 105-1. See also Paul Seabury and Walter A. McDougall, eds., *The Grenada Papers* (San Francisco: Institute for Contemporary Studies Press, 1984), 263.

72. US Departments of State and Defense, *Grenada Documents*, doc. 105-1; Seabury and McDougall, *The Grenada Papers*, 263.

73. US Departments of State and Defense, *Grenada Documents*, doc. 111-6; Seabury and McDougall, *The Grenada Papers*, 278.

74. US Departments of State and Defense, *Grenada Documents*, doc. 112-13.

75. US Departments of State and Defense, *Grenada Documents*, doc. 112-14; Seabury and McDougall, *The Grenada Papers*, 292.

76. Ibid.

77. US Departments of State and Defense, *Grenada Documents*, doc. 112-21.

78. As Richard Hart ("Introduction," in Searle, *In Nobody's Backyard*, xxix) puts it, it was clear that what James had in mind was "a far more fundamental solution to the problems created by the leader's generally acknowledged weaknesses. James' proposal went further than simply helping Bishop to overcome these weaknesses."

79. The only straight objection to the proposal came from George Louison, who maintained that the Central Committee should instead put pressure on Bishop to reform his conduct and "personal discipline": US Departments of State and Defense, *Grenada Documents*, doc. 112-23.

80. Ibid., doc. 112-29.

81. Ibid. See also Hart, "Introduction," xxx.

82. US Departments of State and Defense, *Grenada Documents*, doc. 112-29.

83. Layne responds interestingly to this "no confidence" idea, saying that "the criticisms were made by all Comrades in the spirit of love for the party, ideological clarity and wanting to build a [genuine Marxist-Leninist] party." Frankness was critical for this process, he urged, ending with the appeal that it "will be sad if the meeting concluded that this was a vote of no confidence": ibid., doc. 112-30.

84. The two other abstentions were Unison Whiteman and Hudson Austin, the latter on the grounds that he had arrived late for the meeting and consequently was unprepared to make an informed decision: ibid., doc. 112-34; Seabury and McDougall, *The Grenada Papers*, 294–95.

85. US Departments of State and Defense, *Grenada Documents*, doc. 112-40.

86. Seabury and McDougall, *The Grenada Papers*, 314–15. Bishop is reported as saying at the end of the meeting that "the entire GM (General Membership) had accepted the CC analysis and decision and this has satisfied his concern. He admitted to the GM that his response to the CC criticism was petit bourgeois. He said that the GM had rammed home that the criticism was correct and so too was the decision. He said, 'I sincerely accept the criticism and will fulfill the decision in practice.'"

87. Ibid., 315.

88. They might have had their own fear about a new cult of leadership: see David Scott, "The Fragility of Memory: An Interview with Merle Collins," *Small Axe*, no. 31 (March 2010): 108–21.

89. See John "Chalky" Ventour, "October 1983: The Missing Link" (1988), in *Truth and Reconciliation Commission Report*, vol. 2 (St. George's: Ministry of Legal Affairs, Labour, and Local Government, 2006), app. 14, 8–9.

90. See ibid., 9.

91. See Hart, "Introduction," xxxv; Meeks, "Grenada," 176–77.

92. Reminiscent of Mao and the Chinese Communist Party, says Hart ("Introduction," xxxiv–xxxv).

93. Meeks, "Grenada," 176.

94. Ibid., 178; Hart, "Introduction," xxxvi.

95. Fidel Castro denied that there was any "interference" in Grenada's affairs. See the extraordinary interview that constitutes, Fidel Castro, *Nothing Can Stop the Course of History* (New York: Pathfinder, 1986), 164–65. I return to this question in chapter 4.

96. Bradley, "Hegel's Theory of Tragedy," 89.

97. See Speight, "Arendt and Hegel on the Tragic Nature of Action."

98. I am obviously thinking of the discussion of action in Arendt, *The Human Condition*, chap. 4. It is, of course, very interesting that while the shadow of tragedy hangs over Arendt's conception of action, and while she seems never not to be invoking the ancient Greeks — and sometimes even the tragedians — she refrains from making a direct connection between action and tragedy. Yet unlike Hegel, who does make an explicit connection, Arendt is a tragic theorist of politics, as Jaspers and Shklar both recognized.

99. The connection between Arendt and Hegel on the question of action and its relation to the tragic is intriguing to consider. Certainly, Arendt does not explicitly acknowledge Hegel's influence in this regard, although it is hard to credit that there is *no* connection. At the same time, of course, they were both fundamentally indebted to Aristotle and to what Taylor calls the "thesis of the inseparability of form and matter" in his non-dualist understanding of action: Taylor, "Hegel and the Philosophy of Action," 3; see also Pirro, *Hannah Arendt and the Politics of Tragedy*, 44–50.

100. See Hannah Arendt, "What Is Freedom?" in *Between Past and Future: Eight Exercises in Political Thought*, enlarged ed. (New York: Penguin, 1968). As Arendt puts it, freedom is not "experienced in the dialogue between me and myself" but in the public interactions between others and myself: ibid., 154.

101. "Every act, seen from the perspective not of the agent but of the process in whose framework it occurs and whose automatism it interrupts, is a 'miracle'— that is, something which could not be expected": ibid., 169.

102. In the opening paragraph of the first chapter of *On Revolution*, Arendt writes,

"Revolutions are the only political events which confront us directly and inevitably with the problem of beginning": see Arendt, *On Revolution*, 21.

103. No wonder, Arendt writes (thinking, no doubt, about the fate of the Hungarian Revolution of 1956), "The periods of being free have always been relatively short in the history of mankind": Arendt, "What Is Freedom?" 169.

104. See Arendt, *On Revolution*; Pirro, *Hannah Arendt and the Politics of Tragedy*, 52–53.

105. Arendt, *The Human Condition*, 220.

106. The phrase is Bradley's: Bradley, "Hegel's Theory of Tragedy," 72.

107. It will, I trust, be clear to the reader that Weber's critique of a one-sided "ethics of conviction" in "Politics as a Vocation" is in the back of my mind here. As Weber writes, "The man who embraces an ethics of conviction is unable to tolerate the ethical irrationality of the world": Weber, "Politics as a Vocation," 85. In contrast to this, Weber commends an "ethics of responsibility" that comprehends and mediates the zealous ethics of conviction. He writes, in a justly famous passage,

> I find it immeasurably moving when a *mature* human being—whether young or old in actual years is immaterial—who feels the responsibility he bears for the consequences of his own actions with his entire soul and who acts in harmony with an ethics of responsibility reaches the point where he says, "Here I stand, I can do no other." That is authentically human and cannot fail to move us. For this is a situation that *may* befall *any* of us at some point, if we are not inwardly dead. In this sense an ethics of conviction and an ethics of responsibility are not absolute antitheses but are mutually complementary, and only when taken together do they constitute the authentic human being who *is capable* of having a "politics of vocation." (Ibid., 92)

Chapter Two. Stranded in the Present

Epigraph: Frank Kermode, "The Sense of an Ending, 1999," in *The Sense of an Ending: Studies in the Theory of Fiction* (Oxford: Oxford University Press, 2000 [1967]), 190.

1. Kermode, *The Sense of an Ending*, 45.

2. Ibid., 28. For a discussion of Kermode, see Margaret Tudeau-Clayton and Martin Warner, eds., *Addressing Frank Kermode: Essays in Criticism and Interpretation* (Chicago: University of Illinois Press, 1991), esp. A. D. Nuttal, "The Sense of a Beginning," 22–37. Kermode, often regarded as the most eminent critic of English literature since F. R. Leavis, died in August 2010 after a long life. For a wonderful collection of recollections, see "Memories of Frank Kermode," *London Review of Books*, vol. 32, no. 18, 23 September 2010, accessed 14 February 2012, www.lrb.co.uk/v32/n18/stefan-collini-and-others/memories-of-frank-kermode.

3. See, e.g., Richard Webster, "Frank Kermode's 'The Sense of an Ending,'" *Critical Quarterly* 16, no. 4 (December 1974): 311–24.

4. Paul Ricoeur, *Time and Narrative*, 3 vols., trans. Kathleen McLaughlin and

David Pellauer (Chicago: University of Chicago Press, 1984–86). The problematic of narrative that Ricoeur outlines as responding to human time and human action in time will seed his later work on memory and forgetting (Paul Ricoeur, *Memory, History, Forgetting*, trans. Kathleen Blamey and David Pellauer [Chicago: University of Chicago Press, 2006]); on the self and its antinomies (Paul Ricoeur, *Oneself as Another*, trans. Kathleen Blamey [Chicago: University of Chicago Press, 1995]); and on justice (Paul Ricoeur, *The Just*, trans. David Pellauer [Chicago: University of Chicago Press, 2003]). It should also be remembered that, as Ricoeur himself insists, *Time and Narrative* is connected to *The Rule of Metaphor* (trans. Robert Czerny [Toronto: University of Toronto Press, 1981]), the book that immediately preceded it. In many respects, Ricoeur's oeuvre can be read as one evolving arc of preoccupations, with each successive theme growing out of and responding to earlier ones: see Charles Regan, *Paul Ricoeur: His Life and His Work* (Chicago: University of Chicago Press, 1998). For a helpful discussion, see David Wood, ed., *On Paul Ricoeur: Narrative and Interpretation* (London: Routledge, 1991).

5. Ricoeur's *Time and Narrative* can indeed be read as a direct response to "Dasein and Temporality," in Martin Heidegger, *Being and Time*, trans. John Macquarrie and Edward Robinson (New York: Harper and Row, 1962 [1927]), in which Heidegger takes up the "within-time-ness" of Dasein: see Paul Ricoeur, "Narrative Time," *Critical Inquiry* 7, no. 1 (Autumn 1980): 169–90, and *Time and Narrative*, 60–64. On the criticism of Kermode and Ricoeur, see David Carr, *Time, Narrative, and History* (Bloomington: Indiana University Press, 1986), 19–20. For Ricoeur's respectful response to Carr (and others), see "Discussion: Ricoeur on Narrative" in Wood, *On Paul Ricoeur*, 179–87. For a reading of Augustine that seeks to connect the literary form of his *Confessions* to his preoccupations with time, see Genevieve Lloyd, *Being in Time: Selves and Narrators in Philosophy and Literature* (London: Routledge, 1993), chap. 1.

6. "Speculation on time is an inconclusive rumination to which narrative activity alone can respond": Ricoeur, *Time and Narrative*, 1:6.

7. Ibid., 1:3.

8. As Ricoeur puts it, one way to articulate the question that will be pursued in his study is "whether the paradigm of order characteristic of tragedy, is capable of extension and transformation to the point where it can be applied to the whole narrative field": ibid., 1:38.

9. Ibid., 1:53. Given this focus on time and emplotment, it is not surprising that Ricoeur's work should bear comparison to the thought of Hayden White. For White on Ricoeur, see "The Metaphysics of Narrativity: Time and Symbol in Ricoeur's Philosophy of History," in Wood, *On Paul Ricoeur*, 140–59. And for Ricoeur's curiously diffident response, see "Discussion: Ricoeur on Narrative," 185. Of course, where White was concerned principally with historical narrative, Ricoeur is interested in both fictional and historical narratives. On fictive

narratives, see Ricoeur, *Time and Narrative*, vol. 2, which is devoted to the configuration of time in fictional narratives.

10. Adam Abraham Mendilow, *Time and the Novel* (New York: Humanities Press, 1965 [1952]), 32. Or again, "In the final analysis, virtually all the techniques and devices of fiction reduce themselves to the treatment accorded to the different time-values": ibid., 63.

11. Mikhail Bakhtin, "Forms of Time and Chronotope in the Novel," in *The Dialogical Imagination: Four Essays*, ed. Michael Holquist, trans. Caryl Emerson and Michael Holquist (Austin: University of Texas Press, 1981), 84–85, 250. It seems odd to me that this significance of time in Bakhtin has been relatively neglected in favor of other Bakhtinian concerns, such as dialogism and heteroglossia and the carnivalesque. See, however, Sue Vice, *Introducing Bakhtin* (Manchester: Manchester University Press, 1998), chap. 5. But even there, it seems to me, the centrality of the problem of time for Bakhtin is severely short-changed. For an excellent discussion of Bakhtin's work as a whole in the context of his eloquently idiosyncratic life, see Katerina Clark and Michael Holquist, *Mikhail Bakhtin* (Cambridge, Mass.: Harvard University Press, 1986), esp. chap. 13.

12. See Bernard Yack, *The Longing for Total Revolution: Philosophic Sources of Social Discontent from Rousseau to Marx and Nietzsche* (Princeton, NJ: Princeton University Press, 1986). I discuss the significance of this work in David Scott, *Conscripts of Modernity: The Tragedy of Colonial Enlightenment* (Durham, NC: Duke University Press, 2004).

13. Clearly, this is a phrase with rich resonance in Kermode's idea of being "stranded in the middle." But I am borrowing it from Lloyd, *Being in Time*. Reflecting on time in Descartes's *Meditations*, Lloyd writes: "The Cartesian self is rescued from being stranded in the present through reflection on its dependence on God": ibid., 46. The phrase is also used as the title of Peter Fritzsche's splendid *Stranded in the Present: Modern Time and the Melancholy of History* (Cambridge, Mass.: Harvard University Press, 2004).

14. Merle Collins, *Angel* (London: Seal, 1987); Merle Collins, *The Colour of Forgetting* (London: Virago, 1995). Subsequent references to page numbers in these editions are in parentheses in the text.

15. To date, Collins has published three volumes of poetry (*Because the Dawn Breaks! Poems Dedicated to the Grenadian People* [London: Karia, 1985], *Rotten Pomerack* [London: Virago, 1992], and *Lady in a Boat* [Leeds: Peepel Tree Press, 2003]) and two collections of short stories (*Rain Darling* [London: Women's Press, 1990], and *The Ladies Are Upstairs* [Leeds: Peepel Tree Press, 2011]). Some of her crucial essays are "Grenada—Ten Years and More: Memory and Collective Responsibility," *Caribbean Quarterly* 41, no. 2 (June 1995): 71–88; "Tout Moun ka Pléwé (Everybody Bawling)," *Small Axe*, no. 22 (February 2007): 1–16; and "Are You a Bolshevik or a Menshevik? Mimicry, Alienation, and Confusion in the Grenada Revolution," *Interventions* 12, no. 1 (2010): 35–45.

16. For a discussion of the making of the novel, see David Scott, "The Fragility of Memory: An Interview with Merle Collins," *Small Axe*, no. 31 (March 2010): 144–51. Collins is not the only novelist of the Grenada Revolution. See Dionne Brand, *In Another Place, Not Here* (Toronto: Knopf Canada, 1996); Maria Roberts-Squires, *October All Over* (Oxford: Heinemann, 2005).

17. See Karl Mannheim, "The Problem of Generations," in *Essays on the Sociology of Knowledge*, ed. Paul Kecskemeti (London: Routledge and Kegan Paul, 1952), 276–320. For more recent thinking, see June Edmunds and Bryan S. Turner, eds., *Generational Consciousness, Narrative, and Politics* (Lanham, Md.: Rowman and Littlefield, 2002).

18. For a discussion of time and generations, see also Ricoeur, *Time and Narrative*, 3:109–16. Ricoeur instructively draws on Alfred Schutz, *The Phenomenology of the Social World* (Evanston, Ill.: Northwestern University Press, 1967), esp. 207–14.

19. In my exploration of the problem of genre, I have found the following books and essays especially helpful: Richard Coe, Lorelei Lingard, and Tatiana Teslenko, eds., *The Rhetoric and Ideology of Genre: Strategies for Stability and Change* (Creskill, NY: Hampton Press, 2002); Heather Dubrow, *Genre* (London: Methuen, 1982); John Frow, *Genre* (London: Routledge, 2006); Adena Rosemarin, *The Power of Genre* (Minneapolis: University of Minnesota Press, 1985); Peter Seitel, "Theorising Genres—Interpreting Works," *New Literary History* 34, no. 2 (2003): 275–97; Terry Threadgold, "The Genre Debate," *Southern Review* 21, no. 3 (1988): 315–30; Terry Threadgold, "Talking about Genre: Ideologies and Incompatible Discourses," *Cultural Studies* 3, no. 1 (1989): 101–27; Tzvetan Todorov, *Genres of Discourse*, trans. Catherine Porter (Cambridge: Cambridge University Press, 1990).

20. In an influential essay, Jacques Derrida, for example, suggests paradoxically that "a text cannot belong to no genre. Every text participates in one or several genres, there is no genreless text, there is always a genre and genres, yet such participation never amounts to a belonging" (Jacques Derrida, "The Law of Genre," in *Acts of Literature*, ed. Derek Attridge [New York: Routledge, 1992 (1980)], 221–52).

21. Mikhail Bakhtin, "The *Bildungsroman* and Its Significance in the History of Realism (Toward a Historical Typology of the Novel)," in *Speech Genres and Other Late Essays*, ed. Caryl Emerson and Michael Holquist, trans. Vern W. McGee (Austin: University of Texas Press, 1986), 21. For a helpful discussion of the genre, see Fritz Martini, "Bildungsroman—Term and Theory," in *Reflection and Action: Essays on the Bildungsroman*, ed. James Hardin (Columbia: University of South Carolina Press, 1991), 1–25. See also Hardin's introduction to the volume: ibid., ix–xxvii. For a useful consideration of debates about the genre, see Tobias Boes, "Modernist Studies and the *Bildungsroman*: A Historical Survey of Critical Trends," *Literature Compass* 3, no. 2 (2006): 230–43.

22. See Franco Moretti, *The Way of the World: The* Bildungsroman *in European Culture*, trans. Albert Spragia (London: Verso, 2000 [1987]), 5. One should remember that in the "genre wars" of the 1980s and 1990s, the canonical status of the Bildungsroman was significantly decentered by critics—principally but not only feminists and postcolonial critics—who pointed to the hegemonic assumptions (about gender, race, and empire) within the fictions traditionally associated with the genre and the exclusions perpetuated by its crucial archive. This criticism is critical to my concerns with Collins's *Angel*. For example, feminists have argued that the Goethean model of gradual and cumulative organic growth depended on a reliably integrative relation between the hero and his society that enabled a progressive realization of personality, which clearly was not adequate for understanding women's narrative fiction and, of course, bore little relation to the material and moral-psychological worlds of women's lives: see Elizabeth Abel, Marianne Hirsch, and Elizabeth Langland, "Introduction," in *The Voyage In: Fictions of Female Development* (Hanover, N.H.: University Press of New England, 1983), 3–19. Similarly, it is unsurprising, given the cultural and historical provenance of the Bildungsroman in Europe of the eighteenth century and nineteenth century, that critics who began to rethink the relation between the novel form and modern colonial history would notice not only the suppressed matrix of empire upon which the Enlightenment processes of *Bildung* depended (the solidifying world of bourgeois cultivation, the enlivened social spaces of personal growth and cosmopolitanism), but also the distinctive uses to which the genre was being put by postcolonial writers. Again, the masculinist, racialized ideals of the classical form clearly would be rejected. But still, even as new thematic concerns were being introduced (the ambivalences of colonial education, the longing for political freedom, the alienation of language, the burdens of racial privilege, the proximity of ethnic violence, and so on), what proved adaptable was a literary form that enabled a humanist story of self-discovery and the gradual emergence of self-knowledge against the background of a conflicted social and historical context. The Bildungsroman provided a platform (naturally not an unambiguous one) on which the postcolonial writer could, on the one hand, challenge existing prejudicial representations of her history and identity and, on the other hand, offer more complex, more compelling, more engaged realist literary explorations of the meaning of decolonization and the project of making new nations and postcolonial subjects. So that just as many critics were declaring the Bildungsroman a literary remnant of a bygone era now being replaced by new modernist forms, postcolonial writers were appropriating and reinvigorating the form, turning it to new and distinctive fictional purposes: see Maria Helena Lima, "Decolonizing Genre: Jamaica Kincaid and the *Bildungsroman*," *Genre* 26 (Winter 1993): 431–59; Jose Santiago Fernandez Vazquez, "Recharting the Geography of Genre: Ben Okri's *The Famished Road* as a Postcolonial *Bildungsroman*," *Journal of Commonwealth Literature*

27, no. 2 (2002): 85–106. And for an instructive and sadly unpublished dissertation devoted to this question, see Ericka Hoagland, "Postcolonizing the *Bildungsroman*: A Study of the Evolution of a Genre," Ph.D. diss., Purdue University, Lafayette, Ind., May 2006.

23. In a well-known essay, Fredric Jameson argued that the Third World novel should be read not only as allegory but more specifically as *national* allegory. The latent text of the postcolonial novel, so it is said, told an allegorical story of the unconscious of the nation: see Fredric Jameson, "Third World Literature in the Era of Multinational Capitalism," *Social Text*, no. 15 (Autumn 1986): 65–88. Needless to say, the essay has been much criticized for this view—for the reductionist or Eurocentric assumption, for example, that there is a unitary unconscious that generates the symptomatic features of the manifest text of *all* such fictions. But see Fredric Jameson, *The Political Unconscious: Narrative as a Socially Symbolic Act* (Ithaca, NY: Cornell University Press, 1981).

24. See Jeremy Tambling, *Allegory* (London: Routledge, 2010), 2. See also Maureen Quilligan, *The Language of Allegory: Defining the Genre* (Ithaca, NY: Cornell University Press, 1979), 33. It would now be difficult to argue, for example, that there is any language (certainly any literary or specifically narrative language) that is not, however minimally or obliquely, infinitely allusive and inclined to polysemy, figuration, or metaphor. Indeed, allegory—saying one thing while saying another (to use the familiar shorthand)—may better be thought of as a *dimension* of all more or less complex uses of language: see, e.g., Angus Fletcher, *Allegory: The Theory of a Symbolic Mode* (Ithaca, NY: Cornell University Press, 1964), 8. Fletcher is taking his cue from Northrop Frye, *Anatomy of Criticism: Four Essays* (Princeton, NJ: Princeton University Press, 1957).

25. Quilligan, *The Language of Allegory*, 42.

26. See Fletcher, *Allegory*, chap. 1.

27. For two seminal and contrasting critical essays, see Sylvia Wynter, "Novel and History, Plot and Plantation," *Savacou*, no. 5 (June 1971): 95–102, and Kenneth Ramchand, "History and the Novel: A Literary Critic's Approach," *Savacou*, no. 5 (June 1971): 103–13. For useful general discussions, see Nana Wilson-Tagoe, *Historical Thought and Literary Representation in West Indian Literature* (Gainesville: University Press of Florida, 1998). Needless to say, these are concerns that also shape other traditions in the Caribbean novel: see Barbara Webb, *Myth and History in Caribbean Fiction: Alejo Carpentier, Wilson Harris, and Edouard Glissant* (Amherst: University of Massachusetts Press, 1992).

28. See Wyndham Lewis, *Time and Western Man*, ed. Paul Edwards (Santa Rosa, Calif.: Black Sparrow, 1993 [1927]), 245–51. Lewis is making a contrast with the "space-school" among whom he classed himself. For an invaluable discussion of Lewis's relation to modernism, and to modernist writing in particular, see Edwards's "Afterword," in ibid., 455–508.

29. For the classic exposition, see Edward Baugh, "The West Indian Writer and His

Quarrel with History," *Small Axe*, no. 38 (July 2012): 60–74. (The essay was original published in *Tapia* in 1977, part 1 in the 20 February issue and part 2 in the 27 February issue.) Needless to say, I do not mean to suggest that it is only in the novel that this preoccupation articulated itself. It inhabits Caribbean poetry and drama, too. For contrasting views, see Derek Walcott, "The Muse of History: An Essay," and Kamau Brathwaite, "Timehri," both in *Is Massa Day Dead? Black Moods in the Caribbean*, ed. Orde Coombs (New York: Doubleday, 1974).

30. See James Joyce, *Ulysses* (New York: Vintage, 1961), 34. See the epigraph to the introduction in George Lamming, *The Pleasures of Exile* (London: Michael Joseph, 1960), 9, and the epigraph in Walcott, "The Muse of History," 1.

31. These, of course, were the themes through which nineteenth-century travel writers evoked the Caribbean, in work such as Anthony Trollope, *The West Indies and the Spanish Main* (London: Chapman and Hall, 1859), and James Anthony Froude, *The English in the West Indies; or, the Bow of Ulysses* (London: Longmans, Green, 1888). Famously, V. S. Naipaul repeats a picture of this theme of the Caribbean's historylessness: "History is built around achievement and creation; and nothing was created in the West Indies": V. S. Naipaul, *The Middle Passage* (London: Andre Deutsch, 1962), 29. The agony of an absence of ruins, though drawn from Walcott's poem "The Royal Palms . . . an Absence of Ruins" (*London Magazine*, February 1962, 12–13), was driven home in Orlando Patterson, *An Absence of Ruins* (London: New Authors, 1967).

32. V. S. Reid, *New Day* (New York: Alfred A. Knopf, 1949), and *Leopards* (New York: Viking, 1958).

33. George Lamming, *Of Age and Innocence* (London: Michael Joseph, 1958), and *Season of Adventure* (London: Michael Joseph, 1960).

34. For an especially acute reading, especially of the yield and limits of Lamming's style and technique, see Wilson Harris, "Tradition and the West Indian Novel," in *Tradition, the Writer, and Society: Critical Essays* (London: New Beacon, 1967).

35. Wilson Harris, *Palace of the Peacock* (London: Faber and Faber, 1960), *The Far Journey of Oudin* (London: Faber and Faber, 1961), *The Whole Armour* (London: Faber and Faber, 1962), and *The Secret Ladder* (London: Faber and Faber, 1963). See also Wilson Harris, "A Note on the Genesis of *The Guyana Quartet*," in *The Guyana Quartet* (London: Faber and Faber, 1985), 7–14.

36. The kind of critical archive there should be on Collins does not exist, but for an insightful discussion of her work, see Carolyn Cooper, "'Sense Mek Befoh Book': Grenadian Popular Culture and the Rhetoric of Revolution in Merle Collins's *Angel* and *The Colour of Forgetting*," in *Arms Akimbo: Africana Women in Contemporary Literature*, ed. Janice Lee Liddell and Yakini Belinda Kemp (Gainesville: University Press of Florida, 1999), 176–88. See also Betty Wilson, "An Interview with Merle Collins," *Callaloo* (Winter 1993): 94–107.

37. See Tagoe-Wilson, *Historical Thought and Literary Representation in West Indian Literature*, chap. 9. But see also Belinda Edmondson, *Making Men: Gender, Literary Authority, and Women's Writing in the Caribbean Narrative* (Durham, NC: Duke University Press, 1999); Donette Frances, *Fictions of Feminine Citizenship: Sexuality and the Nation in Contemporary Caribbean Literature* (New York: Palgrave, 2010).

38. See Evelyn O'Callaghan, *Woman Version: Theoretical Approaches to West Indian Fiction by Women* (London: Macmillan, 1993).

39. Michelle Cliff, *No Telephone to Heaven* (New York: Plume, 1987); Grace Nichols, *Whole of a Morning Sky* (London: Virago, 1986); Margaret Cezair-Thompson, *The True History of Paradise* (New York: E. P. Dutton, 1999); V. S. Naipaul, *Mimic Men* (London: Andre Deutsch, 1967); V. S. Naipaul, *Guerrillas* (New York: Alfred A. Knopf, 1975).

40. Erna Brodber, *Myal* (London: New Beacon Books, 1988), *Louisiana* (London: New Beacon Books, 1994), and *The Rainmaker's Mistake* (London: New Beacon Books, 2007).

41. I borrow the phrase from Mendilow, *Time and the Novel*, 33.

42. Mendilow writes, "Of the four degrees of relationship of truth to life into which works of fiction may be graded, the impossible, the improbable, the possible and the probable, the novel proper claimed from the beginning to have eliminated from its field the first two, and so to have clearly marked itself off from the romance. The third was at first held by many to be legitimate, but the greater novelists maintained that they were writing within the limits only of the fourth": ibid., 40.

43. On this period of Grenada's social history, see A. W. Singham, *The Hero and the Crowd in a Colonial Polity* (New Haven, Conn.: Yale University Press, 1968), chap. 1; Beverly Steele, *Grenada: A History of Its People* (London: Macmillan, 2003), chaps. 11–12.

44. For a general account of the postemancipation transformation of labor conditions in the British Caribbean, particularly for women, see Bridget Brereton, "Family Strategies, Gender, and the Shift to Wage Labour in the British Caribbean," in *The Colonial Caribbean in Transition: Essays on Postemancipation Social and Cultural History*, ed. Bridget Brereton and Kevin Yelvington (Gainesville: University Press of Florida, 1999), 77–107.

45. M. G. Smith, "Structure and Crisis in Grenada, 1950–1954," in *The Plural Society in the British West Indies* (Berkeley: University of California Press, 1965), 270–71. See also, more generally, M. G. Smith, *Stratification in Grenada* (Berkeley: University of California Press, 1965).

46. For a discussion of the politics of Crown Colony rule in Grenada, see Singham, *The Hero and the Crowd in a Colonial Polity*, chap. 3; Pat Emmanuel, *Crown Colony Politics in Grenada, 1917–1951* (Bridgetown: Institute for Social and Eco-

nomic Research, 1978). For a discussion broadly as part of British colonial policy in the West Indies, see Gordon K. Lewis, *The Growth of the Modern West Indies* (New York: Monthly Review Press, 1968), chap. 4.

47. On this shift throughout the British colonial world, see Catherine Hall, *Civilizing Subjects: Metropole and Colony in the English Imagination, 1830–1867* (Chicago: University of Chicago Press, 2002).

48. See the vivid and moving portrait of the Grenadian peasantry in M. G. Smith, *Dark Puritan* (Kingston: Institute for Social and Economic Research, 1963).

49. See William Macmillan, *Warning from the West Indies: A Tract for Africa and the Empire* (London: Faber, 1936). See also Arthur Lewis, *Labour in the West Indies: The Birth of a Workers' Movement* (London: New Beacon Books, 1977 [1938]); Nigel Bolland, *On the March: Labour Rebellions in the British Caribbean, 1934–39* (Kingston: Ian Randle, 1995).

50. Smith, "Structure and Crisis in Grenada," 280. See also Singham, *The Hero and the Crowd in a Colonial Polity*, 150.

51. On the Moyne Commission and the region, see the classic work of Lewis, *The Growth of the Modern West Indies*, chap. 3.

52. Smith, "Structure and Crisis in Grenada," 262.

53. The classic work on Gairy remains Singham, *The Hero and the Crowd in a Colonial Polity*, chaps. 4–6, conclusion.

54. On Jamaica during these years, see Obika Gray, *Radicalism and Social Change in Jamaica, 1960–1972* (Knoxville: University of Tennessee Press, 2007).

55. See Mannheim, "The Problem of Generations."

56. For a discussion of the making of the novel, see Scott, "The Fragility of Memory," 154–60.

57. There is another crucial allegorical dimension of Thunder's genealogy. His father, Ned, is from the "Nigger Yard." (Collins here draws an intertextual connection to Martin Carter's great poem "I Come From the Nigger Yard.") This connects Ned, a descendant of slaves as well as of indentured Indian workers who replaced the slaves on the sugar plantations, to the continued history of sugar-plantation work rather than the peasantry.

58. For a neat discussion of Benjamin and allegory, see Howard Caygill, "Walter Benjamin's Concept of Allegory," in *The Cambridge Companion to Allegory*, ed. Rita Copeland and Peter T. Struck (New York: Cambridge University Press, 2010), 241–53.

Chapter Three. Generations of Memory

Part epigraph: Paul Ricoeur, *Memory, History, Forgetting*, trans. Kathleen Blamey and David Pellauer (Chicago: University of Chicago Press, 2004), 89. *Chapter epigraph*: Sigmund Freud, "Mourning and Melancholia," in *The Standard Edition of the Complete Psychological Works of Sigmund Freud* (hereafter, *Standard Edition*), trans. and ed. James Strachey (London: Hogarth Press, 1955), 14:243.

1. Ibid., 237–58. Between 1914 and 1917, Freud elaborated a number of concepts that were more or less implicit in *The Interpretations of Dreams* (1900), especially on narcissism, repression, instincts, and the unconscious: see Sigmund Freud, "On Narcissism: An Introduction" (1914), "Instincts and Their Vicissitude" (1915), "Repression" (1915), and "The Unconscious" (1915), all in Strachey, *Standard Edition*, 14:67–102, 109–40, 141–58, 159–215.

2. Freud was famously preoccupied with the war: see Sigmund Freud, "Thoughts for the Times on War and Death" (1915), in Strachey, *Standard Edition*, 275–300. More generally on the European memory of the war, see Jay Winter, *Sites of Memory, Sites of Mourning: The Great War in European Cultural History* (Cambridge: Cambridge University Press, 1995). Stéphane Mosès writes that the year "1914 marked the end of an epoch of universal history, for the political collapse of Europe also signified the collapse of values on which its civilization had rested until then": Stéphane Mosès, *The Angel of History: Rosenzweig, Benjamin, Scholem*, trans. Barbara Harshav (Stanford, Calif.: Stanford University Press, 2009), 21.

3. See Sigmund Freud, "Remembering, Repeating, and Working Through" (1914), in Strachey, *Standard Edition*, 12:145–56.

4. Freud, "Mourning and Melancholia," 14:245.

5. Ibid.

6. Ibid., 14:249.

7. See "The Ego and the Id" (1923), in Strachey, *Standard Edition*, 19:3–66, in which Freud revises the topological structure of the psyche.

8. It is perhaps necessary to acknowledge the suggestive intervention some years ago of David Eng and David Kazanjian, eds., *Loss: The Politics of Mourning* (Berkeley: University of California Press, 2003), because its concerns are very close to mine. In their introduction, "Mourning Remains" (1–25), Eng and Kazanjian urge a "Benjaminian" rereading of Freud's "Mourning and Melancholia" that inflects the *political* accent in the direction of a positive appreciation of melancholia over mourning. As opposed to mourning, which "abandons lost objects by laying their histories to rest, melancholia's continued and open relation to the past finally allows us to gain new perspectives on and new understandings of lost objects": ibid., 4. I can see, I think, what the hoped for uptake is of this move. But in my view, it both misreads Freud's idea of mourning as presuming a past that can be *finally* and absolutely overcome and, at the same time, dissolves his essential insight into what is psychically corrosive about melancholia—namely, the narcissistic-regressive structure that fuels self-torment and undermines futurity.

9. See Young Leaders, *Under the Cover of Darkness* (St. George's: Presentation Brothers College, 2002).

10. I take up the trial in chapter 4.

11. The colleagues said to have been "executed" with Maurice Bishop that day were

Fitzroy Bain, Norris Bain, Evelyn Bullen, Jacqueline Creft, Keith Hayling, Evelyn Maitland, and Unison Whiteman. Another colleague, Vincent Noel, was killed earlier in the crossfire with soldiers. See also the account in Maurice Paterson, *Big Sky, Little Bullet: A Docu-Novel* (St. George's: Maurice Paterson, 1992), chap. 21.

12. Quoted in Young Leaders, *Under the Cover of Darkness*, 21–23.

13. This story, particularly the account of Bernard reading the death sentence" from a piece of paper, was more or less repeated by Fabian Gabriel, a former corporal in the People's Revolutionary Army, who was given a "conditional pardon" in exchange for testimony against his former comrades: see Callistus Bernard, *They Could Only Kill Me Once* (London: Hibiscus, 2006), 114–17. Other "eyewitness" accounts were also offered in court, some with macabre details, such as Beverly Ann Charles's account of Lester Redhead slitting Bishop's throat and slicing off of his ring finger: see ibid., 127–28. See also Paterson, *Big Sky, Little Bullet.*

14. In addition to Callistus Bernard, the seventeen who were convicted were Hudson Austin, Dave Bartholomew, Bernard Coard, Phyllis Coard, Leon Cornwall, Liam James, Vincent Joseph, Ewart Layne, Kamau McBarnette, Andy Mitchell, Cecil Prime, Lester Redhead, Cosmos Richardson, Selwyn Strachan, Christopher Stroude, and John Ventour.

15. See Bernard, *They Could Only Kill Me Once*, 126.

16. "In the resulting chaos which followed the end of the shoot-out, Maurice Bishop and seven of our colleagues were tragically killed": ibid., 5.

17. Richard Hart, *The Grenada Trial, a Travesty of Justice* (Kingston: Foundation for Phyllis Coard, 1996), 13–14; Richard Hart, *The Grenada Revolution: Setting the Record Straight*, Socialist History Occasional Paper Series, no. 20 (London: Caribbean Labour Solidarity and Socialist History Society, 2005), 56; Allan Scott, "The Quest for Justice: The Case of the Grenada 17" (St. George's: Committee for Human Rights in Grenada, n.d.), chap. 4.

18. This is part of a larger story of the crumbling of an era in the monumental collapse of the modernist dreamscape of mass utopia of which the idea of socialism was one instance: see Susan Buck-Morss, *Dreamworld and Catastrophe: The Passing of Mass Utopia in East and West* (Cambridge, Mass.: MIT Press, 2000); James Scott, *Seeing like a State: How Certain Schemes to Improve the Human Condition Have Failed* (New Haven, Conn.: Yale University Press, 1998).

19. For a useful discussion of dead bodies and the rupture of political time, see Katherine Verdery, *The Political Lives of Dead Bodies: Reburial and Postsocialist Change* (New York: Columbia University Press, 1999). I do not exactly share Verdery's framing question—namely, why the postsocialist period has been accompanied by so much dead-body politics—nor am I especially interested in the "re-enchantment" of the study of the political (although I am sympathetic in large measure). What I do find stimulating is her idea that a politics of corpses can be about "cosmologies and practices relating the living and the dead" and,

specifically, that "dead-body politics can be part of a larger process whereby fundamental changes are occurring in conceptions of time": ibid., 26–27. In the postsocialist world, Verdery argues, history is "not simply being rewritten with new/old characters and a different plot line—for instance a plot that replaces a communist radiant future with a narrative of tyranny overthrown and resistance triumphant. Rather, the very notions of time that underlie history are thrown open to question": ibid., 115. This is a very crucial insight.

20. The boys—Andre Bierzynski, Eddy Charles, Keith Fraser, Valentine Swaney Jr., and Asa Ventour—won the Grenada leg of the competition but came second in the regional competition.

21. Brother Robert Fanovitch, interview by the author, St. George's, Grenada, 17 December 2007.

22. For a very poignant sense of the vengeful grief of one victim's parent, see Sylvia Belmar, "The Truth of October 19, 1983," *Grenada Today*, 26 May 2000, 19, 21. Belmar's daughter, Gemma, died a few days after 19 October 1983 from gunshot wounds sustained that day. See also "Liars and Murderers," editorial, *Grenada Today*, 29 October 1999, 4.

23. In all, seventeen bodies were accounted for at Fort Rupert. This, in fact, was one of the great achievements of the research of the Young Leaders—namely, to have arrived at a plausible estimate of the number of persons who died as a consequence of the shooting at the fort: see Young Leaders, *Under the Cover of Darkness*, chap. 2.

24. The pathology report is in the *Truth and Reconciliation Commission Report* (St. George's: Ministry of Legal Affairs, Labour, and Local Government, 2006), sec. 8, accessed 12 March 2012, www.thegrenadarevolutiononline.com /trcreport5-8-1.html.

25. This last remark about photographs is not exactly accurate, since the Young Leaders reproduce a photograph with the caption "US soldiers recovering bodies from grave at Camp Fedon, Calivigny in early November, 1983": Young Leaders, *Under the Cover of Darkness*, 35. If this photograph exists, might there not be others?

26. "Armed Forces Pathology Report," in *Truth and Reconciliation Commission Report*, sec. 8.

27. The remains were moved around quite a bit. On Thursday, 10 November, they were taken to the hospital in St. George's to be X-rayed, and on Friday, 11 November, they were returned to St. George's University: see Young Leaders, *Under the Cover of Darkness*, 43.

28. Ibid., 36.

29. Ibid., 37–38.

30. Fanovitch interview.

31. Young Leaders, *Under the Cover of Darkness*, 40.

32. Robert Jordan granted the students two interviews. He seems to have kept a

diary; therefore, the students had good reason to suppose that his memory of the content and sequence of events was accurate: see ibid., 42.

33. Ibid., 41.

34. Ibid., 42.

35. See ibid., 50–51.

36. Ibid., 49.

37. Ibid.

38. Salimbi Gill, "Foreword," in ibid., 7. Gill is a prominent lawyer and politician in Grenada.

39. Ibid.

40. See Young Leaders, *Under the Cover of Darkness*, chap. 6.

41. The United States also fought an unexpectedly protracted battle there against the Cuban construction workers building the airport. The Reagan administration, it will be remembered, asserted that the airport was to be used as a staging ground for a generalized communist assault in the Caribbean.

42. There is also a monument to the American liberators at the US medical school, St. George's University, True Blue. Called "A Page of History," this bronze memorial (by the sculptor Ken Clark and brought from the United States) bears the following inscription: "Here inscribed on this monument are the signatures of the United States servicemen who gave their lives in the evacuation of the students of St. George's University School of Medicine, October 25th, 1983."

43. "Memory is never shaped in a vacuum. . . . The motives of memory are never pure": James Young, *The Texture of Memory: Holocaust Memorials and Meaning* (New Haven, Conn.: Yale University Press, 1993), 2.

44. See W. James Booth, *Communities of Memory: On Witness, Identity, and Justice* (Ithaca, NY: Cornell University Press, 2006).

45. I take the phrase "new colonialism" from Merle Collins, "Grenada, Ten Years and More: Memory and Collective Responsibility," *Caribbean Quarterly* 41, no. 2 (June 1995): 76. But see also David Scott, "The Fragility of Memory: An Interview with Merle Collins," *Small Axe*, no. 31 (March 2010): 160–63. See also Paterson, *Big Sky, Little Bullet*, 295.

46. Reinhart Koselleck, *Futures Past: On the Semantics of Historical Time*, Keith Tribe, trans. (Cambridge: MIT Press, 1985), xxiv.

47. Sylviane Agacinski, *Time Passing: Modernity and Nostalgia*, trans. Jody Gladding (New York: Columbia University Press, 2003), 10.

48. See Marianne Hirsch, *Family Frames: Photography, Narrative, and Postmemory* (Cambridge, Mass.: Harvard University Press, 1997). See also, more recently, Marianne Hirsch, "The Generation of Postmemory," *Poetics Today* 29, no. 1 (2008): 106–11.

49. Young Leaders, *Under the Cover of Darkness*, 8.

50. See Merle Collins, "Shame Bush," in *Lady in a Boat* (Leeds: Peepal Tree Press, 2003), 50–52: "All the quiet that surround us is the silence of pain / Is the quiet

of caution; this destruction mustn't happen again / Is the quiet of those who criticize a leader that popular / Never thinking that would mean a sentence of murder / Is the silence of those who confused when invasion reach / Their own act like the devil so they welcome marines to the beach."

51. Verdery, *The Political Lives of Dead Bodies*, 115–24.

52. Young Leaders, *Under the Cover of Darkness*, 10–16.

53. Walter Benjamin, "Left-Wing Melancholy," in *Selected Writings, Volume 2, Part 2, 1931–1934*, ed. Michael W. Jennings, Howard Eiland, and Gary Smith (Cambridge, Mass.: Harvard University Press, 1999), 423–27.

54. Ibid., 425.

55. Wendy Brown, "Resisting Left Melancholia," in Eng and Kazanjian, *Loss*, 458–65.

56. This is the Stuart Hall, of course, of *The Hard Road to Renewal: Thatcherism and the Crisis of the Left* (London: Verso, 1988).

57. Brown, "Resisting Left Melancholia," 463–64.

Chapter Four. Evading Truths

Epigraph: Judith Shklar, *Faces of Injustice* (New Haven, Conn.: Yale University Press, 1992), 83.

1. For a forceful and now canonical formulation of the tension between law and justice, see Martha Minow, *Between Vengeance and Forgiveness: Facing History after Genocide and Mass Violence* (Boston: Beacon, 1998). See also Martha Minow, *Breaking the Cycles of Hatred: Memory, Law, and Repair* (Princeton, NJ: Princeton University Press, 2003).

2. The idea of "political evil"—drawing inspiration sometimes from various of the writings of Hannah Arendt—has become a commonplace in the contemporary post–Cold War rhetoric of liberalism's new vindicationist autobiography. For one instance of this contemporary rhetoric, see Alan Wolfe, *Political Evil: What It Is And How to Combat It* (New York: Knopf, 2011). What is endlessly illuminating about books such as Wolfe's is how they insulate—implicitly, more often than not—the actions of liberal regimes or liberal leaders from being characterized as "political evil." Political evil belongs primarily to the actions of liberalism's others. On Arendt on evil, see George Kateb, *Hannah Arendt: Politics, Conscience, Evil* (New York: Rowman and Littlefield, 1987). For a different approach from Wolfe's to the whole question, see Robert Meister, *After Evil: A Politics of Human Rights* (New York: Columbia University Press, 2011).

3. This, notably, is not the story Jon Elster tells in his continuous history of trials and purges and so on going back two millennia: Jon Elster, *Closing the Books: Transitional Justice in Historical Perspective* (New York: Cambridge University Press, 2004).

4. See Francis Fukuyama, *The End of History and the Last Man* (New York: Free Press, 1992); Bruce Ackerman, *The Future of Liberal Revolution* (New Haven,

Conn.: Yale University Press, 1992); Samuel Huntington, *The Third Wave: De-mocratization in the Late Twentieth Century* (Norman: University of Oklahoma Press, 1993).

5. I borrow the term "social imaginary" from Charles Taylor, *Modern Social Imagi-naries* (Durham, NC: Duke University Press, 2003), to evoke the semiotic field in which a political project articulates itself.

6. Perhaps definitive here for the early Cold War reframing of the liberal idea was the conference on totalitarianism organized by Carl Friedrich under the aus-pices of the American Academy of the Arts in March 1953: see Carl Friedrich, *Totalitarianism* (New York: Grosset and Dunlap, 1954). See also Abbott Glea-son, *Totalitarianism: The Inner History of the Cold War* (New York: Oxford Uni-versity Press, 1997).

7. For an enthusiast's account, see Michael Ignatieff, *The Rights Revolution* (Toronto: House of Anansi, 2000), and *Human Rights as Politics and Idolatry* (Princeton, NJ: Princeton University Press, 2003). See also Lynn Hunt, *Invent-ing Human Rights: A History* (New York: W. W. Norton, 2008). For a more nu-anced and critical account of the emergence of the contemporary hegemony of human rights, see Samuel Moyn, *The Last Utopia: Human Rights in History* (Cambridge, Mass.: Harvard University Press, 2010).

8. On this period of the drafting of the Universal Declaration of Human Rights and particularly of the role of the Soviet Union, see Mary Ann Glendon, *A World Made New: Eleanor Roosevelt and the Universal Declaration of Human Rights* (New York: Random House, 2002).

9. For a discussion of the "right to democracy," see Thomas Franck, "The Emerg-ing Right to Democratic Governance," *American Journal of International Law* 46, no. 1 (January 1992): 46–91, and "Democracy as a Human Right," in *Human Rights: An Agenda for the Next Century*, ed. Louis Henkin and John Lawrence Hargrove (Washington, DC: American Society for International Law, 1994), 73–101.

10. See Martti Koskenniemi, *The Gentle Civilizer of Nations: The Rise and Fall of International Law, 1870–1960* (New York: Cambridge University Press, 2004), and, more recently, *The Politics of International Law* (Oxford: Hart, 2011).

11. I am thinking here principally of the role of John Rawls, *A Theory of Justice* (Cam-bridge, Mass.: Harvard University Press, 1971), and, subsequently, *Political Lib-eralism* (New York: Columbia University Press, 1993), in shaping the resurgence of a confident rights-based liberalism. In the later *Law of Peoples* (Cambridge, Mass.: Harvard University Press, 2001), Rawls sought to address himself to the wider global implications of his liberal theory, how "decent societies" should behave toward one another.

12. See Guillermo O'Donnell, Philippe C. Schmitter, and Laurence Whitehead, *Tran-sitions from Authoritarian Rule, Volume 1: Southern Europe* (Baltimore: Johns

Hopkins University Press, 1986); Guillermo O'Donnell, Philippe C. Schmitter, and Laurence Whitehead, *Transitions from Authoritarian Rule, Volume 2: Latin America* (Baltimore: Johns Hopkins University Press, 1986); Guillermo O'Donnell, Philippe C. Schmitter, and Laurence Whitehead, *Transitions from Authoritarian Rule, Volume 3: Comparative Perspectives* (Baltimore: Johns Hopkins University Press, 1986); Guillermo O'Donnell and Philippe C. Schmitter, *Transitions from Authoritarian Rule, Volume 4: Tentative Conclusions about Uncertain Democracies* (Baltimore: Johns Hopkins University Press, 1986).

13. O'Donnell and Schmitter, *Transitions from Authoritarian Rule*, 3.
14. See Patricia Haynor, *Unspeakable Truths: Facing the Challenge of Truth Commissions* (New York: Routledge, 2002), 10.
15. *Nunca Mas (Never Again): A Report by Argentina's National Commission on Disappeared People* (London: Faber, 1986).
16. The conferences in question here are the Aspen Institute conference in 1988 and the conference in South Africa in 1994. In the wake of Neil Kritz, ed., *Transitional Justice: How Emerging Democracies Reckon with Former Regimes*, 3 vols. (Washington, DC: US Institute of Peace, 1995), the number of references to "transitional justice" rose significantly. For a very helpful account of the emergence of the "field" of transitional justice, see Paige Arthur, "How 'Transitions' Reshaped Human Rights: A Conceptual History of Transitional Justice," *Human Rights Quarterly* 31 (2009): 321–67.
17. See Minow, *Between Vengeance and Forgiveness*.
18. John Gray has usefully characterized liberalism as showing two rival "faces"—one concerned with achieving a rational consensus on the best way to live, and the other with the peaceful coexistence among different forms of life. On the former account, the protection of what are deemed "universal rights" requires a global projection of liberal values. As Gray points out, however, this is only "a species of liberal fundamentalism": John Gray, *Two Faces of Liberalism* (New York: New Press, 2000), 110. I am indebted to Gray for this useful contrast, but I have a number of reservations. One concerns the ambiguity about whether, in the end, value pluralism and modus vivendi for him are not ways to rescue liberalism from itself. Another concerns the extent to which Euro-America defines the geopolitical parameters of his thinking about liberalism and thus obscures from him the place of transitional justice in shaping *one* of the defining faces of contemporary liberalism.
19. The Grenada 17 typically acted, and represented themselves, as a *whole*. But it is important to recognize that the burden of their "case" has been directed at the party and army leadership.
20. See Shklar, *The Faces of Injustice*.
21. The thirteen named in the appeal were Hudson Austin, Dave Bartholomew, Callistus Bernard, Bernard Coard, Leon Cornwall, Liam James, Ewart Layne,

Colville McBarnette, Cecil Prime, Lester Redhead, Selwyn Strachan, Christopher Stroude, and John Ventour. Phyllis Coard was not named because she had been granted leave in 2000 to seek medical treatment in Jamaica.

22. See paragraph 32 of the judgment: "Coard & Ors v. The Attorney General (Grenada) [2007] UKPC 7 (7 February 2007)": http://www.bailii.org/uk/cases /UKPC/2007/7.html (accessed 7 June 2013), http://www.privy-council.org.uk /output/Page535.asp. The entire judgment is worth serious study.

23. On the Cold War, see Fred Halliday, *The Making of the Second Cold War*, 2d rev. ed. (London: Verso, 1989). On the Reagan doctrine and the beginnings of the neoconservative movement, see, variously, John Erhman, *The Rise of Neoconservatism: Intellectuals and Foreign Affairs, 1945–1994* (New Haven, Conn.: Yale University Press, 1995); David Harvey, *The New Imperialism* (New York: Oxford University Press, 2003); Stefan Haler and Jonathan Clarke, *America Alone: Neo-Conservatives and the Global Order* (New York: Cambridge University Press, 2004).

24. See Arthur, "How 'Transitions' Reshaped Human Rights," 329.

25. Ruti Teitel, *Transitional Justice* (Oxford: Oxford University Press, 2000).

26. The trial was covered extensively in the regional media but perhaps most comprehensively in the Barbadian daily, the *Nation* in December 1986.

27. Teitel, *Transitional Justice*, 3.

28. Ibid.

29. Ibid., 6.

30. Ibid.

31. I am, of course, thinking of the essay *On Liberty* (1859), in which John Stuart Mill cautions that settled liberty depends on a certain level of civilization, and those peoples who have yet to attain that level will need to be urged along the road of progress, by a coercive hand, if necessary.

32. For some discussion, see Uday Singh Mehta, *Liberalism and Empire: A Study in Nineteenth Century Liberal Thought* (Princeton: Princeton University Press, 1999).

33. See Diane F. Orentlicher, "Settling Accounts: The Duty to Prosecute Human Rights Violations of a Prior Regime," *Yale Law Review* 100 (1991): 2537–2615.

34. Teitel, *Transitional Justice*, 28–29.

35. Ibid., 29.

36. Ibid., 30.

37. See Hart, *The Grenada Trial: A Travesty of Justice* (Kingston: Foundation for Phyllis Coard, 1996).

38. Amnesty International, "The Grenada 17: The Last of the Cold War Prisoners?" report no. AMR 32/001/2003, 22 October 2003. Not surprisingly, the report was criticized by the government of the day: see Amnesty International, "Open Letter to the Prime Minister and People of Grenada Concerning the 'Grenada 17,'" report no. AMR 32/006/2003, 4 November 2003.

39. Amnesty International, "The Grenada 17," 4.

40. On the desire of the United States to suggest a sharp opposition between Bishop and Coard, see Richard Hart, "Introduction," in *In Nobody's Backyard: Maurice Bishop's Speeches, 1979–1983: A Memorial Volume*, ed. Chris Searle (London: Zed, 1984), xxxviii. On Castro's views of the events of 19 October 1983, see Fidel Castro, *A Pyrrhic Military Victory and a Profound Moral Defeat* (Havana: Editora Politica, 1983).

41. US Departments of State and Defense, *Grenada Documents: An Overview and Selection*, ed. Michael Ledeen and Herbert Romerstein (Washington, DC: US Government Printing Office, 1984). An overlapping selection of papers was released as Paul Seabury and Walter A. McDougall, eds., *The Grenada Papers* (San Francisco: Institute for Contemporary Studies Press, 1984).

42. Amnesty International, "The Grenada 17," 4. It appears that there was no formal detention of Bishop and that therefore the idea of "house arrest" is misleading, once more giving the impression of a calculation rather than an evolving and fluid situation: see John "Chalky" Ventour, "October 1983: The Missing Link" (1988), in *Redeeming the Past: A Time for Healing*, report of the Grenada Truth and Reconciliation Commission, 2 vols. (St. George's: Ministry of Legal Affairs, Labour, and Local Government, 2006), 2:23–25.

43. See Fidel Castro, *Nothing Can Stop the Course of History: Interview with Jeffrey M. Elliot and Mervyn M. Dymally* (New York: Pathfinder, 1986), 162, 165. On the dubious role of the Cubans generally, see Ventour, "October 1983."

44. Amnesty International, "The Grenada 17," 4.

45. In fact, Amnesty International recognizes this: see ibid., n. 1.

46. Ibid., 2.

47. Ibid., 4. See also Robert A. Pastor, "The Invasion of Grenada: A Pre- and Post-Mortem," in *The Caribbean after Grenada: Revolution, Conflict, and Democracy*, ed. Scott B. McDonald, Harold M. Sandstrom, and Paul B. Goodwin Jr. (New York: Praeger, 1988), 104.

48. Amnesty International, "The Grenada 17," 9–13. See also Richard Hart, *The Grenada Trial*, 10–14. For a firsthand account, see Callistus Bernard, *They Could Only Kill Me Once* (London: Hibiscus, 2006), chap. 2.

49. Notably, the revolutionary government was in the process of drafting a new constitution at the time of its collapse. In June 1983, the PRG announced the establishment of a Constitution Commission. It consisted of three lawyers, Alan Alexander, Ashley Taylor, and Richard Hart: see Richard Hart, *The Grenada Revolution: Setting the Record Straight*, Socialist History Society Occasional Paper, no. 20 (London: Caribbean Labor Solidarity, 2005), 4–6. Hart's book was a critical response to the account of the revolution written by Sir Paul Scoon, governor general of Grenada during the time of the PRG: see Paul Scoon, *Survival for Service: My Experiences as Governor General of Grenada* (London: Macmillan, 2003).

50. For a fascinating discussion of some of the legal issues at stake, see Simeon C. R. McIntosh, *Kelsen in the Grenada Court: Essays on Revolutionary Legality* (Kingston: Ian Randle, 2008).

51. Amnesty International, "The Grenada 17," 14.

52. Ibid., 15.

53. As though this was deemed insufficient to ensure the necessary verdict, there was one last piece of intimidation. As the jury members were about to retire, they were handed a "verdict sheet" on which each had to indicate the verdict he or she arrived at in each of the counts. In other words, any juror who found "not guilty" would be known by name.

54. This caused an angry response from the judge: see "Genesis and Development of the Unconstitutional Court System (and the Jury Selection Procedures) Used to Try the Grenada 17," in *Redeeming the Past*, 2:11–12; Bernard, *They Could Only Kill Me Once*, 108–10. The head of the defense team, Ian Ramsey, wrote to the Heads of Commonwealth Governments, "As lawyers trained in England and brought up in the principles of the common law, we are unable to take part, nay prohibited, from legitimising in any way a trial by an admittedly unconstitutional court": quoted in Amnesty International, "The Grenada 17," 18.

55. Amnesty International, "The Grenada 17," 19.

56. Quoted in ibid.

57. Ibid., 21.

58. "The evidence of Cletus St. Paul is very important evidence in this trial. . . . The Prosecution is relying on it to lay the factual basis for you to find that the ten accused persons at the time at Fort Frederick instigated or commanded the soldiers to go to Fort Rupert to cause the deaths that they did": see ibid., fn. 39, 21–22.

59. Ibid., 21.

60. See Hart, "The Grenada Trial," 9.

61. Amnesty International, "The Grenada 17," 22; Hart, "The Grenada Trial," 7, 21; Ventour, "October 1983," 10–11.

62. See Minow, *Between Vengeance and Forgiveness*, chaps. 3–4; Haynor, *Unspeakable Truths*, chap. 3.

63. See Haynor, *Unspeakable Truths*, chap. 2.

64. Teitel, *Transitional Justice*, 69.

65. Ibid., 70.

66. Ibid.

67. Ibid. I leave aside the question of how far this is a plausible reading of either Nietzsche or Foucault.

68. Keith Mitchell, the sixth prime minister since the death of Maurice Bishop, came to power with the victory of his New National Party on 20 June 1995, winning eight of fifteen parliamentary seats. In the elections of January 1999,

Mitchell and his party affirmed their hold on power when they swept all fifteen seats. Mitchell was subsequently reelected for a third term in November 2003, although this time by a narrow margin. In 1997, in the wake of the decision of the Mercy Committee not to accede to the request from the Conference of Churches to release Phyllis Coard and Colville McBarnette on medical grounds, Mitchell announced his intention—and then withdrew it—to establish a truth and reconciliation committee.

69. See, e.g., "U.S. Body Bags Found with Human Remains," *Grenada Informer*, 7 January 2000, 3; "The Body Finders," *Grenada Today*, 7 January 2000, 1, 21.

70. See, e.g., "Reflections and Apologies to All Ex-Detainees of the PRG from Some Former Leaders of the NJM," *Grenadian Voice*, 8 February 1997, and Bernard Coard, "Apology to the Families of the Victims of the October 1983 Crisis, and to the Grenadian People," both in *Redeeming the Past*, vol. 2, app. A, apps. 4–5. See also "The Apology of Ewart Layne," *Grenadian Voice*, 9 October 1999, 3.

71. Leslie Pierre became a tireless campaigner for the release of the Grenada 17 from prison. He had been central in seeking to enable them to tell their side of the story, arranging, importantly, for four of the seventeen—Bernard Coard, Ewart Layne, Leon Cornwall, and Selwyn Strachan—to be interviewed on nationwide television in October 1999: see *Grenadian Voice*, 9 October 1999. I had the opportunity to meet with Pierre on two occasions in St. George's, Grenada, to talk about 1983 and its aftermath.

72. Dullah Omar (1934–2004) was an antiapartheid activist and lawyer who served in the South African cabinet from 1994 until his death in 2004.

73. *Redeeming the Past*, vol. 2, app. A, 5–6.

74. Clearly, with such vague and toothless terms of reference as these, the commission could not have been expected to accomplish much. Not surprisingly, from the beginning there was a good deal of suspicion that Mitchell's regime was being entirely cynical and therefore that, despite the grand-sounding gestures, little was to be expected from the commission. Although it is valuable, the report itself is a shoddy piece of work.

75. *Redeeming the Past*, vol. 2, app. A, 5–6.

76. Ibid.

77. Ibid., 1:8.

78. This is the celebrated language of Desmond Tutu, *No Future without Forgiveness* (New York: Image, 1999). For a criticism of the whole idea of forgiveness as exemplified by Tutu and the South African Truth and Reconciliation Commission, see Thomas Brudholm, *Resentment's Virtue: Jean Améry and the Refusal to Forgive* (Philadelphia: Temple University Press, 2008).

79. *Redeeming the Past*, 2:24–26.

80. Ibid., 1:37.

81. Ibid., vol. 2, app. 1.

82. It appears that no contact was made with the Grenada 17 until 4 February 2002 (that is, a full six months after the appointment of the commission), and then contact was made by way of a summary announcement that they communicated verbally to the commissioner of prisons that the commissioners of the TRC would be visiting the Richmond Hill Prison in a matter of hours to hear their testimonies. Needless to say the Grenada 17 were much taken aback and much aggrieved by this manner of communication and requested (as was of course their right) that any further contacts be made through their legal counsel. It would take a further two and a half months before this contact was made. In view of this—and given the crucial fact that the commission had no legal authority to grant amnesty to the Grenada 17 who were, after all, still in a legal battle to overturn their convictions—it is hard to see what reason they could have had to rest any confidence in the sincerity and impartiality of the TRC commissioners.

83. *Redeeming the Past*, 1:37.

84. Ibid., 1:36.

85. Ibid., 1:39. Their cautious recommendation reads, "It is in the context of this perspective, therefore, and having regard to the need for both victims of wrong doing and the alleged wrong doers to feel satisfied that justice is done to their respective causes for reconciliation to take place, that the Commission would prefer to see the State provide an appropriate opportunity for the 'Grenada 17' to access existing or established Courts within the legal system and which would studiously ensure the process of fair trial, regardless of the outcome": ibid., 1:40.

86. Ibid., 1:12.

87. Ibid.

88. Ibid., 1:7.

89. In a number of letters written to the two-man committee set up to form the commission and to the commission itself, the Grenada 17 set out its argument and suggestions, as well as its doubts: see, e.g., ibid., vol. 2, apps. 1–2.

90. For an account of the origin of his invaluable document, see Ventour, "October 1983," 3–5.

91. Ibid., 8–9. Louison was subsequently expelled from the NJM at the general meeting of 13 October 1983.

92. Castro has denied that he knew anything about the crisis in advance of Bishop's death: see Castro, *Nothing Can Stop the Course of History*, 162, 165.

93. Ventour, "October 1983," 19–20.

94. See Castro, *Nothing Can Stop the Course of History*, 164–65.

95. Ewart Layne, "A Travesty of Justice: How 10 NJM Leaders of the Grenada Revolution Were Convicted by One Lie," *Redeeming the Past*, vol. 2, app. 8, 1–22.

96. Ibid., 3. St. Paul's evidence had been suspected as flawed by Justice J. O. F. Haynes, president of the Court of Appeal, but Haynes died in December 1988, before he could call St. Paul to give an account of his several conflicting state-

ments. The matter was simply shelved on the appointment of the new president of the court.

97. For some of the provisions of the Commissions of Inquiry Act governing the appointment and parameters of the Grenada TRC, see *Redeeming the Past*, 1:17.

Epilogue

Hannah Arendt, *The Human Condition* (Chicago: University of Chicago Press, 1958), 237.

1. "The discoverer of the role of forgiveness in the realm of human affairs was Jesus of Nazareth": Arendt, *The Human Condition*, 238. This is why love is a close affiliate of forgiveness, "for love, although it is one of the rarest occurrences in human lives, indeed possesses an unequaled power of self-revelation and an unequaled clarity of vision for the disclosure of *who*, precisely because it is unconcerned to the point of total unworldliness with *what* the loved person may be, with his qualities and shortcomings no less than with his achievements, failings, and transgressions": ibid., 242. Undoubtedly, in this passage Arendt must have had Heidegger in mind. For a fascinating account of her friendship with, and forgiveness of, Heidegger, see Daniel Maier-Katkin, *Stranger from Abroad: Hannah Arendt, Martin Heidegger, Friendship, and Forgiveness* (New York: W. W. Norton, 2010).

2. Arendt, *The Human Condition*, 240.

3. Ibid., 239, 241. Forgiving, it is true, is always an "eminently personal (though not necessarily individual or private) affair"; ibid., 241. That, Arendt suggests, is why it "has always been deemed unrealistic and inadmissible in the public realm": ibid., 243.

4. Ibid., 241.

5. The literature is vast. It ranges from work that takes up the issue of the aftermaths of New World slavery (e.g., Roy L. Brooks, *Atonement and Forgiveness: A New Model for Black Reparations* [Berkeley: University of California Press, 2004]) to work that takes up the case of South Africa (e.g., Desmond Tutu, *No Future without Forgiveness* [New York: Image, 1999]).

6. See, e.g., Jeffrie G. Murphy "Forgiveness and Resentment," in Jeffrie G. Murphy and Jean Hampton, *Forgiveness and Mercy* (Cambridge: Cambridge University Press, 1988), 14–34.

7. Ibid., 15.

8. Ibid., 24–26. See also Jeffrie G. Murphy, *Getting Even: Forgiveness and Its Limits* (Oxford: Oxford University Press, 2003). The political theorist Peter Digeser takes a different approach: see Peter Digeser, *Political Forgiveness* (Ithaca, NY: Cornell University Press, 2001). Seeking to evade the psychological and theological baggage of many conceptions of forgiveness, he maintains that forgiveness essentially is an "illocutionary act of self-disclosure." What counts here

are "not motives or sentiments but whether the actor is pursuing a desired end by publicly subscribing to a set of moral practices and rules": Digeser, *Political Forgiveness*, 4.

9. See "Nadia Bishop Speaks of 'Forgiveness and Reconciliation,'" *Grenada Today*, 12 January 2008, accessed 9 April 2012, www.belgrafix.com/gtoday/2008news /Jan/Jan12/Nadia-Bishop-speaks-of-forgiveness-and-reconciliation.htm.

10. Jacques Derrida, "On Forgiveness," in *On Cosmopolitanism and Forgiveness*, trans. Mark Dooley and Michael Hughes (New York: Routledge, 2001), 39.

11. Ibid., 44.

12. See Murphy, "Forgiveness and Resentment," 31; Derrida, "On Forgiveness," 58.

13. See "Reflections and Apologies to All Ex-Detainees of the PRG from Some Former Leaders of the NJM," *Grenadian Voice*, 8 February 1997. See also "The Apology of Ewart Layne" *Grenadian Voice*, 9 October 1999, 3.

14. Of interest here is Thomas Brudholm, *Resentment's Virtue: Jean Améry and the Refusal to Forgive* (Philadelphia: Temple University Press, 2008).

15. Some met the release with condemnation—for example, Cheddi Jagan Jr., son of the late Guyanese Prime Minister Cheddi Jagan, who founded the People's Political Party. In a letter to the *Stabroek News*, he said, in part, "The release of Bernard Coard and his associates from prison in Grenada is a slap in the face of all West Indians who believe in justice, democracy and good over evil. Here we have a truly evil man who ordered the brutal killing of a true West Indian patriot, Maurice Bishop, his pregnant girlfriend and other patriotic Grenadians. It is simply amazing that not one of our leaders in this region sees the need to condemn the release of Coard, who should really have been hanged for his heinous crimes": see Cheddi Jagan Jr., "Bernard Coard Should Not Have Been Released," letter to the editor, *Stabroek News*, 10 September 2009, accessed 14 December 2009, www.stabroeknews.com/2009/letters/09/10/bernard-coard-should-not -have-been-released.

INDEX

Trinidad, 81, 109
Trotman, Donald, (Grenada TRC), 153
truth and reconciliation, 14, 28, 117, 133, 135, 150, 153; truth commissions, 151, 162. *See also* Grenada TRC

Universal Declaration of Human Rights, 129
Universal History, 6, 12
University of the West Indies, 84

Ventour, John, 20, 53, 132–33, 148, 158–59, 168
Verdery, Katherine, 123, 202–3n
Victor, Teddy, 40

Weber, Max, 34, 183n, 192n
White, Hayden, 2, 177n
Whiteman, Unison, 15, 17, 40, 58, 105, 112, 132, 142
Williams, Raymond, on tragedy and revolution, 22, 35–36, 43, 63; *Modern Tragedy*, 35, 36, 184n, 185n; *The Long Revolution*, 35
Woodrow Wilson International Center for Scholars, 130

Young Leaders, 25, 104, 109, 112–14, 116, 120–21, 123, 126; *Under the Cover of Darkness*, 25, 103, 104, 115–17, 120–123, 126, 152